D0292138

Measuring ROI in Healthcare

Measuring ROI in Healthcare

Tools and Techniques to Measure the Impact and ROI in Healthcare Improvement Projects and Programs

VICTOR V. BUZACHERO
JACK PHILLIPS, PhD
PATRICIA PULLIAM PHILLIPS, PhD
ZACK L. PHILLIPS, RRT, MHA

New York   Chicago   San Francisco   Lisbon   London   Madrid   Mexico City
Milan   New Delhi   San Juan   Seoul   Singapore   Sydney   Toronto

Copyright © 2013 by Victor Buzachero, Jack Phillips, Patti Pulliam Phillips, and Zack L. Phillips. All rights reserved. Printed in the United States of America. Except as permitted under the United States Copyright Act of 1976, no part of this publication may be reproduced or distributed in any form or by any means, or stored in a data base or retrieval system, without the prior written permission of the publisher.

2 3 4 5 6 7 8 9 0 DOC/DOC 1 9 8 7 6 5 4 3

ISBN 978-0-07-181271-9
MHID 0-07-181271-7

e-ISBN 978-0-07-181272-6
e-MHID 0-07-181272-5

McGraw-Hill books are available at special quantity discounts to use as premiums and sales promotions or for use in corporate training programs. To contact a representative, please e-mail us at bulksales@mcgraw-hill.com.

This book is printed on acid-free paper.

Library of Congress Cataloging-in-Publication Data

Phillips, Jack J.
  Measuring ROI in healthcare : tools and techniques to measure the impact and ROI in healthcare improvement projects and programs / by Jack Phillips, Victor Buzachero, Patricia Phillips, and Zack Phillips.
    pages cm
  Includes bibliographical references and index.
  ISBN 978-0-07-181271-9 (alk. paper) — ISBN 0-07-181271-7 (alk. paper) 1. Medicine—Practice—Finance. 2. Medical offices—Management. I. Buzachero, Victor. II. Phillips, Patricia Pulliam. III. Phillips, Zack. IV. Title. V. Title: Measuring return on investment in healthcare.
  R728.P386 2013
  610.68'1—dc23   2013002299

I would like to dedicate this book to my wife Nancy Buzachero.
—V.B.

This is dedicated to our healthcare clients who are using this methodology to transform their organizations.
—P.P.P. and J.P.

I dedicate this book to my parents Don and Ellen and my extended family. Thanks for your unconditional love, kindness, and hospitality over the years.
—Z.L.H.

Contents

Preface

Healthcare expenditures will continue to grow in the next two decades. Showing the value for the expenditures in terms that resonate with all stakeholders is imperative. Changes in payment methods from a fee for service (utilization) to a more quality-centered, pay-for-performance product will reward providers that show improvement in quality and efficiency. Centers for Medicare and Medicaid Services (CMS) and others will likely award contracts and favorable revenue arrangements to providers that demonstrate value via the outcomes. All healthcare systems are working toward building internal systems that not only deliver better outcomes but also prove them.

Executives are now asking for the return on investment (ROI) on major healthcare projects in technology, quality, patient satisfaction, procurement, process improvement, case management, staffing, compliance, innovation, marketing, and other functional areas. Using the method outlined in this book, you will be able to deliver the ROI in a credible, reliable way.

THE NEED FOR THIS BOOK

The ability to connect the dots and show bottom-line accountability while maintaining quality and efficiencies will be the key to survival in the healthcare industry. When the measurement processes in healthcare are examined, it becomes apparent that no method is consistently used to show the value of various projects and programs. The ROI Methodology, developed and refined over two decades, has worked its way into the healthcare field with dramatic results. "Show me the ROI" is the familiar response from individuals asked to invest (or continue to invest) in major projects. At times, this response is appropriate. At other times, it may be misguided; measures not subject to monetary conversion are also important, if not critical, to most projects. However, excluding the ROI from a successful profile is unacceptable in this age of the "show me" generation. The ROI is often required before a project is approved. Sometimes, it is needed as the project is being designed and developed. Other times, it is needed after project implementation.

This issue is compounded by concern that most projects today fail to live up to expectations. A systematic process is needed that can identify barriers to and enablers of success and can drive organizational improvements. The challenge lies in doing it—developing the measures of value, including monetary value, when they are needed and presenting them in a way so that stakeholders can use them.

A GUIDE TO MEASURING ROI

This book is a basic guide for anyone involved in implementing healthcare improvement projects—systemwide medical procedures, technology implementations, systems integration, new quality processes, physician engagement, nurse retention, risk management, leadership development, or any other type of project where significant expenditures of time and money are at stake. Strategies to assist in forecasting the value of the project in advance and in collecting data during and after project implementation are presented. This book uses a results-based approach to project evaluation, focusing on a variety of measures that are categorized into six data types:

1. Reaction

2. Learning

3. Application and Implementation

4. Impact

5. Return on Investment

6. Intangibles

This book offers a step-by-step guide to identifying, collecting, analyzing, and reporting all six types of data in a consistent manner that leads to credible results.

CREDIBILITY IS KEY

This unique book focuses on building a credible process—one that will generate a balanced set of data that are believable, realistic, and accurate, particularly from the viewpoint of sponsors and key stakeholders. More specifically, the methodology presented in this book approaches credibility head-on through the use of:

- A balanced set of data

- A logical, systematic process

- Guiding Principles, a conservative set of standards

- A proven methodology based on thousands of applications

- An emphasis on implementing the methodology within an organization to ensure that the process is sustained

- A procedure accepted by sponsors, clients, and others who fund projects

The book explores the challenges of measuring the hard-to-measure and placing monetary values on the hard to value. It clarifies much of the mystery surrounding the allocation of monetary values. Building on a tremendous amount of experience, application, practice, and research, the book draws on the work of many individuals and organizations, particularly those who have attained the ultimate levels of accountability using the ROI Methodology. Developed in an easy-to-read format and fortified with examples, CEO highlights, and quick summaries, this guide is made for audiences who seek to understand more about bottom-line accountability and use of evaluation data to improve future outcomes.

TARGET AREAS FOR PROJECTS

This book is geared toward a variety of functional areas in healthcare organizations where projects are implemented. These areas include (but are not limited to) projects in:

- Human resources, education, talent management

- Learning and development, performance improvement

- Technology, IT systems

- Medical meetings, events, and conferences

- Leadership, development, coaching

- Marketing, promotion

- Risk management, compliance

- Public relations, community affairs, government relations

- Quality, Six Sigma

- Operations, methods, logistics

- Case management

- Research and development, innovation

- Finance, control, accounting

- Procurement, distribution, supply chain

- Public policy projects

- Charitable projects

More than 3,300 individuals have become a certified ROI professional (CRP) through the ROI Institute. Although many books tackle accountability in a certain function or process, this book shows a method that works across all types of projects.

Acknowledgments

FROM JACK AND PATTI PHILLIPS

At last count, we have had the pleasure of working with more than 300 healthcare organizations during the last two decades. Although much of that work began in the HR and learning and development areas, many of the projects have covered technology, marketing, quality processes, and more recently, all types of processes, systems, and medical procedures. Some of the early efforts involved work at Banner Healthcare, VA Health Systems, Baptist Hospital chains, and Scripps Health. With the VA, we've enjoyed more than a decade of ROI use, and they have done a marvelous job of sustaining the use of ROI as a tool in their large, complex system.

We have learned much from our clients in this important field. We appreciate their willingness to invite us in to share their projects with them. It has allowed us to develop capability in their organizations for the sustained use of ROI. Without our clients, this book would not be developed.

We would like to thank Vic Buzachero and Zack Phillips for their willingness to collaborate on this project. They each bring tremendous operational experience in the healthcare field and know firsthand the applicability of the ROI Methodology to healthcare organizations.

We owe much appreciation to Rachel Robinson, who, as senior editor, has guided this project from the very beginning. She is an outstanding editor and project manager, which makes her a valuable asset well beyond her publishing responsibilities. Thank you, Rachel, for your contribution to this publication and the many others we send your way.

FROM VIC BUZACHERO

We would like to acknowledge Scripps Health for providing information and background on the organization, performance management process, and decision-making systems. In addition, thanks to Nancy Buzachero who provided support and for the time I spent distracted from her during vacation, grandbaby showers, and valuable evening hours after a day at work. Her patience and understanding were cherished.

FROM ZACK PHILLIPS

I would like to thank Jack, Patti, and Vic for the opportunity to be involved in this project and Rachel Robinson for her tireless efforts in editing this book. I would also like to thank my parents Don and Ellen for their love and support. I am privileged to be associated with everyone connected with this project and look forward to a bright future showing the ROI in healthcare.

CHAPTER 1

Healthcare Performance Improvement Trends and Issues

Few topics stir emotions to the extent that healthcare does. The mention of the topic often elicits strong feelings and opinions about costs, quality, access, and a host of other issues. Healthcare touches everyone, and it represents one of the largest expenditures in almost any economy, particularly in the United States. The cost to provide healthcare is growing much faster than the cost of other goods and services. Although the quality of healthcare has improved, safety and consistent quality outcomes still remain a concern. Access to quality healthcare is still an issue (particularly for those individuals who cannot afford it), as is the patient experience, which is rarely addressed appropriately.

Because of its tremendous cost and importance, the healthcare industry has been a target for many types of measurement efforts. Healthcare (the treatment of the health of people) is one of the most highly regulated and measured of all industries. All types of monitoring, recording, and measuring have entered into the healthcare arena, some with success and others not as successful due to the "practice of medicine." The practice of medicine is not an exact science, but one of discovery. Meanwhile, all types of healthcare performance improvement projects have been undertaken, and unfortunately, many of them have failed to live up to expectations. What is needed is a systematic approach to improving the healthcare industry, using a proven measurement process that generates credible outcomes.

These important challenges must be addressed for a sustainable healthcare system in the United States and around the world. This opening chapter describes the issues and challenges that the healthcare industry faces and builds the case for major changes in the ways that healthcare improvement projects are initiated, delivered, and evaluated. The following opening stories highlight the dramatic changes that are occurring in healthcare and what healthcare organizations must do to survive in the future. Scripps has spent years preparing for the future and they will be able to address the tremendous changes that will occur. Metropolitan Foundation Hospital more than likely will not be able to survive and will be a candidate for consolidation, merger, or acquisition.

OPENING STORIES

METROPOLITAN FOUNDATION HOSPITAL

Metropolitan Foundation Hospital has enjoyed a successful 30 years of service in a major metropolitan area. With several locations in the city, the nonprofit healthcare provider is operating at a modest but manageable deficit. Executives are active in their community as part of their corporate social responsibility program. The hospital only accepts patients who do not have health insurance to meet the minimally acceptable legal requirement. Fees charged are based on the cost of services.

As the top executives plan for the future, they see substantial changes in the healthcare area as Medicare switches from *pay for services* to *pay for value* or bundled payments for service (capitation). Commercial payers are also migrating in the same direction. One analysis shows that based on Medicare reimbursement rates, the hospital would have to reduce prices by $1,200 per average case rate, which obviously would be devastating financially for the healthcare firm.

As the top executives address this issue, they have reviewed the current status with some of the key areas. Although they have collected patient satisfaction data, they have not taken any particular actions because of them. Further, identifying the cost of processes and procedures has not been routine and systematic. Although patient quality and outcomes are loosely tracked, little effort has been made to show related cost of that patient quality. Efforts to improve physician and nurse engagement have been limited at best. Top executives recognize that too much waste occurs and the staff seems to be inefficient, but they struggle with commitment to make changes. These challenges present executives with some critical obstacles in the future of healthcare.

SCRIPPS HEALTH

Scripps Health is a not-for-profit, San Diego–based healthcare system that is successful on any dimension. The system, which includes five hospitals and 23 outpatient facilities, treats almost 2 million patients annually. Scripps employs more than 13,000 employees and has been named one of "America's 100 Best Companies to Work For" every year since 2008. The system also includes clinical research and medical education programs.[1]

Having enjoyed success over the past 80 years, Scripps is a financially sound and stable organization with AA-rated bonds, one of only four healthcare organizations in California to hold this distinction. The "people" part of their process is managed extremely well, enabling Scripps to provide efficient, quality healthcare. Scripps regularly appears on lists of admired organizations, the best places to work, and the best employer for certain groups. Executives place specific emphasis on corporate social responsibility with more than $370 million contributed to community service and charity care. Scripps is considered among the top providers of healthcare. For example, Scripps was named by Thomson Reuters as one of the Top 10 health systems in the nation for providing high quality, safe and efficient patient care.

The success of Scripps rests on the quality of its leadership and the systems and processes in place to make it an outstanding healthcare delivery organization. Scripps focuses significant efforts on sound financial processes, process improvement projects, and a variety of initiatives to improve the quality of healthcare. Among the processes used by Scripps is the ROI Methodology, a process that shows the success of healthcare improvement projects using six types of data with standards and a process model. At least 20 of Scripps professional team members have achieved the designation of Certified ROI Professional as they continue to conduct ROI studies on a variety of processes to ensure that they are delivering value and quality healthcare and achieving a positive financial outcome.

NEW ERA IN HEALTHCARE

Healthcare reform is front and center in American society, the economy, and political arenas. Costs have grown annually, outpacing general inflation for decades, compounding the healthcare concern. The weight of this cost trend on Medicare has led Congress to pass landmark legislation that may, in fact, be the legacy of the Obama Administration. The legislation addresses coverage for the uninsured, affordable health insurance for small businesses, and coverage for minors and preexisting conditions. This legislation is sweeping in nature and has far-reaching implications.

SUBSTANTIAL COST IMPACT

To pay for expanded coverage for the millions of uninsured Americans, a series of cuts in Medicare reimbursement to hospitals, physicians, and other providers from current levels will be used as "prepayment" for this coverage. The expanded coverage and payments for the uninsured will forestall the current practice of cost shifting by hospitals to commercial carriers to cover the uninsured. Hospitals have used the shifting of the cost of providing uninsured care to commercially insured payers via increased pricing.

Healthcare reform also allows employers and individuals to purchase coverage through state-run insurance exchanges that bid competitively at lower prices to offer coverage. These declining prices toward Medicare rates, which generally do not cover costs in most hospitals, will have a devastating impact on the viability of healthcare operations. As illustrated by Figure 1.1, hospitals of all sizes will need to reduce costs by as much as 17 percent to break even on Medicare reimbursement.

CHANGING THE RULES OF THE GAME

Payment for services has traditionally been based on a fee for service model in healthcare. Healthcare reform includes modification to the model by shifting to pay for value added via value-based purchasing, penalties for readmissions, and prices that do not cover excessive utilization but instead reward providers for managing population health. The overall concept of the "triple aim" focuses on the following:

1. Decreased costs

2. Higher value through improved outcomes and services

3. Expanded coverage to care for a population or communities' health[2]

The "triple aim" approach is a radical modification of the current model for the healthcare enterprise. The healthcare model will shift accordingly with emphasis on accountable care as described in Figure 1.2.

RETHINKING ORGANIZATION OF CARE

Currently, analysts claim $365 billion of waste occurs in the system today.[3] This waste is largely avoidable; however, it is difficult to avoid in the current fragmented system. This system is characterized with payers that cover the cost of care for users (patients) provided by an independent fragmented market of providers (physicians and hospitals) that are not integrated with care models, information, or costs. The system is full of redundancies and inefficiencies of over- and undertreatment due to excessive,

FIGURE 1.1   Percent of Costs That Must Be Cut Due to Medicare

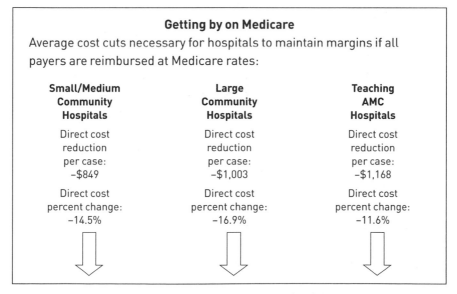

Source: Adapted from Sg2 INSIGHT database, CY 2010, Sg2 Analysis (2010).

FIGURE 1.2 Emphasis on Accountable Care

Acccountable Care Organizations

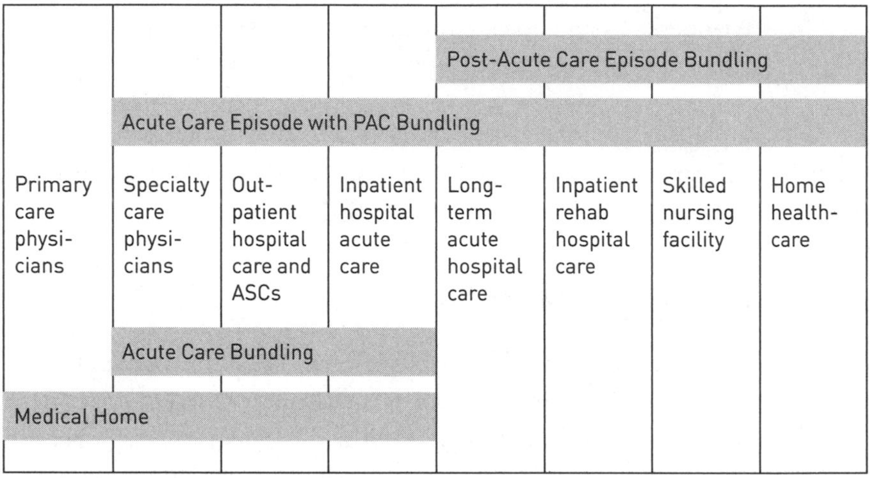

Primary care physicians	Specialty care physicians	Out-patient hospital care and ASCs	Inpatient hospital acute care	Long-term acute hospital care	Inpatient rehab hospital care	Skilled nursing facility	Home health-care
				Post-Acute Care Episode Bundling			
	Acute Care Episode with PAC Bundling						
	Acute Care Bundling						
Medical Home							

Source: American Hospital Association.

overlapping, and nonintegrated processes, tests, and treatments. Decisions for improvement are made in today's current environment incrementally by fragmented groups (physicians, hospitals, insurers, ambulatory centers, etc.), each maximizing returns at the expense of the others and at the expense of the patients in the system. Each exploits the other at the expense of the whole to maximize individual gains. This action drives costs of care up in a never-ending spiral. Each group also seeks larger scale to leverage negotiations, again at the expense of the others and the patient.

Generally, the system is comprised of tax-exempt organizations complemented with public institutions and independent physicians. Physicians are, however, rapidly moving away from independent practice and joining larger groups as shown in Figure 1.3.

These larger groups focus on the patient with a "do no harm" perspective with little or no business acumen in decision making. This process, therefore, makes limited use of financial or mathematical models to determine value added even when investments are made with financial objectives.

FIGURE 1.3 Independent and Dependent Physicians

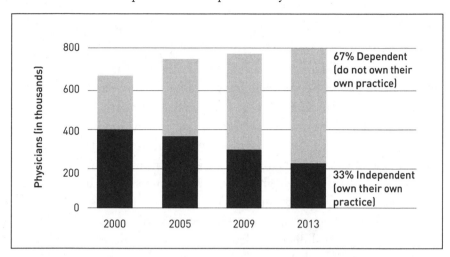

Source: Adapted from Accenture, Medical Group Management Association, and American Medical Association.

POST HEALTHCARE REFORM

As noted previously, healthcare reform legislation creates an industry with a "triple aim" driven by a new reimbursement model. Increasing value via the "triple aim" mandates lower costs through entirely new systems and processes that produce better patient quality, outcomes, and experiences. This three-pronged approach helps executives lead quality initiatives by improving the health of the population, enhancing the patient care experience, and reducing or controlling per capita costs. In essence, the industry will not survive in its current form and must reinvent itself with new business models, systems of care, and processes. The system will evolve from care per incident, or pay for procedure, to care for a population and pay for value.[4] This evolution will require a model with lower cost structures, medical management of care, intelligent information systems, and integrated networks of care and physicians, all accountable for population health.

The Challenges

Marshall Goldsmith's book titled *What Got You Here Won't Get You There: How Successful People Become Even More Successful* is especially appropriate for the healthcare industry.[5] This industry must transform fundamentally during a time when demand will increase significantly due to aging baby boomers who are turning 65 in unprecedented numbers each year. This aging population puts enormous pressures on federal Medicare programs and radically shifts the mix of payers in the healthcare industry. As the baby boomers age, they enter the phase of life where the average individual consumes the majority of medical resources a person uses in a lifetime. They also demand high quality of care.

More demand, lower prices, and higher expected outcomes and experiences require new skills in leadership and tools to permit the industry to determine added value of initiatives, interventions, and new methods. The American Hospital Association, among others, has highlighted topics and key skills for success, including physician relations, community health, critical thinking, financial and quality integration, and risk assumption. At the organizational level, boards of directors and trustees must apply knowledge and skills in healthcare delivery and performance, business and finance, and human resources. After all, success is achieved through people, and the cost of employees is the largest healthcare expenditure. To misjudge the impact and importance of these critical skills will negatively affect an organization's ability to survive during this time of accelerated transition.

HOW THIS BOOK WILL HELP

This book serves as an important tool and describes a process that will help meet these challenges. It offers a results-based methodology that focuses on how to make healthcare improvement projects successful by achieving proper alignment of organizational outcomes, delivering value following a step-by-step process, and using conservative standards in the collection and analysis of data. With these elements, projects are successful in meeting the needs of various stakeholders including the CEO, CFO, and a variety of payer networks.

THE VALUE EVOLUTION

"Show me the value." There's nothing new about the statement, especially in business. Organizations of all types want value for their investments. What's new is the method that organizations can use to get there. While "showing the money" is the ultimate report of value, organization leaders recognize that value lies in the eye of the beholder; therefore, the method used to show the money must also show the value as perceived by all stakeholders. Just as important, organizations need a methodology that provides data to help improve investment decisions. This book presents an approach that does both: it measures the value that organizations receive for investing in programs and projects, and it develops data to improve those programs.

But first, a discussion about the evolution of value—moving from activity-focused value to the ultimate value, return on investment (ROI).

THE VALUE SHIFT

"Show me the money" represents the newest value statement. In the past, program, project, or process success was measured by number of patients served, number of procedures, length of stay and money spent, activities and processes. Some consideration was given to patient outcomes, but little consideration was given to the monetary benefits derived from these activities. Today the value definition has shifted: value is defined by outcomes versus activity. More frequently, value is defined as monetary benefits compared with costs. Although the methodology to "show the money" described in this book had its beginnings in the 1970s, it has expanded in recent years to become the most broadly comprehensive approach to demonstrating the value of project investment.

Even as projects, processes, and programs are implemented to improve the social, environmental, and economic climates, the monetary value is often sought to ensure that resources are allocated appropriately and that investments reap a return. No longer is it enough to report the number of procedures performed, equipment used, technology employed, number of participants or volunteers, or the money generated through a fundraising effort. Stakeholders at all levels—including executives, shareholders, managers and supervisors, taxpayers, project designers, and participants—seek the outcomes and, in many cases, the monetary values of those outcomes.

The Importance of Monetary Values

While some people are concerned that too much focus is placed on economic value, it is economics, or money, that allows organizations and individuals to contribute to the greater good or continue to meet community health needs. Monetary resources are limited, and the goal is to put them to best use rather than under- or overusing them. Organizations, governments, and individuals have choices about where they invest these resources. To ensure that monetary resources are put to best use, they must be allocated to programs, processes, and projects that yield the greatest return.

For example, if a healthcare improvement initiative is implemented to improve efficiencies, and it does improve efficiencies, one might assume that the initiative was successful. But if the initiative costs more than the efficiency gains are worth, has value been added to the organization? Could a less-expensive process have yielded similar or even better results, possibly reaping a positive ROI? These questions and others like them are, or should be, asked on a routine basis. No longer will activity suffice as a measure of results. A new generation of decision makers is defining value in a new way.

The "Show Me" Generation

Figure 1.4 illustrates the requirements of the new "show me" generation. "Show me" implies that stakeholders want to see impact data (i.e., numbers and measures). This concept accounted for the initial attempt to see value in programs, which evolved into "show me the money," a direct call for financial results. But financial results alone do not provide the needed evidence to ensure that projects add value. Often, a connection between a healthcare project and value is assumed, but that assumption soon must give way to the need to show an actual connection. Hence, "show me the real money" was an attempt at establishing credibility. This phase, though critical, still left stakeholders with an unanswered question: "Do the monetary benefits linked to the project outweigh the costs?" This question is the mantra for the new "show me" generation: "Show me the real money, and make me believe it." This new generation of project sponsors also

FIGURE 1.4 The "Show Me" Evolution

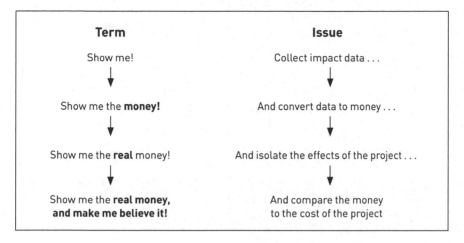

recognizes that value is more than just a single number: value is what makes the entire organizational system tick—hence the need to report value based on various definitions.

In the past, managers, directors, and administrators of many support functions in government, nonprofit, and private healthcare organizations had no business experience. Today things have changed. Many of these managers have a business background, a formal business education, or a business focus. Mike Warren, for example, the CEO of Children's Hospital in Birmingham, Alabama, had a successful career as CEO of an energy company prior to becoming involved in the healthcare industry. These new, enlightened executives are more aware of bottom-line issues in the organization and are more knowledgeable of operational and financial concerns. They often take a business approach to their processes, with ROI being a part of that strategy. Because of their background, ROI is a familiar term. They have studied the use of ROI in their academic preparation, where ROI was used to evaluate purchasing equipment, building new facilities, or buying a new company. Consequently, they understand and appreciate ROI and are eager to apply it in other areas.

EVIDENCE-BASED OR FACT-BASED MANAGEMENT

A recent important trend indicates a move to fact-based or evidence-based management. Although many key decisions are still based on instinctive input and gut feelings, more managers are now using sophisticated and detailed processes to show value. Quality decisions must be based on more than gut feelings or the blink of an eye. With a comprehensive set of measures, including financial ROI, better organizational decisions regarding people, services, projects, and processes are possible. When taken seriously, evidence-based management can change how every manager thinks and acts. It is a way of seeing the world and thinking about the craft of management. Evidence-based management proceeds from the premise that using better, deeper logic and facts to the extent possible helps leaders do their jobs better. It is based on the belief that facing the hard facts about what works and what doesn't work, and understanding and rejecting the nonsense that often passes for sound advice, will help organizations perform better.[6] This move to fact-based management makes expanding measurement to include ROI easier.

VALUE DEFINED

The changes in perspective on value and the shifts that are occurring in healthcare have led to a new definition of value. Value is not defined as a single number or single category of data, rather it's composed of a variety of different types of data, often collected within different time frames, and representing both qualitative and quantitative data.

THE VALUE EQUATION

The focus on paying for value from Medicare and other providers leads to a simplified definition for value. Experts and organizations suggest that the value equation shown in Figure 1.5 is the most accurate way to reflect value. In this equation, value is quality divided by payment. Quality is a composite of patient outcomes, safety, and experiences, while payment is the cost of healthcare from the perspective of all purchasers. It is, in essence, the way that Medicare and others define value, in that it must pay for the quality delivered. This concept applies to anyone wanting to receive value in proportion to the cost for specific purchases. For example, if the cost of a club sandwich is $35, the purchaser can certainly deduce that the value is not represented accurately by the cost. Conversely, if the club sandwich cost $5, the purchaser can probably say that its value is equal to its cost. The difficulty with this equation is in calculating the monetary value of quality.

FIGURE 1.5 The Value Equation Reconsidered for Healthcare

$$\text{Value} = \frac{\text{Quality}^1}{\text{Payment}^2}$$

1. A composite of patient outcomes, safety, and experiences
2. The cost to all purchasers of purchasing care

Source: Adapted from Healthcare Financial Management Association, "The Value in Healthcare: Current State and Future Directions" (2010).

Medicare has not defined every quality indicator that should be included. Limited definitions have included the outcome metrics that are currently employed as the ultimate indicators of quality, emphasizing either mortality or readmission rates within a certain time frame. These indicators come with a cost regardless of whether the rate is higher or lower than expected standards. This equation will evolve in terms of what providers define as the value. The challenge is to develop this numerator so that it is credible and represents the true definition of value.

Cost

When the cost of healthcare is considered, including the amount paid by the patient, the employer, or government purchases, the numbers are staggering. From the macro perspective, the primary problem with the payment is the current state of the purchasing/payment streams. The purchaser who initiates the purchase of healthcare (the patient) will often have little or no sense of the total price of the services purchased. Figure 1.6 shows the healthcare payment streams.[7] For the provider of healthcare, the services rendered must have a cost equal to or less than the payment received in order to survive. From the perspective of the healthcare provider, the costs are the fully loaded costs in all categories to deliver a certain type of service or healthcare. This figure highlights the different perspectives from which the value must be developed. For example, an ROI calculation must be based on this perspective because of the different purchasers in the stream. In a purchaser-centered value equation, the provider's cost is relevant to the

FIGURE 1.6   Defining Value: Healthcare Payment Streams

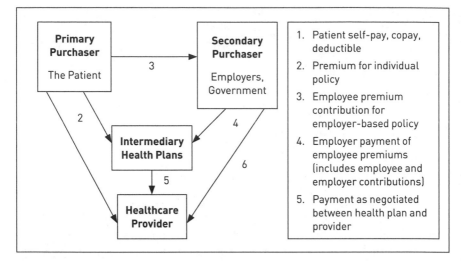

Source: Data from The Healthcare Financial Management Association, The Value in Healthcare: Current State and Future Directions (2010).

purchaser only to the extent that it drives the amount of the payment. From the provider perspective, the total costs must be absorbed. Ideally they should receive payments in excess of the cost for survival and sustainability.

At the micro level, for individual projects, the message is clear. All of the costs must be included. When a new medical procedure is established, a new IT project is implemented, or a new scheduling system for overtime is initiated, it must reap benefits that cover all of the fully loaded costs of the project, program, or initiative.

BENEFITS

Benefits can be defined in a variety of ways, such as access and availability; perception; knowledge and capability; actions, processes, and implementation; impact; and determination of financial benefit.

ACCESS AND AVAILABILITY

Access to healthcare is the first concern for patients according to the Healthcare Financial Management Association (HFMA) as depicted in

FIGURE 1.7   Defining Value: Patient Perspectives on Quality

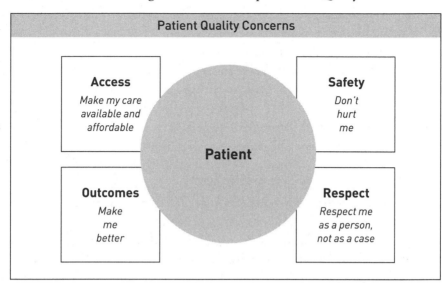

Source: Data from Healthcare Financial Management Association, "The Value in Healthcare: Current State and Future Directions" (2010).

Figure 1.7. Making healthcare both available and affordable to the individual are the baseline requirements for bringing the patient into the healthcare delivery process. According to HFMA, during the healthcare delivery process, the patient has three primary concerns with the quality of care: safety, outcomes, and respect. Essentially, access and availability of healthcare define the input to the process. They do not reflect outcomes of the healthcare delivery system.

PERCEPTION

Before outcomes can be generated in healthcare processes, those processes must receive proper reactions from those directly involved in them. When a new healthcare initiative is implemented, such as a new system, a new procedure, a new technique, or new equipment, the reaction to the process is the first set of outcome data. If the reaction is negative, then the project will likely be unsuccessful. The reactions of the various stakeholders, particularly those who are charged with making the process work, represent an important part of value. When these data are collected and adjustments are made, it can make a world of difference in the success of a project.

KNOWLEDGE AND CAPABILITY

To improve processes in an organization, the individuals involved must know how to make it work and have the capability to carry through with the processes to achieve results. This value stream is largely ignored with most projects and programs. Value in terms of knowledge and capability determines the extent to which those involved actually have the ability and the appropriate skills to deliver what the project intends. Knowledge and capability represent value from the perspective of those who organize the project and for those who are actually involved in it.

ACTIONS, PROCESSES, AND IMPLEMENTATION

Actions, processes, and implementation needed to make a project work are the greatest areas of measurement and together form an important category of value. They consist of the specific activities and actions that individuals undertake to deliver efficient, effective healthcare. As a new procedure is implemented, this category of value indicators measures the degree to which the users are using the procedure properly. As a new procedure is implemented, these measures determine the extent to which the procedure is being followed. As a new scheduling system is implemented, these measures gauge the extent to which the system is being utilized. These important value streams indicate whether things are working properly and moving in the right direction, and whether participants are doing what they are supposed to be doing.

IMPACT

Perhaps the most powerful and significant value category is the impact of the healthcare initiative. Most of these measures focus directly on patient outcomes and cover the three measures of quality care shown in Figure 1.7: outcomes, safety, and respect. In fact, this category can be subdivided as tangible and intangible data. The tangibles are those measures that can be easily and credibly converted to money and the end results will enter into the financial calculation. Tangibles are the healthcare outcomes in which patients improve faster and with better results, as well as outcomes of minimizing, reducing, or eliminating incidents or accidents that could derail the process or have an adverse effect on patients. Intangibles are those outcomes that are more challenging to convert to money, but are important just the same. They include measures such as patient satisfaction, nurse engagement, teamwork, employee satisfaction, and physician engagement. They may also consist of measures such as reputation, image, stress, brand awareness, and other softer processes.

DETERMINATION OF FINANCIAL BENEFIT

The ultimate measure of accountability is the financial ROI, which is the measure of the costs versus the benefits. Financial ROI can be described in two different ways. One is the benefit/cost ratio and the other is the ROI expressed as a percent. The benefit/cost ratio is the benefits divided by the costs, and the ROI is the net benefits (benefits minus the costs) divided by the costs, times 100. These are accepted measures in the financial community and can be applied to any healthcare project.

CRITERIA

When these values are developed in healthcare organizations, they must meet certain criteria. First, they should be balanced; no project should be evaluated with only a single measure such as ROI. The balanced set of data, representing a variety of different qualitative and quantitative measures, both financial and nonfinancial should be used. A balanced profile is consistent with the use of ROI in finance and accounting. In fact, more than 200 years ago, the original developers of ROI suggested that an ROI calculation for capital expenditure is an imprecise measure and it should not be used alone to make a decision. Other types of measures must be examined, especially in today's healthcare organizations.

The value presented must be credible for those who respect and need it. These individuals must see the value as coming from people or processes that are accurate, conservative, and reliable. Also, it must be efficient in terms of its collection and use. If the process is inefficient or takes too much effort, it will not be used.

The data in these different categories must represent both tactical and strategic issues. Tactical data provide the bases for making changes and improvements along the way. Strategic measures show how projects or programs are linked to strategy and important outcomes. Finally, the data and the calculation must represent different perspectives. In healthcare delivery, the many perspectives include not only the variety of individuals who pay for the program, but others who are involved in various other aspects as

TABLE 1.1 Value Defined

Value is defined as:
- access and availability
- perceptions
- knowledge and capability
- actions, processes, and implementation
- impact, tangible and intangible
- financial benefit

When value is developed, it must be:
- balanced
- credible
- efficient
- tactical and strategic
- representative of different perspectives

---

well. Table 1.1 shows the definition of and the criteria for developing measures of value.

MODELS

When the different categories of value are considered, they must be linked in some way. Dozens of models have been developed to show connection between different types of data. Michael Porter, in his classic work, *Redefining Healthcare*, developed the model shown in Figure 1.8. In this model, Porter indicates the initial condition of patients that leads to processes, which lead to indicators and, in turn, to health outcomes.

This model is important because it shows the chain of impact that occurs through the process. The indicators are the actual measures that define the outcomes. The inputs and access are assumed for this particular model. Porter's model can be refined to insert two other important data sets, perceptions (reaction) and learning (knowledge and capability). As mentioned earlier, these issues can make a difference in the success or failure of the project's outcome. In other words, an adverse reaction, or failure to develop capability to make the project successful, will mean the project does not deliver appropriate value. When measured and used to make improvements, these issues can enhance the success of a project.

FIGURE 1.8 Measuring Value in Healthcare

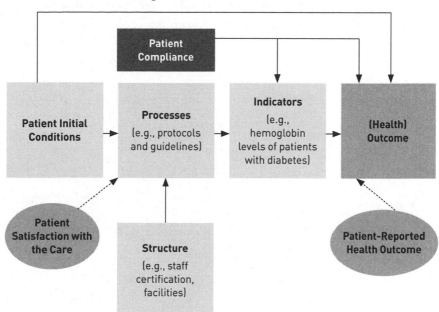

Source: Data from Michael E. Porter, "What Is Value in Healthcare?" *The New England Journal of Medicine* 363 (2010): 2477–480.

When these adjustments are made, the chain of impact is refined to reflect the model shown in Figure 1.9. In this model, two categories of input data and five types of outcome data are represented. This shows the chain of impact that must exist as patients have access to the system. Services are provided at a reasonable cost, and a positive reaction is developed along the way. Individuals who are delivering the service develop the capability to make it work, and the project is implemented properly. When the impact has occurred, it results in a variety of patient and organizational outcomes. Finally, the ROI can be developed, which is the ultimate level of accountability.

This enhanced model of Porter's chain of impact is the basis for the ROI process model presented in this book. It is a modification of the classic logic model applied in many government, science, education, and healthcare systems. In this case, the outcomes on the logic model are enhanced to show five different outcome categories, whereas most of the logic model presentations show immediate outcomes, intermediate outcomes, and impact.

FIGURE 1.9 Defining Value as a Chain of Impact

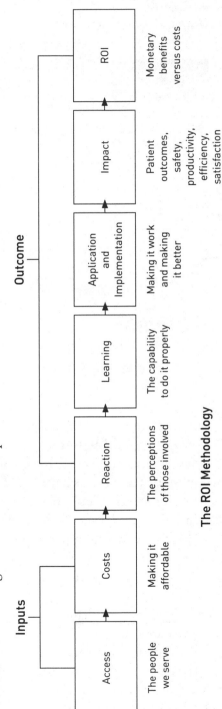

The ROI Methodology

CHALLENGES ALONG THE WAY

The journey to increased accountability and the quest to show monetary value, including ROI, are not going unchallenged. This movement represents a tremendous cultural shift for employees, a systemic change in processes, and often a complete rethinking of the initiation, delivery, and maintenance of improvement processes in organizations.

COMMITMENT

Commitment is the key to successful implementation of ROI. Many hope to obtain an immediate ROI using the ROI Methodology, but it is, as previously mentioned, more than a simple calculation. To achieve success, commitment to making changes when the data reveal that the change needed is imperative, as is commitment to using the information the process provides. Executives in the healthcare field often know what they should be doing to improve outcomes and show the value of programs, but accepting accountability to move through the process is a challenge for them.

PREPARATION AND SKILLS

Although interest in showing value and measuring ROI is now heightened and much progress has been made, these issues still challenge even the most sophisticated and progressive functions. The problem often lies in the lack of preparation and skills necessary to conduct these types of analyses. Rarely do the curricula in degree programs or the courses in a professional development program include processes and techniques to show accountability at this level. Consequently, these skills must be developed by the organization, using a variety of resources, so that they are in place for successful implementation.

FEAR OF ROI

Few topics stir up emotions to the degree that ROI does. For a few narrowly focused executives, the conclusion behind the ROI value is simple: if it is negative, they kill the program; if it is an extremely positive value, they do not believe it. The potential for this response from executives causes some healthcare professionals to avoid the issue altogether. A familiar reaction emerges: "If my project or program is not delivering value, the last thing I want to do is publish a report for my principal sponsor." Unfortunately, if the project is not delivering value, the sponsor probably already knows it, or at least someone in the organization does. The best thing to do is to show the value using a systematic, credible process, in advance of a request.

Another fear is of abuse of the data. Will the data be used to punish some people, reward others, or improve processes? Ideally, results should be used to improve processes. The challenge is to ensure that data are not misused or abused. The fear of ROI can be minimized when the individuals involved understand the ROI Methodology, how it is designed and delivered, and the value that it can bring from a positive perspective.

TIME FOR ANALYSIS

Thorough analysis takes time. Many practitioners and some sponsors are restless and do not want to take the time to do the appropriate analyses. In a fast-paced work environment where decisions are often made quickly and with little input or data, some executives question the time and the effort involved in this type of analysis. What must be shown, however, is that this effort is necessary and appropriate, and will ultimately payoff. When the process is implemented, the individuals involved usually see that the value of the increased effort and activity far outweighs the cost of the time.

POWER AND POLITICS

Having appropriate data represents power to many individuals. How that power is used is important. If used for constructive purposes or to improve processes, data are perceived as valuable. If data are used for destructive or political purposes, they may be seen as less valuable. The important issue is that if the information is based on credible facts, then it generates power. If it is based on opinions or gut feelings, then the person who provides those opinions is more influential than the opinions themselves. Essentially, facts create a level playing field for decision making. As one executive said, "If a decision is based on facts, then anyone's facts are equal as long as they are relevant; however, if it must be based on opinions, then my opinion counts a lot more." This underscores the power of having credible data for making decisions.

Sustainability

The final challenge is sustaining such a radical shift in accountability. The implementation of the ROI Methodology must consist of more than just conducting one or two studies to show the value of healthcare projects or programs. It must represent a complete change in processes so that future projects and programs focus on results. This change will require building capability, developing consistent and compelling communication, involving stakeholders, building the process into projects, creating expectations, and using data for process improvements. This approach is the only way to sustain any change for the long term; otherwise, it becomes a one-shot or short-term project opportunity.

SO MANY TOOLS, NOT ENOUGH TIME

The healthcare field has enjoyed the application and use of many tools to monitor costs, control quality, and understand the financial aspects of the organization. Here is a brief review of some of the important tools that have entered this field.

Measurements and Monitoring

Perhaps no other industry has enjoyed measurement processes as much as healthcare. Almost every facet of healthcare is monitored, documented, recorded, and ultimately reported. This scrutiny starts with the patient record, which includes full recording of a patient's condition and concludes with documentation for billing to demonstrate effective delivery of care. A measurement culture generates a tremendous database of all types of data, including patient satisfaction, patient medical histories, supplies, procedures, billing, financial, outcomes, risks, and other data. Tables 1.2 and 1.3 illustrate the vast amount of data that is recorded and made available. Table 1.2 represents measures categorized as hard

TABLE 1.2   Examples of Hard Data in Healthcare Organizations

Output	Costs
Inpatient revenue	Operating expense
Outpatient revenue	Treatment costs
Bed occupancy	Expense per discharge
Capacity	Budget variances
Clinician productivity	Unit costs
New patients	Cost by account
Forms processed	Variable costs
Discharges	Fixed costs
Screenings	Overhead cost
Inventory turnover	Operating costs
Patients served	Accident costs
ER visits	Program costs
Inpatient surgeries	Marketing expense
Tasks completed	Bad debts
Output per hour	Cost per case
Productivity	Supply chain savings
Reimbursements	
Work backlog	**Time**
Births	Length of stay
Project completions	Cycle time
	Equipment downtime
Quality	Overtime
Payment denials	On-time schedules
Nurse turnover	Time to project completion
Risk-adjusted mortality	Processing time
Risk-adjusted complications	Time to proficiency
Unplanned readmission rate	Assessment time
Medication event rate	Time to bill
Unscheduled returns	Response rate
Nosocomial infections	Patient wait times
Bloodstream infections	Efficiency
Error rates	Work stoppages
Accidents	Order response
Rework	Chart time
Shortages	Late reporting
Deviation from standard	Lost-time days
Inventory adjustments	
Incidents	
Compliance discrepancies	
Agency fines	

data. Table 1.3 represents data categorized as soft data. For the most part, these data sets are impacts—consequences of particular actions and activities. For this reason, lack of data is not necessarily an issue in the healthcare field.

TABLE 1.3   Examples of Soft Data in Healthcare Organizations

Work Climate/Satisfaction	**Customer Service**
Grievances	Patient complaints
Discrimination charges	Patient satisfaction
Employee complaints	Market share
Employee satisfaction	Patient loyalty
Physician satisfaction	Patient retention
Organization commitment	
Employee engagement	**Employee Development/Advancement**
Nurse engagement	Promotions
Physician engagement	Capability
Employee loyalty	Intellectual capital
Intent to leave	Requests for transfer
Stress	Performance appraisal ratings
	Readiness
Initiative/Innovation	Networking
Creativity	
Innovation	**Image**
New ideas	Brand awareness
Suggestions	Reputation
New products and services	Leadership
Trademarks	Social responsibility
Copyrights and patents	Environmental friendliness
Process improvements	Social consciousness
Partnerships/alliances	Diversity
	External awards
	Community awareness

BALANCED SCORECARD

The Balanced Scorecard was created by Kaplan and Norton.[8] This measurement system shows managers how to use data to mobilize people to fulfill an organizational mission. The balanced scorecard was championed as a management system that can channel the energies, abilities, and specific knowledge held by people throughout the organization into achieving long-term strategic goals. The measurement system divides data into four categories: financial performance, customer knowledge, internal business processes, and learning and growth. These four categories were designed to align individual, organizational, and cross-departmental initiatives and to identify entirely new processes for meeting customer and shareholder objectives. Table 1.4 shows the typical scorecard for a hospital.

A concern about the balanced scorecard is that it was created initially for banking, oil, insurance, and retail companies, although it has since

TABLE 1.4   Typical Balanced Scorecard for a Hospital

Organizational Health
- Turnover rate as a percentage of the national average
- Vacancy rate as a percentage of the national average
- Physician satisfaction percentile
- Med/surg 1:6 nursing ratio maintained

Quality and Process Improvements
- Patient satisfaction percentile—inpatient
- Patient satisfaction percentile—emergency department patients
- Nosocomial pressure ulcers
- Emergency department treat and release patients <120 minutes
- Emergency department patients admitted <4 hours
- Percentage of physician orders entered electronically

Volume and Market Share Growth
- Volume
- Market share

Financial Health
- Operating margin

worked its way into healthcare. Healthcare has modified the balanced scorecard under the concept of strategic pillars; however, the scorecard lacks precise measurement or alignment to business needs. Its typical use has been to track the measures that matter in these four categories, but sometimes without the efforts to improve the measures. Tracking the measures alone provides little value because unless effort is made to improve the measures, the needed changes in healthcare will not happen. The most important value comes from these efforts to improve the measures or to continue measures that are already exceptional. Although Kaplan and Norton focus much of their attention on performance improvement, organizations did not necessarily follow through in these efforts.

Costing Models

Because of the significant cost of healthcare, much focus goes into capturing, monitoring, controlling, and properly allocating cost. A variety of

FIGURE 1.10 Current State: Business Intelligence Differences in Costing Methods

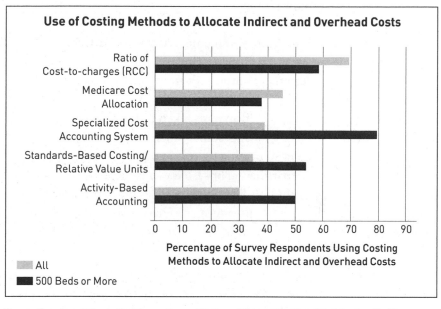

Use of Costing Methods to Allocate Indirect and Overhead Costs

Percentage of Survey Respondents Using Costing Methods to Allocate Indirect and Overhead Costs

All

500 Beds or More

Source: Data from *Value in Healthcare: Current State and Future Directions* (Westchester: Healthcare Financial Management Association, June 2011). Accessed from www.hfma.org, January 19, 2012.

costing processes such as activity-based costing have been implemented. Activity-based costing provides a more accurate assignment of both direct and indirect costs of hospital procedures and services. Figure 1.10 shows the current state of business intelligence differences in costing models, based on a survey conducted by the Healthcare Financial Management Association (HFMA). In this example, 69 percent of respondents report using the ratio of cost to charges (RCC); in contrast, only 30 percent report using activity-based costing. The difference narrows for larger facilities, where almost 50 percent are using activity-based costing.[9]

Process Improvement

All types of organizations have been bombarded with process improvement techniques, tools, and approaches. Sometimes labeled *reengineering, process improvement, reinventing, transformation*, or simply *performance improvement*, a proliferation of tools have been developed, all aimed at making projects, departments, functions, and organizations better. Most of the tools use a systematic process to analyze needs, recommend solutions, and implement those solutions to achieve results. These techniques have shown tremendous promise if they are managed properly, supported sufficiently, and adjusted regularly.

These projects are sometimes implemented on a departmental, cross-department, or system-wide basis, depending on the situation. Still others have used them to redesign care processes from end-to-end. Figure 1.11 shows the status of performance improvement in healthcare organizations.

As the figure shows, most efforts are taken at the departmental level with more than 90 percent having some experience with departmental studies. Slightly fewer than 90 percent report significant or some experience in implementing cross-departmental or system-wide initiatives. Experience levels drop off significantly, however, for care redesign that moves beyond facilities' walls to the cross-continuum initiative. Although healthcare extensively measures activity, defining the right things to measure has yet

FIGURE 1.11 Current State of Performance Improvement

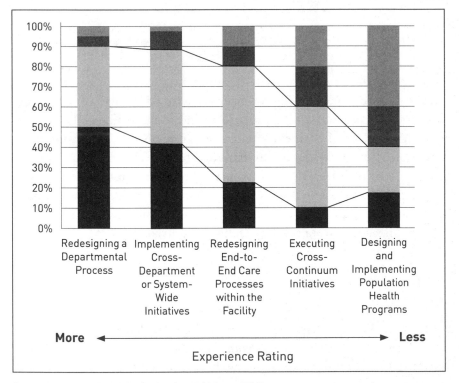

Source: Data from HFMA Value Project Survey (January 2011).

to be accomplished. Few facilities are working with designing and implementing population health programs.

VARIATION IN HEALTHCARE

The variation in healthcare is ironic considering that it is set in an industry driven by a scientific process that exists to discover and identify issues concerning the human body and to create solutions for or treat the identified pathology that causes the issues. This paradox is driven by the scientists themselves and the variation that exists with each human body. The scientists (physicians) gather volumes of data about the human body that is driven by a unique combination of DNA for each person. These data for all individuals, whether outcome measures or from prior observation, do not reside in a single database; therefore, discovery or recall is dependent upon the expertise or knowledge of each individual physician. It is literally impossible for physicians to individually retain such a database. The physicians themselves are subject to human error due to fatigue, distraction, or other factors. Variation is even further complicated when one considers that no standard approaches or methods exist to guide the discovery and treatment processes.

A second major cause of variation occurs with the human subjects themselves. Humans, by their very nature, communicate differently due to individual motivation. Therefore, the subjects themselves do not always disclose full information, or comply with directives provided, due to their own self-interest. They will often seek input from others for treatment and not disclose any of this to the physician.

On a third level, the environment itself is fragmented with each department, treatment unit, hospital, or care setting using unique and differing systems, processes, equipment, or technology, all causing variation. Comparisons of outcomes from unit to unit are difficult to say the least. As a result, healthcare is a target-rich environment for improvement with as much as 30 percent of all expenditures viewed as waste, redundant, or even unnecessary or inappropriate.

QUALITY AND WASTE

Because of concerns about quality, particularly patient care quality, an abundance of quality processes have entered the healthcare area. These processes have been implemented under the names of continuous quality improvement, total quality management, patient quality, Six Sigma, and even Lean Six Sigma. These processes focus on quality and often begin with calculating the cost of mistakes, errors, and waste. The processes are aimed at improving quality and minimizing waste.

In healthcare environments, waste exists in abundance. Waste in supplies, waste in excess procedures, waste in inappropriate procedures, waste due to redundancies by physicians and other providers who are unable to tap databases of patient information concerning prior procedures, treatments, and outcomes are all areas of excessive waste. It is common for each physician to have his or her own workup of a patient in related treatments that are not available to other physicians unless they practice together and/or have a common electronic medical record.

Outcomes due to poor and virtually nonexistent information systems can cause readmissions due to uncoordinated and unplanned care or even noncompliance by the patient. Wrong-site surgery, medication errors, and other "never" events concerning patient care occur, again, from a lack of common practice, procedures, and processes.

Costs of healthcare and medical errors, along with consumer expectations and expectations of large purchasers of healthcare like employers and the government, all demand that the system change. The "system" must change to reduce costs. It must change to deliver error-free outcomes and produce a reliable result. It must change to improve overall services and add value to the patient experience.

Too Many Tools, Too Much Information: What's a Leader to Do?

The tools available within the healthcare setting are vast. Performance improvement tools such as techniques used in Lean or Six Sigma efforts abound. Scientific methods and metric-driven scorecards all produce information overload with insufficient intelligence to take action. The time required to use these tools, each time, is overwhelming. Even in business planning processes, tools such as computing internal rate of return or the capital asset pricing model used for capital allocation are helpful, but lack quantifiable information of "true value." Assumptions, incremental/differential accounting, and anecdotal information are compiled to influence decisions. Little from these data determines actual value, rather most of this information is directional in nature. Applying clinical process improvement to operation processes is meaningful for best practice development and dissemination as described in Figure 1.12, but it has limitations. We may know things get better or worse, but we do not always know whether process improvement initiatives "make a difference" that actually matters to the decision makers and others.

FIGURE 1.12   Applying Clinical Process Improvement to Operational Process Improvement

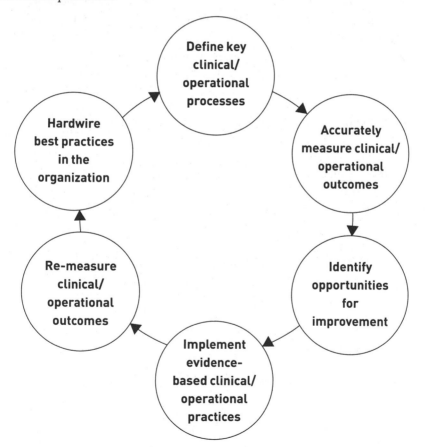

Source: Adapted from American Hospital Association Committee on Performance Improvement, Jeanette Clough, Chairperson. *Hospitals and Care Systems of the Future* (Chicago: American Hospital Association, September 2011).

Enter ROI

The ROI Methodology provides a standard approach through which data are collected and analyzed following a set of principles that ensure reliable information. This information represents actionable intelligence. Actionable intelligence provides the decision-making information to determine whether and how value is created from the action. Using this process provides healthcare executives intelligence to prioritize their focus on the highest value efforts to achieve the aspirations of the "triple aim" required to survive the next decade.

Determining the ROI of projects and programs permits decision makers to deal with four forces shaping future margins. Figure 1.13 provides descriptions of these forces as provided by the Healthcare Advisory Board. Payoff from using ROI will come from investments in new models of care. These models will use new skill sets in financial and health delivery integration to create value for the system and not suboptimize for the components.

ISSUES WITH HEALTHCARE IMPROVEMENT INITIATIVES

As mentioned earlier, a wealth of healthcare improvement processes have been aimed at making healthcare organizations more productive, efficient, and quality-focused. These processes are often initiated by interdepartmental or cross-functional projects.

Unfortunately, too many healthcare projects and initiatives fail. They fail for a variety of reasons. Understanding those reasons helps us to have success with our own projects. The methodology introduced in this book is a way to measure the success of improvement projects throughout the healthcare life cycle. When things are not working as well as they should, data are available to make necessary adjustments. When they are working well, data are available to explain why. The ROI Methodology focuses on results of the project, ensuring that the project delivers the appropriate value for the client. This approach helps ensure that projects will not fail in the future. But what causes failure? Here are a few reasons.

Lack of Business Alignment

Unfortunately, too many projects are "fuzzy" when it comes to their alignment with specific business measures. This fuzziness seems odd when

FIGURE 1.13   Four Forces Shaping Future Margins

Dramatic Shifts Within Financial and Clinical Profiles:	
Decelerating Price Growth • Federal and state budget pressures constraining public payer price growth • Payments subject to quality, cost-based risks • Commercial cost shifting stretched to the limit	**Continuing Cost Pressure** • No sign of slower cost growth ahead • Drivers of new cost growth largely nonaccretive
Shifting Payer Mix • Baby boomers entering Medicare rolls • Coverage expansion boosting Medicaid eligibility • Most demand growth over the next decade comes from publicly insured patients	**Deteriorating Case Mix** • Medical demand from aging population threatening to crowd out profitable procedures • Incidence of chronic disease, multiple comorbidities rising

Source: Adapted from Healthcare Advisory Board interviews and analysis.

one considers that most projects start with a business need (e.g., improve patient outcomes). Even still, the alignment between the business need and the project is often vague. Examples of projects might be the implementation of a leadership development program, a medical conference, a new system for automating physician records, a new hospital department, or a wellness and fitness program for the staff. The specific business measures these projects target may be unclear. Without a clear connection to the business, their success in terms of driving business value may be limited or nonexistent. Therefore, one of the first steps to improving key outcomes is to ensure that the project is connected to those outcomes, driving specific business measures. For example, in many healthcare organizations today, acquisition of physician practices is important because the physicians are hospital admitters. However, acquisitions of practices that do not align with business needs make little sense and have no ROI. If a hospital acquires an obstetrics group when the labor and delivery unit is already full and cannot

FIGURE 1.14 Lack of Alignment

Measurement and Use of Business Intelligence			
To what extent does your organization measure and use business intelligence related to value in the following areas?			
	None	Measure	Manage
Costs of Adverse Events	43%	37%	20%
Margin Impact of Readmissions	38%	42%	20%
Cost of Waste in Care Processes	50%	29%	21%

None: We do not measure.
Measure: We have measured the impact, but do not manage the metrics.
Manage: We manage to these measures (e.g., data drives actions to reduce costs or improve margin).

Source: Data from HFMA Value Project Survey (January 2011).

assume any more volume, that acquisition would be a decision that is not aligned to the business.

Unfortunately, all too many healthcare organizations are not taking steps to identify the needs of their business and act accordingly. Figure 1.14 demonstrates this fact. Results of the HFMA survey show that 43 percent do not measure the cost of adverse events, and 37 percent measure it but do not act on it. Only 20 percent of respondents calculate the cost of adverse events and act on them. Likewise, only 20 percent are measuring and acting on the calculations involving the margin impact of readmissions. Fifty percent are not calculating the cost of waste in care processes, and only 21 percent are calculating the cost and using the data. These data indicate a lack of business alignment in healthcare organizations, due in part to failure to gather and use the intelligence necessary to identify the real business needs.[10]

INAPPROPRIATE SOLUTION TO A PROBLEM

Some improvement projects are designed to implement a particular solution to a problem. It may involve an existing solution, the purchase of new software, the implementation of a new quality system, or the installation of a workforce management system. These prepackaged solutions may not always be appropriate to address the problem (i.e., the solution itself will not drive the business measures that must change). For example, many healthcare organizations implement solutions to reduce premium pay and outside labor. However, by doing so, sometimes they slow down throughput of patients and increase length of stay. It may be an improper solution because when length of stay is increased, more errors are introduced, patient satisfaction is reduced, and costs are increased.

PARTICIPANTS ARE NOT ENGAGED

To be successful, participants in programs and projects must be fully engaged. The participants are the individuals who must make the project work. They must clearly understand the need and rationale for the project. Lack of explanation or lack of persuasion can create an adverse reaction to the project in the early stages, dooming it to failure. Expectations must be clearly outlined so that the engagement occurs early. At each stage of the process, participants are involved, their inputs are respected, and they are held accountable for results. In many circumstances, healthcare is so complex, with so many concurrent activities, that having someone's full attention and active engagement is a challenge. The lack of a clear agenda causes healthcare professionals to struggle with engagement. For example, in the midst of community disaster, a large part of the organization will focus on the task at hand, but doctors and nurses in specific disciplines must stay focused on their daily work (OB doctors will still have babies to deliver so their attention is diverted and routine or scheduled surgeries must still be performed).

Figure 1.15 shows the extent of engagement in organizations, taken from the HFMA survey. Only 26 percent of the responding organizations actively engage the physician in decision making with regard to department budget and resource allocation. If the same level of engagement exists with healthcare improvement projects, it is no wonder so many projects fall short.

LACK OF FOCUS ON BUSINESS RESULTS

Participants sometimes lack a clear vision of the ultimate objective for a project. The reason for their involvement in the project is unclear. Business measures and their targets for improvement should be translated into impact objectives. Process and action steps should be reflected in application objectives. Communicating these objectives to all stakeholders

FIGURE 1.15 Engaging Physician Leaders in Department Budgeting/ Resource Allocation Processes

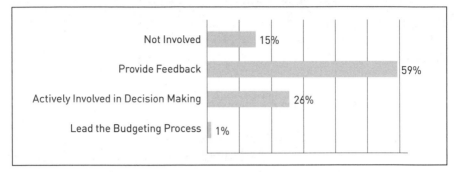

Source: Data from HFMA Value Project Survey (January 2011).

provides focus throughout the project, ensuring that business alignment exists. Routinely monitoring the success with these objectives provides information useful in making adjustments—better positioning the project for success.

FAILURE TO PREPARE THE ENVIRONMENT FOR THE PROJECT

Projects are usually implemented in the work environment. Implementation often involves change, and change must be accepted and supported in that work unit. An important part of a project is to understand the environment in which it is implemented. Any impediments to the success of the project or barriers to implementation must be addressed early and often. Ideally, part of project planning will be the identification of inhibiting factors to the success of the project and tackling those issues before they become barriers to success.

LACK OF ACCOUNTABILITY WITHIN THE PROJECT

Too often, project participants and other stakeholders do not feel that success is their responsibility. If no one accepts responsibility, then no one is accountable, and the project will fail as a consequence. Ideally, every person involved must understand his or her responsibility, clearly defined with expectations and specific objectives at different levels. It should be apparent to the healthcare project manager and other stakeholders that the participants are meeting the objectives, standards, and expectations. Without that commitment, the project can easily drift and ultimately fail.

One of the problems with accountability is that pay is not tied to many of these projects. When executives receive bonuses or incentives or their overall pay is connected to the performance of these projects and processes they may take more responsibility for results. Although a trend of linking pay to performance is growing, it is not yet common. In the last few years, hospitals have connected executive pay to patient satisfaction, clinical outcomes, employee satisfaction, or physician satisfaction. Still, not enough organizations use this connection.[11]

FAILURE TO ISOLATE THE EFFECTS OF THE PROJECT

Often, factors apart from the healthcare project end up influencing the impact measures linked to the project. External factors can also influence success of the impact measures linked to the project. An important challenge is to sort out what has caused the results, isolating the success to individual factors. This step provides the sponsors, who fund the project, a clear understanding of how well the project contributed to improvement in key measures. The good news is that this step can be achieved credibly in any project setting. The disappointing news is that it frequently is not addressed appropriately in most projects, leaving the success of the project in doubt.

LACK OF INVOLVEMENT WITH KEY MANAGERS

Other managers, outside the project team, also support the project and make it successful. Sometimes they are the managers of the participants involved in the project. At other times, they are the managers of the support team for the project. In either case, their support and reinforcement are essential for the project's success. These managers must be identified early and steps must be taken to ensure that they live up to their roles and responsibilities, providing the proper reinforcement and support needed to make the project successful. Without their support, the project could fail.

Perhaps no executive is more important than the chief financial officer. The HFMA study shows that most of a CFO's time is spent on volume, revenue growth, cost reduction, and efficiency (60%), leaving 40 percent for clinical outcomes, quality improvement, and patient satisfaction. Experts suggest that these figures should be reversed, with perhaps a vast majority of effort focused on clinical outcomes and patient satisfaction. The involvement of this key manager in projects targeting clinical outcomes and patient satisfaction, as well as others, can position any project for success.

FAILURE TO TAKE THE PROJECT TO MONEY

Top executives sometimes fixate on the monetary value of measures. They want to see the value of contribution in terms of revenue, costs, or costs avoided. They need to see money because money can clarify the extent of the problem. Monetary values normalize measures, so they are weighted in a manner less subjective than when left as intangibles. Figure 1.16 shows data from the HFMA study that indicate most survey respondents see only some or limited connection between quality improvement and cost. Only 22 percent see this connection clearly. More process improvement projects need to clearly show the connection between working on quality, waste, and patient outcomes, and their relative costs. Such clarification requires that measures of quality, waste, and patient outcomes be converted to money so that the opportunities for improvement are evident.

THE CHAIN OF IMPACT FOR HEALTHCARE PROJECTS

Sometimes it is helpful to think about the success of a healthcare project in terms of a chain of impact (or chain of value) that must occur if the project is successful in terms of business contribution. After all, without a business contribution, it is unlikely the project will be implemented. The chain of impact includes the five categories of outcomes discussed in general terms previously. These categories, also referred to as levels are: Reaction (Level 1), Learning (Level 2), Application and Implementation

FIGURE 1.16   Making the Quality/Cost Connection

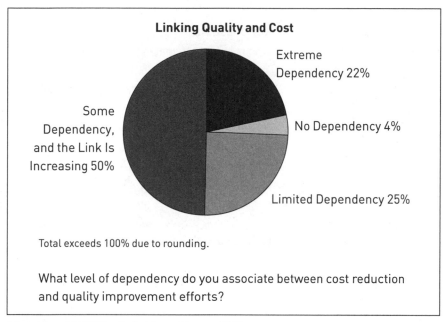

Total exceeds 100% due to rounding.

What level of dependency do you associate between cost reduction and quality improvement efforts?

Adapted from: HFMA Value Project Survey (January 2011).

(Level 3), Impact (Level 4), and ROI (Level 5). Together, these five levels form a chain of impact that occurs as projects are implemented. Figure 1.17 illustrates this chain of impact that occurs through the implementation of healthcare projects and key questions asked at each level.

This chain of impact begins with the inputs to the process. Inputs, referred to as Level 0, define the people involved in the project, how long it will take it to work, the cost, resources, and efficiencies. Obviously, these data are essential to move forward with a project, but they do not represent the success of the project. It is through reaction, learning, and application of knowledge, skill, and information that a positive impact on business measures will result.

Reaction is the first level of outcomes. Participants involved in the project must see the value in it. They must perceive the project is important, necessary, useful, and practical. If the reaction is adverse, the project will not likely deliver business value.

FIGURE 1.17 The Chain of Impact for Healthcare Projects

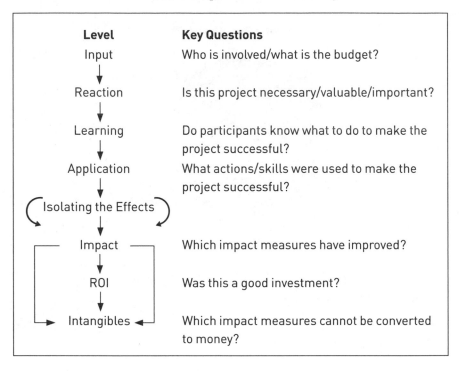

Next is Learning (Level 2). With any project, learning must occur for the project to be successful. Acquisition of knowledge, skill, or information is necessary when implementing most new technology, systems, procedures, processes, and regulations. Participants must understand the issue itself, they must know what they need to do and what is involved in the project, and they must be aware of the project's potential success.

Level 3 is Application and Implementation, which represents action on the part of the participants involved in the project. They must change their habits, take action, use new technology, or change procedures. This activity (i.e., tasks, action, behavior) is essential for the project to be successful. Unfortunately, it is at this level that projects usually fail. Participants often do not do what they need to do to make the project successful. The many barriers to success with application must be identified and either removed, minimized, or circumvented. In addition to barriers, enablers exist to support successful application. These also must be identified and then enhanced to allow participants to fully engage in projects and have success with them.

Level 4 is Impact. What participants know and what they do with what they know lead to a consequence, or impact, on key measures. When participants are involved in healthcare improvement projects, they want to know why they should participate. What will be the impact? Will a cost savings result? Will waste be reduced? What improvement can be realized? How will it help patient care? As project implementation succeeds, changes should occur in productivity, efficiencies, healthcare quality, process times, and cost reduction or avoidance. In addition, long-term impacts, such as patient satisfaction, job engagement, and job satisfaction, should improve. These impact measures, which are available in organizational record systems, represent the most important data set for top executives, leaders, and administrators. It is at this level that a step is always taken to isolate the effects of the project from other influences.

Finally, Level 5, ROI, the ultimate evaluation, is a comparison of the costs versus benefits. If the monetary benefits exceed the costs of the project it is perceived as a good investment, economically. Positive economic returns are critical to the continuation of many projects.

Another data set (not level) that is critical in this chain of impact is the intangibles. Even though they are not a new level of outcome measures, intangibles are the impact measures that cannot be converted to money credibly with minimum resources. They are important and often provide the rationale for many of the early projects an organization selects. Image, reputation, and brand are powerful measures, even without the monetary value tied to them.

PROBLEMS WITH CURRENT MEASUREMENT SYSTEMS IN HEALTHCARE—AND HOW TO IMPROVE THEM

For the most part, the current systems of measuring and evaluating healthcare projects fall short of providing the proper system for accountability, process improvement, and results generation. As we examine the ways in which projects are evaluated, ten areas for improvement surface. Table 1.5 lists each problem or issue and presents what is needed for improvement. It also shows how the ROI Methodology presented in this book addresses all ten of these areas.

TABLE 1.5 Problems and Opportunities with Current Measurement Systems

Topic	Problem or Issue	What Is Needed	ROI Methodology
Focus of use	Audit focus; punitive slant; surprise nature	Process improvement focus	The number one use for the ROI Methodology
Standards	Few, if any, standards exist	Standards needed for consistency and credibility	Twelve standards accepted by users
Types of data	Only one or two data types	Need a balanced set of data	Six types of data representing quantitative, qualitative, financial, and nonfinancial data
Dynamic adjustments	Not dynamic; does not allow for adjustments early in the project cycle	A dynamic process with adjustments made early and often	Adjusts for improvement at four levels and at different time frames
Connectivity	Not respectful of the chain of impact that must exist to achieve a positive impact	Data collected at each stage of the chain	Every stage has data collection and a method to isolate the project's contribution
Approach	Activity based	Results based	Twelve areas for results-based processes
Conservative nature	Analysis not very conservative	A conservative approach is needed for buy in	Very conservative: CFO and CEO friendly
Simplicity	Not user friendly; too complex	User friendly, simple steps	Ten logical steps
Theoretical foundation	Not based on sound principles	Should be based on theoretical framework	Endorsed by hundreds of professors and researchers; grounded in research and practice
Acceptance	Not adopted by many organizations	Should be used by many	More than 5,000 organizations using the ROI Methodology

FOCUS OF USE

Sometimes evaluation looks like auditing. Usually during a surprise visit, someone checks to see whether the project is working as planned, and a report is generated (usually too late) to indicate that a problem exists.

Evaluation of many capital expenditures, for example, is often implemented this way. The project is approved by the board, and after it is completed, a board-mandated follow-up report is produced by internal auditors and presented to the board. This report points out how things are working and/or not working, often at a point that is too late to make any changes. Even in government, social sciences, and education, the evaluations are often structured in a similar way. For example, our friends in the British government tell us that when new projects are approved and implemented, funds are set aside for evaluation. When the project is completed, an evaluation is conducted and a detailed report is sent to appropriate government authorities. Unfortunately, these reports reveal that many of the programs are not working, and it is too late to do anything about them. Even worse, the people who implemented the project are either no longer there or no longer care. When accountability issues are involved, the evaluation reports usually serve as punitive information to blame the usual suspects or serve as the basis for performance review of those involved.

It is not surprising that auditing with a punitive twist does not work with healthcare projects. These project evaluations must be approached with a sense of process improvement—not performance evaluation. If the project is not working, then changes must take place for it to be successful in the future.

Standards

Unfortunately, many of the approaches to evaluate healthcare projects lack standards unless the project is a capital expenditure, in which case the evaluation process is covered by Generally Accepted Accounting Principles (GAAP). However, most healthcare projects are not capital expenditures. In these instances, standards must be employed to ensure consistent application and reliable results. Overall, the standards should provide consistency, conservatism, and cost savings as the project is implemented. Use of standards allows the results of one project to be compared to those of another and the project results to be perceived as credible.

Types of Data

The types of data that must be collected vary. Unfortunately, many projects focus on impact measures alone, showing cost savings, less waste, improved productivity, or improved patient care. These measures will change if this project is implemented. The types of measures also include intangibles.

What is needed is a balanced set of data that contains financial and nonfinancial measures as well as qualitative and quantitative data. Multiple types of data not only show results of investing in healthcare projects, but help explain how the results evolved and how to improve them over time. To effectively capture the return on investment, six types of data are needed: reaction, learning, application, impact, ROI, and intangible benefits.

Dynamic Adjustments

As mentioned earlier, a comprehensive measurement system must allow opportunities to collect data throughout project implementation rather than waiting until it has been fully completed (perhaps only to find out it never worked from the beginning). Reaction and learning data must be captured early. Application data must be captured when project participants are applying knowledge, skills, and information routinely. All these data should be used to make adjustments in the project to ensure success, not just to report postprogram outcomes at a point that is too late to make a difference. Impact data are collected after routine application has occurred and represent the consequences of implementation. These data should be connected to the project and must be monitored and reviewed in conjunction with the other levels of data. When the connection is made between impact and the project, a credible ROI is calculated.

Connectivity

For many measurement schemes, such as the balanced scorecard, it is difficult to see the connection between a healthcare project and the results. It is often a mystery as to how much of the reported improvement is connected to the project or even whether a connection exists.

Data need to be collected throughout the process so that the chain of impact is validated. In addition, when the business measure improves, a method is necessary to isolate the effects of the project on the data to validate the connection to the measure.

APPROACH

Too often, the measurement schemes are focused on activities. People are busy. They are involved. Things are happening. Activity is everywhere. However, activities sometimes are not connected to impact. The project must be based on achieving results at the impact and ROI levels. Not only should the project track monetary results, but also, the steps and processes along the way should focus on results. Driving improvement should be inherent to the measurement process. By having a measurement process in place, the likelihood of positive results increases. A complete focus on results versus activity improves the chances that people will react positively, change their attitude, and apply necessary actions, which lead to a positive impact on immediate and long-term outcomes.

CONSERVATIVE NATURE

Many assumptions are made during the collection and analysis of data. If these assumptions are not conservative, then the numbers are overstated and unbelievable, which decreases the likelihood of accuracy and buy in. The results, including ROI, should be CFO and CEO friendly.

SIMPLICITY

Too often, measurement systems are complex and confusing for practical use, which leaves users skeptical and reluctant to embrace them. The process must be user-friendly, with simple, logical, and sequential steps. It must be void of sophisticated statistical analysis and complicated financial information, at least for the projects that involve participants who lack statistical expertise. It must be user-friendly, even to those who do not have statistical or financial backgrounds.

THEORETICAL FOUNDATION

Sometimes measurement systems are not based on sound principles. They use catchy terms and inconvenient processes that make some researchers and professors skeptical. A measurement system must be based on sound principles and theoretical frameworks. Ideally, it must use accepted processes as it is implemented. The process should be supported by professors and researchers who have used the process with a goal of making it better.

ACCEPTANCE

A measurement system must be used by practitioners in all types of organizations. Too often, the measurement scheme is presented as theoretical but lacks evidence of widespread use. The ROI Methodology, first described in publications in the 1970s and 1980s (with an entire book devoted to it in 1997[12]), now enjoys more than 5,000 users. It is used in all types of projects and programs from technology, quality, marketing, and human resources, among others. In recent years it has been adopted for green projects and sustainability efforts.

The success of the ROI Methodology will be highlighted in detail throughout this book with examples of applications. It is a comprehensive process that meets the important needs and challenges of those striving for successful healthcare projects.

THE ELUSIVE ROI

Without a doubt, the concept of ROI has entered the healthcare field. In recent literature, it is mentioned regularly, and often with a lot of passion, but some issues coincide with ROI. Sometimes individuals and executives use the term *ROI* to reflect a benefit or value instead of the financial definition of ROI. In other terms, they are using cost effectiveness to show that if they lower costs, they have positive ROI. In other cases, it is considered cost recovery, which may help the ROI definition, but sometimes does not. Sometimes terms such as *return on expectation* or *return on inspiration (ROE/ROI)* are used, which have dramatically different meanings for finance and accounting executives than they do for those who make up such acronyms.

Profits can be generated through increased revenue or cost savings. In practice, more opportunities can be found for cost savings than for increased revenue. Cost savings can be realized when improvements in productivity, quality, efficiency, cycle time, or actual cost reduction occur. In a review of almost 500 studies, the vast majority of which were based on cost savings, approximately 85 percent of the studies used a payoff based on cost savings from output, quality, efficiency, time, or a variety of soft data measures. The others used a payoff based on revenue increases, where the earnings were derived from the profit margin. Cost savings are important for non-profits and public-sector organizations, where opportunities for profit are often unavailable. Most projects or programs are connected directly to cost savings; ROI can still be developed in these settings.

The formula should be used consistently throughout an organization. Deviations from, or misuse of, the formula can create confusion, not only among users, but also among finance and accounting staff. The chief financial officer (CFO) and the finance and accounting staff should become partners when evaluating programs for ROI. The staff must use the same financial terms as those used and expected by the CFO. Without the support, involvement, and commitment of these individuals, widespread use of ROI will be unlikely.

Table 1.6 shows some financial terms that are misused in literature. Terms such as *return on intelligence* (or *information*), abbreviated as ROI, do nothing but confuse the CFO, who assumes that ROI refers to the return on investment as described earlier. Sometimes *return on expectations* (ROE), *return on anticipation* (ROA), and *return on client expectations* (ROCE) are used, also confusing the CFO, who assumes the abbreviations refer to return on equity, return on assets, and return on capital employed, respectively. The use of these terms in the payback calculation of a project will also confuse and perhaps lose the support of the finance and accounting staff. Other terms such as *return on people, return on resources, return on technology, return on web, return on marketing, return on objectives,* and *return on quality* are often used with almost no consistency in terms of financial calculations. The bottom line: don't confuse the CFO. Consider this person an ally, and use the same terminology, processes, and concepts when applying financial returns for projects.

NEEDED: RESULTS-BASED LEADERSHIP

What makes a healthcare project successful? When the issues described in this chapter are addressed throughout the healthcare life cycle, success is almost guaranteed. To achieve success is to avoid the pitfalls that cause

TABLE 1.6 Misused Financial Terms

Term	Misuse	CFO Definition
ROI	Return of information Return of intelligence	Return on investment
ROE	Return on expectation	Return on equity
ROA	Return on anticipation	Return on assets
ROCE	Return on client expectation	Return on capital employed
ROP	Return on people	?
ROR	Return on resources	?
ROT	Return on technology	?
ROW	Return on web	?
ROM	Return on marketing	?
ROO	Return on objectives	?
ROQ	Return on quality	?

failure, understanding those issues and making sure that they are working with the project instead of against it.

Strong leadership is necessary for this to work. Leaders must ensure that healthcare improvement projects are designed to achieve results. Table 1.7 shows the twelve actions necessary to provide effective, results-based management, which is critical to delivering results at the ultimate level, ROI. However, only one of the items involves data collection and evaluation (number 11). The remaining leadership areas represent steps and processes that must be addressed throughout the healthcare process and project cycle. These actions were developed after observing, studying, conducting, and reviewing thousands of ROI studies. We know what keeps projects, programs, and systems working and what makes them successful. Following these twelve leadership rules can ensure project success.

TABLE 1.7   Leadership for Results

1. Allocate appropriate resources for healthcare improvement projects and programs.
2. Assign responsibilities for projects and programs
3. Link projects to specific business needs.
4. Address performance issues involving the key stakeholders for the project identifying the behavior/actions that must change.
5. Understand what individuals must know to make projects successful, addressing the specific learning needs.
6. Develop objectives for the projects at multiple levels including reaction, learning, application, impact, and ROI.
7. Create expectations for success of the project with all stakeholders involved, detailing roles and responsibilities for the project's success.
8. Address barriers to successful projects early in the project so that they can be removed, minimized, or diminished.
9. Establish the level of evaluation needed for each project at the beginning so that participants will understand the focus.
10. Develop partnerships with key administrators and managers who can make the project successful. (For many, this is the manager or the person who is the participant in the project.)
11. Ensure that measures are taken and the evaluation is complete with collection and analysis of a variety of data.
12. Communicate project results to the appropriate stakeholders as often as necessary to focus on process improvement.

THE APPROACH OF THIS BOOK

The remainder of this book focuses on the proper use of the ROI Methodology. The following issues about the approach will provide additional insight as to what you can expect in the book.

Audience

The primary audience for this book includes managers and executives concerned with the valuation of projects, programs, processes, and people.

Executives generally are strongly committed to their projects; however, they need to see value in terms they can appreciate and understand—money.

This book is also intended for professionals, analysts, and practitioners who are responsible for evaluating the success of a project. It shows how the various types of data are collected, processed, analyzed, and reported.

PROFESSIONAL APPLICATIONS IN WHICH ROI HAS BEEN MEASURED

The ROI Methodology is geared toward a variety of professional areas in healthcare organizations. These areas include (but are not limited to) the following:

- Human resources, human capital
- Learning and development, performance improvement
- Technology, IT systems
- Medical meetings and events
- MD practice acquisition
- Medical equipment evaluation and replacement
- Clinical process redesign
- Sales, marketing
- Public relations, community affairs, government relations
- Project management solutions
- Quality, Six Sigma
- Medical procedures
- Medical process improvements
- Compliance, ethics
- Logistics, distribution, supply chain
- Public policy initiatives

- Social programs
- Charitable projects

The Difference

Although other books attempt to address accountability in these and other functional areas, *Measuring ROI in Healthcare* presents a methodical approach that can be replicated throughout an organization, enabling comparisons of results. The process described in this book is the most documented method in the world, and its implementation has been phenomenal, with more than 4,000 organizations currently using it in one function or another. Many books tackle accountability in a certain function or process, but this book shows a method that works across all types of processes, ranging from new procedures to the implementation of new technology and from educational programs to public policy initiatives.

Terminology: Projects, Programs, Solutions

In *Measuring ROI in Healthcare*, the terms *project* and *program* are used to describe a variety of processes that can be evaluated using the ROI Methodology. This issue is important because readers may vary widely in their perspective. Healthcare professionals involved in technology applications may use the terms *system* and *technology* rather than *program*. In public policy on the other hand, the word *program* is prominent. For a medical meetings and events planner, the word *program* may not be particularly pertinent, but in human resources, *program* fits quite well. Finding one term that fits all these situations would be difficult. Consequently, the terms *project* and *program* are used interchangeably. Table 1.8 lists these and other terms that may be used to refer to an initiative undergoing evaluation using the ROI Methodology.

FINAL THOUGHTS

So what? What does all this mean? Given the dramatic changes in healthcare and the need to lower costs, improve patient quality, increase access,

TABLE 1.8 Terms and Applications

Term	Example
Program	Leadership development for senior administrators
Project	A workforce management project for the sleep center
System	A new portal for physicians
Initiative	A faith-based effort to reduce infant mortality
Policy	A new policy for physician engagement
Procedure	A new procedure to reduce bloodstream infections
Event	A medical trade show
Meeting	Innovations in healthcare conference
Process	A quality control process
People	Staff additions in the patient care center
Tool	A new values-based selection tool for the nursing staff

and enhance care, substantial changes are essential. This chapter makes the case for having a more comprehensive, credible process to show the value of healthcare projects. Some important stakeholders are demanding, requiring, or suggesting more accountability up to and including ROI. "Show me the money" has become a common request—and is being made now more than ever. A variety of forces have created this current focus on results, leaving healthcare planners with only one recourse: to step up to the accountability challenge, create a process that can measure success, develop data that please a variety of important stakeholders, and use a process that improves projects and programs in the future. The remainder of the book will focus directly on the ROI Methodology and how it is being applied in the healthcare field.

CHAPTER 2

ROI Methodology Basics

The process of developing monetary value, including ROI, represents a comprehensive, systematic methodology that includes defining the types of data, conducting an initial analysis with objectives, forecasting value (including ROI), using the ROI process model, and implementing and sustaining the process. This chapter describes the approach for achieving the level of accountability needed for project evaluation in today's healthcare climate.

OPENING STORY

A group of hospitals in the Birmingham, Alabama, metro area participated in adopting new procedures to reduce bloodstream infections in the intensive care unit. Participating hospitals comprised a mix of religious-affiliated, government-owned (city, county, and state), university-affiliated, and private-sector organizations. These hospitals were concerned about the excessive number of central line blood infections that were occurring as a result of a central vascular catheter, inserted into a large vein in the chest, introducing infection.

As participants implemented a new set of procedures for reducing the number of infections, they realized that the procedures represented a cultural shift in the way they operated. It required participants to use checklists, gain knowledge, double check, and speak up. In order for the new procedures to be successful, various levels of data were needed beyond the traditional monitoring of infections, length of stay, and costs associated with these infections. Successive sets of data were needed that would examine the team's reaction to the new procedures, the learning of new processes and procedures, and correct application of new information and tools, all of which are aimed at the impact: infections, mortality rates, length of stay, and operating costs. This group envisioned sets of data that represented a chain of impact that must be present for the project to be effective. These sets represent four levels of outcome data (reaction, learning, application, and impact). A fifth level, financial ROI is possible and is sometimes necessary to calculate in today's environment. Collecting data along these levels and using a method to isolate the effects of this program from other factors provides comprehensive data that show the impact of this program. Figure 2.1 shows the types of data from this study, according to *The Birmingham News*.[1]

TYPES OF DATA

The richness of the ROI Methodology is inherent in the types of data monitored during the implementation of a particular project. These data are categorized by levels. Figure 2.2 shows the types and levels of data that represent value. Subsequent chapters provide more detail on each level.

Level 0 represents the input to a project and details the number of people and hours, the focus, and the cost of the project. These data represent the activity around a project versus the contribution of the project. Level 0 data represent the scope of the effort, the degree of commitment, and the support for a particular project. For some, these data equate to value. However, the costs and efforts for a project are not evidence that the organization is reaping value from it.

Reaction (Level 1) marks the beginning of the project's outcome value stream. Reaction data capture the degree to which the participants involved in the project, including the stakeholders, react favorably or unfavorably. The key is to capture the measures that reflect the perceived value of the

FIGURE 2.1 Example of Levels of Evaluation

Project: The Comprehensive Unit Based Safety Program	
Description: Infections in the bloodstream can be dangerous and hard to treat. According to the Centers for Disease Control and Prevention, almost 250,000 occur in U.S. hospitals each year, often in patients who have a central vascular catheter, a tube inserted into a large vein in the chest, which may be used to provide medication or fluids or check blood oxygen levels and other vital signs. The catheters are very important in treatment but inserting them correctly and keeping the entry site and dressings clean can be complicated.	
The Comprehensive Unit Based Safety Program is focused on reducing central blood line infections in intensive care units. The hospital instituted a checklist system that sets up specific steps for doctors, nurses, and technicians to take when inserting and managing a central line. The checklists give nurses explicit permission to challenge their superiors—including doctors—if they don't follow the steps without fear of reprisal. They also require workers to assess each day whether a central line catheter needs to remain in place or can be removed, which reduces the patient's risk of infection.	
Level 0—Input	• All doctors, nurses, and technicians (participants) in the intensive care units are involved.
Level 1—Reaction	All participants must see this program as: • Necessary. • Important. • Feasible. • Practical.
Level 2—Learning	• All participants must demonstrate knowledge of the checklist and new procedures. • Participants must practice "speak up" conversations with colleagues and visitors.
Level 3—Application	• Checklist will be monitored. • The use of new procedures will be observed. • Extent of "speak up" conversations will be collected.
Level 4—Impact	• Central line bloodstream infections will be reduced by 50% in six months. • Mortality rates reduced by 5%. • Days in hospital reduced by 2%. • ICU Costs reduced by 3%.
Level 5—ROI	• ROI objective is 25%.

Source: Data from Alabama Hospital Association/*The Birmingham News*/ROI Institute, Inc.

project, or the satisfaction or acceptance of the change as a perceived value, focusing on issues such as usefulness, relevance, importance, and appropriateness. Data at this level provide the first sign that project success may be achievable. These data also present project leaders with information they need to make adjustments to help ensure positive results.

FIGURE 2.2 Types and Levels of Data

Level	Measurement Focus	Typical Measures
0: Inputs ↓	Inputs into the project, including indicators representing project's scope, efficiency, and costs.	Types of projects, number of projects, number of people involved, hours of involvement, cost of projects.
1: Reaction ↓	Reaction to the project, including perceived value of the project.	Relevance, importance, usefulness, fairness, appropriateness, motivational, necessity.
2: Learning ↓	Learning to use the project content, materials, and system, including the confidence to make the project successful.	Skills, knowledge, capacity, competencies, confidence, contacts.
3: Application and Imple- mentation ↓	The actions taken, use of project content, materials, and system in the work environment, including progress with implementation.	Extent of use, task completions, frequency of use, actions completed, success with use, barriers to use, enablers to use.
4: Impact ↓	The consequences of action. The consequences of the use of the project content, materials, and system expressed as business impact measures of output, quality, cost, and time.	Productivity, patients served, patient revenue, patient outcomes, quality, wait times, cost per case, efficiency, patient satisfaction, employee engagement.
5: ROI ↓	Comparison of project's monetary benefits from project to project costs.	Benefits/costs ratio (BCR) ROI (%) Payback period

The next level is Learning (Level 2); every process or project involves a learning component. For some—such as projects for new technology, new systems, and new competencies—this component is substantial. For others, such as a new policy or new simple procedure, learning may be a small part of the process but is still necessary to ensure successful execution. In either case, measurement of learning is essential to success. Measures at this level focus on skills, information, knowledge, capacity, competencies, confidence, and networking contacts.

Application and Implementation (Level 3) measures the extent to which the project is properly used, applied, or implemented. Effective implementation is a must if impact is the goal. This is one of the most important data categories, and most project breakdowns occur at this level. Research has consistently shown that in almost half of all projects, participants and users are not doing what they should to make the project successful. At this level, data collection involves measures such as the extent of use of information, task completion, frequency of use of skills, success with use, and actions completed, as well as barriers and enablers to successful application. This level provides a picture of how well the system supports the successful transfer of knowledge and skills for project implementation.

Level 4, Impact, is important for understanding the business consequences of the project. At this level, data are collected that attract the attention of sponsors and other executives. This level shows the important impacts such as patient productivity, patient revenue, quality, patient safety, wait time, cost per case, efficiencies, and patient satisfaction connected with the project. For some, this level reflects the ultimate reason the project exists: to show the impact within the organization on various groups and systems. From an executive's perspective, success cannot be achieved without this level of data. Achieving this level of measurement helps to isolate the effects of the project on the specific measures. Without this extra step, alignment with the business cannot occur.

ROI (Level 5) is calculated next. It specifies the monetary value of the impact measures compared with the cost of the project. This calculation is typically stated in terms of either a benefit/cost ratio, ROI as a percentage, or a payback period. This level of measurement requires two important steps: first, the impact data (Level 4) must be converted to monetary values; second, the cost of the project must be captured.

Along with the five levels of results (Levels 1–5) and the initial level of Input (Level 0), a sixth type of outcome data—not a sixth level— is developed through this methodology. It consists of the intangible benefits—impact measures that are not converted to money but nonetheless constitute important measures of success.

The measures described in Figure 2.1 demonstrate the project value stream using this concept of levels.

THE INITIAL ANALYSIS

Research suggests that the number one reason for project failure is the project's lack of alignment with the business. The first opportunity to obtain business alignment is in the initial analysis. Several steps ensure that the project is absolutely necessary. As shown in Figure 2.3, these steps constitute the beginning of the complete, sequential model representing the ROI Methodology. The first step in this analysis examines the potential payoff of solving a problem or taking advantage of an opportunity. Is it a problem worth solving, or is the project worthy of implementation? For some situations the answer is obvious: Yes, the project is worthy because of its critical nature, its relevance to the issue at hand, or its effectiveness in tackling a major problem affecting the organization. Employment gaps are a problem worth pursuing. To address employment gaps, healthcare organizations recruit primary care physicians, which will, in turn, increase referrals to specialists.

The next step is to ensure that the project is connected to one or more business measures. The measures that must improve as a reflection of the overall success of the project are defined. Sometimes the measure is obvious; at other times it is not.

Next, the performance needs are examined with the question "What must change to influence the business measures previously defined?" This step aligns the project with the business and may involve a series of analytical tools to solve the problem, analyze the cause of the problem, and ensure that the project is connected with business improvement in some way. This step appears to be quite complex, but the approach is simple. A series of questions helps: What is keeping the business measure from being where it needs to be? If it is a problem, what is its cause? If it is an opportunity, what is hindering it from moving in the right direction? This step is critical because it provides the link to the project solution. Problems such as decreased volume patient days, poor case mix, decreased revenues, and increased costs must be addressed immediately and effectively.

When performance needs have been determined, the learning needs are examined by asking: What specific skills, knowledge, or information

FIGURE 2.3 Business Alignment Model

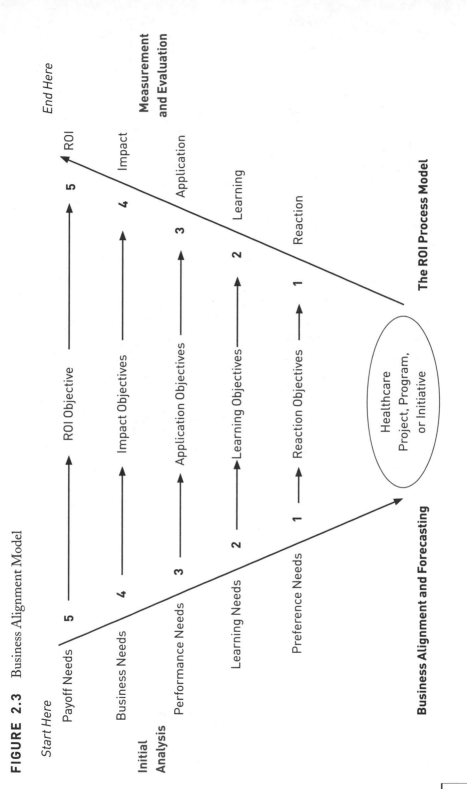

Start Here

End Here

Payoff Needs **5** → ROI Objective **5** → ROI

Initial
Analysis

Business Needs **4** → Impact Objectives **4** → Impact

Performance Needs **3** → Application Objectives **3** → Application

Learning Needs **2** → Learning Objectives **2** → Learning

Preference Needs **1** → Reaction Objectives **1** → Reaction

Healthcare
Project, Program,
or Initiative

Measurement
and Evaluation

The ROI Process Model

Business Alignment and Forecasting

must be acquired or improved so that performance can change? Every solution involves a learning component, and this step defines what the participants or users must know to make the project successful. The needed knowledge may be as simple as understanding a policy, or as complicated as learning many new competencies.

The next step is identifying the preferences for the proposed project. How best can the information be presented to ensure that the necessary knowledge will be acquired and job performance will change to meet the business need? This level of analysis involves issues surrounding the importance, value, necessity, and feasibility for project implementation and delivery.

The final step is to identify the input needs, defining the individuals who will be involved, for how long, and at what costs. Location, timing, and scheduling issues are also determined before the project is launched.

Collectively, these levels clearly define the issues that lead to initiation of the project. When these preliminary steps are completed, the project can be positioned to achieve its intended results.

Understanding the need for a project is critical to positioning it for success. Positioning a project requires the development of clear, specific objectives that are communicated to all stakeholders. Objectives should be developed for each level of need and should define success, answering the question "How will we know the need has been met?" If the criteria of success are not communicated early and often, participants will go through the motions, with little change resulting. Developing detailed objectives with clear measures of success will position the project to achieve its ultimate objective. More detail on the initial analysis and objectives are contained in the next chapter.

Before a project is launched, forecasting the outcomes is important to ensure that adjustments can be made or alternative solutions can be investigated. This forecast can be simple, relying on the individuals closest to the situation, or it can be a more detailed analysis of the situation and expected outcome. Recently, forecasting has become a critical tool for project sponsors who need evidence that the project will be successful before they are willing to plunge into a funding stream for it. Because of its importance, forecasting is a focus of the book by Jack and Patti Phillips, *The Consultant's Guide to Results-Driven Business Proposals: How to Write Proposals That Forecast Impact and ROI* (McGraw-Hill).

THE ROI PROCESS MODEL

The next challenge for many project leaders is to collect a variety of data along a chain of impact. Figure 2.4 displays the sequential steps that lead to data categorized by the five levels of results.[2] This figure shows the ROI Methodology, a step-by-step process beginning with the objectives and concluding with reporting of data. The model assumes that proper analysis is conducted to define need before the steps are taken.

Planning the Evaluation

The first phase of the ROI Methodology is evaluation planning. This phase involves several procedures, including understanding the purpose of the evaluation, determining the feasibility of the planned approach, planning data collection and analysis, and outlining the details of the project.

EVALUATION PURPOSE

Evaluations are conducted for a variety of reasons:

- To improve the quality of projects and outcomes
- To determine whether a project has accomplished its objectives
- To identify strengths and weaknesses in the process
- To enable the cost-benefit analysis
- To assist in the marketing of projects in the future
- To determine whether the project was the appropriate solution
- To establish priorities for project funding

The purposes of the evaluation should be considered prior to developing the evaluation plan because the purposes will often determine the scope of the evaluation, the types of instruments used, and the type of data collected. As with any project, understanding the purpose of the evaluation will give it focus, and will also help gain support from others.

FIGURE 2.4 The ROI Process Model

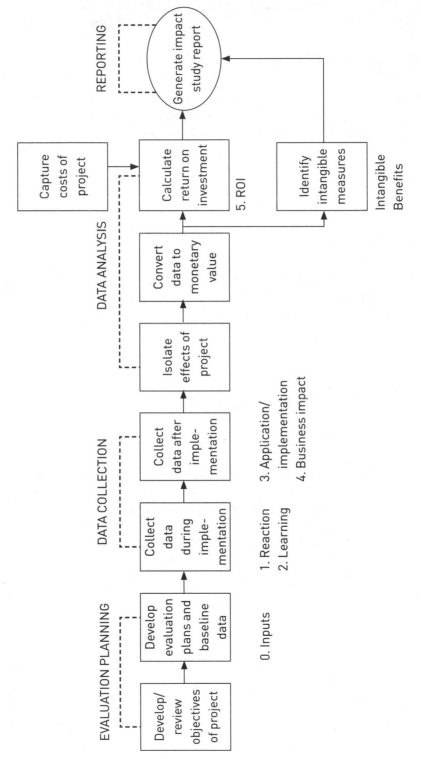

FEASIBILITY

An important consideration in planning the ROI impact study is the determination of the levels at which the project will be evaluated. Some evaluations will stop at Level 3, Application, where the evaluation will determine the extent to which participants are using what they have learned. Others will be evaluated to Level 4, Impact, where the consequences of applications are monitored and measures directly linked to the project are examined. If the ROI calculation is needed, the evaluation will proceed to Level 5. To reach this level of measurement, two additional steps are required. The Level 4 impact data must be converted to monetary values, and the costs of the project must be captured so that the ROI can be developed. Evaluation at Level 5 is intended for projects that are expensive, high profile, and have a direct link to business needs.

OBJECTIVES

The initial analysis, which defines the needs along the five levels, also defines the objectives at these levels. Projects need clear direction, and the objectives provide this clarity. Objectives, when defined precisely, provide the participants and other stakeholders with the direction they need to make the project successful. The objectives are defined along the same five levels as the needs assessment:

- Reaction objectives

- Learning objectives

- Application and implementation objectives

- Impact objectives

- ROI objectives

Having specific objectives, particularly at the higher levels, takes the mystery out of what the project should accomplish. On occasion, the initial analysis may stop with Level 2 objectives, excluding the application and impact objectives that are needed to direct the higher levels of evaluation. If application and impact objectives are not available, they must be developed using input from participants, analysts, project developers, subject matter experts, and team leaders.

Three planning documents are developed next: the data collection plan, the ROI analysis plan, and the project plan. These documents should be completed during evaluation planning and before the evaluation project is implemented—ideally, before the project is designed or developed. Appropriate up-front attention will save time later, when data are actually collected.

DATA COLLECTION PLAN

Figure 2.5 on pages 66–67 shows a completed data collection plan for a project to implement a flexible work system for employees. The project is designed to allow certain administrative employees who process claims to work at home instead of the office.

This document provides a place for the major elements and issues regarding data collection. The initial objectives (at different levels) are appropriate for planning. Specific detailed objectives are developed later, before the project is designed. Entries in the Measures column define the specific measure; entries in the Method/Instruments column describe the technique used to collect the data; in the Sources column, the source of the data is identified; and the Timing column indicates when the data are collected.

ROI ANALYSIS PLAN

Figure 2.6 on page 68 shows a completed ROI analysis plan for the same project. This planning document captures information on key items necessary for developing the actual ROI calculation. In the first column, significant data items are listed. Although these items are usually Level 4 impact data, in some cases this column includes Level 3 items. These items will be used in the ROI analysis.

The method employed to isolate the project's effects is listed next to each data item in the second column. The method of converting data to monetary values is included in the third column. The cost categories that will be captured for the project are outlined in the next column. Normally, the cost categories will be consistent from one project to another. The intangible benefits expected from the project are outlined in the fifth column. This list is generated from discussions about the project with sponsors and subject matter experts. Communication targets are outlined in the sixth column. Finally, other issues or events that might influence project implementation and its outputs are highlighted in the last column. Typical items include the capability of participants, the degree of access to data sources, and unique data analysis issues.

The ROI analysis plan, when combined with the data collection plan, provides detailed information for calculating the ROI, illustrating how the evaluation will develop from beginning to end.

PROJECT EVALUATION PLAN

The final plan developed for the evaluation planning phase is a project evaluation plan, as shown in Figure 2.7 on page 69. A project plan consists of a description of the project and the timeline of the project evaluation, from the planning of the study through the final communication of the results. This plan becomes an operational tool to keep the project evaluation on track.

Collectively, the three planning documents provide the direction necessary for the ROI impact study. Most of the decisions regarding the process are made as these planning tools are developed. The remainder of the project becomes a methodical, systematic process of implementing the plan. In this crucial step in the ROI Methodology, valuable time allocated to this process in the beginning will save precious time later.

COLLECTING DATA

Data collection is central to the ROI Methodology. Both hard data (representing output, quality, cost, and time) and soft data (including job satisfaction and patient satisfaction) are collected. Data are collected using a variety of methods, including the following:

- Surveys
- Questionnaires
- Tests
- Observations
- Interviews
- Focus groups
- Action plans
- Performance contracts
- Performance monitoring

FIGURE 2.5 Completed Data Collection Plan

Data Collection Plan
Evaluation Purpose: Measure Success of Program
Program: Flexible Work System Project **Responsibility:** HR/Consultants **Date:** March 30

Level	Broad Program Objective(s)	Measures	Data Collection Method/Instruments	Data Sources	Timing
1	**Reaction** • Employees should see the flexible work system project as satisfying, important, rewarding, and motivational. • Managers must see this project as necessary, appropriate, and important.	• Rating scale (4 out of 5)	• Questionnaires • Interviews	• Participants • Managers	• 30 days • 30 days
2	**Learning** • Employees must know the realities of working at home, the conditions, roles, and regulations. • Employees must have the discipline and tenacity to work at home. • Managers must be able to explain company policy and regulations for working at home. • Managers must be able to manage remotely.	• Rating scale (4 out of 5)	• Questionnaires • Interviews	• Employees • Managers	• 30 days • 30 days
3	**Application** • Managers should conduct a meeting with direct reports to discuss policy, expected behavior, and next steps. • At least 30 percent of eligible employees should volunteer for at-home assignments within one month.	• Checklist • Sign Up	• Data monitoring • Data monitoring	• Company records • Company records	• 30 days • 30 days

#	Objective	Measure	Data Collection Method	Source	Timing
	• At-home offices are built and properly equipped. • The at-home workplace should be free from distractions and conflicting demands. • Managers will properly administer the organization's policy. • Managers should effectively manage the remote employees.	• Rating Scale (4 out of 5)	• Questionnaires	• Participants • Managers	• 90 days • 90 days
4	**Impact** • Commute time should be reduced to an average of 15 minutes per day. • Office expense per person should reduce by 20 percent in six months. • Productivity should increase by 5 percent in six months. • Employee turnover should reduce to 12 percent in six months. • Stress should be reduced. • Carbon emissions should be reduced. • The organization's image as green should be enhanced. • Employee engagement should improve.	• Direct costs • Claims per day • Voluntary turnover • Rating scale (4 out of 5) • Rating scale (4 out of 5)	• Business performance monitoring • Survey	• Company records • Participants • Managers	• 6 months • 6 months • 6 months • 90 days • 90 days
5	**ROI** Achieve a 25% return on investment.	Baseline Data:			

FIGURE 2.6 Completed ROI Analysis Plan

Program: Flexible Work Systems Project **Responsibility:** HR/Consultants **Date:** March 30

Data Items (Usually Level 4)	Methods for Isolating the Effects of the Program/Process	Methods of Converting Data to Monetary Values	Cost Categories	Intangible Benefits	Communication Targets for Final Report	Other Influential Issues During Application
• Office expenses • Productivity • Turnover	• Control group • Expert estimates • Control group • Participant estimates	• Standard value based on costs • Standard values • External values	• Initial analysis and assessment • Forecasting impact and ROI • Project development • IT support and maintenance • Administration and coordination • Materials • Facilities and refreshments for meetings • Salaries plus benefits for employee and manager time in meetings • Evaluation and reporting	• Reduced commuting time • Reduced carbon emissions • Reduced fuel consumption • Reduced sick leave • Reduced absenteeism • Improved job engagement • Improved community image • Improved image as environmentally friendly • Enhanced corporate social responsibility • Improved job satisfaction • Reduced stress • Improved recruiting image	• Participants • Managers • HR team • Executive group • Consultants • External groups	• Must observe marketing and economic forces • Search for barriers/obstacles for progress

FIGURE 2.7   Project Evaluation Plan

	A	M	J	J	A	S
Decision to conduct ROI study	▓					
Evaluation planning complete	▓	▓				
Instruments designed	▓	▓				
Data collected			▓			
Data tabulation/Preliminary summary				▓		
Analysis conducted					▓	
Report written					▓	
Report printed					▓	
Results communicated						▓
Improvements initiated						▓
Implementation complete						▓

The important challenge in data collection is to select the method or methods appropriate for the setting and the specific project, within the time and budget constraints of the organization. Data collection methods are covered in more detail in Chapters 4 through 6.

Isolating the Effects of the Project

An often overlooked issue in evaluations is the process of isolating the effects of the project, sometimes labeled attribution. In this step, specific strategies are explored that determine the amount of the impact that is directly related to the project. This step is essential because many factors will influence impact data. The specific strategies of this step pinpoint the amount of improvement directly related to the project, resulting in increased accuracy and credibility of ROI calculations. The following techniques have been used by organizations to tackle this important issue:

- Control groups
- Trend line analysis
- Forecasting models
- Participant estimates

- Managers' estimates
- Senior management estimates
- Experts' input
- Customer input

Collectively, these techniques provide a comprehensive set of tools to handle the important and critical issue of isolating the effects of projects. Chapter 7 is devoted to this important step in determining the ROI of projects.

Converting Data to Monetary Values

To calculate the return on investment, Level 4 impact data are converted to monetary values and compared with project costs, which requires that a value be placed on each unit of data connected with the project. Many techniques are available to convert data to monetary values. The specific technique selected depends on the type of data and the situation. The techniques include the following:

- Use of standard value for output data
- Use of standard value for the cost of quality
- Time savings converted to participants' wage and employee benefits
- Analysis of historical costs from records
- Use of internal and external experts to provide input
- Use of external databases
- Participant estimates
- Manager estimates
- Soft measures mathematically linked to other measures

This step in the ROI model is important and necessary in determining the monetary benefits of a project. The process is challenging, particularly with soft data, but can be methodically accomplished using one or more of these strategies. Because of its importance, this step in the ROI Methodology is described in detail in Chapter 8.

IDENTIFYING INTANGIBLE BENEFITS

In addition to tangible monetary benefits, intangible benefits—those not converted to money—are identified for most projects. Intangible benefits include items such as:

- Improved patient satisfaction

- Increased employee engagement

- Increased brand awareness

- Improved networking

- Enhanced reputation

- Enhanced image

- Reduced stress

- Reduced conflicts

During data analysis, every attempt is made to convert all data to monetary values. All hard data—such as output, quality, and time—are converted to monetary values. The conversion of soft data is attempted for each data item. However, if the process used for conversion is too subjective or inaccurate, and the resulting values lose credibility in the process, then the data are listed as an intangible benefit with the appropriate explanation. For some projects, intangible nonmonetary benefits are extremely valuable and often carry as much influence as the hard data items. Chapter 9 is devoted to the nonmonetary intangible benefits.

TABULATING PROJECT COSTS

An important part of the ROI equation is the calculation of project costs, which are found at Level 0, input. Tabulating the costs involves monitoring or developing all the related costs of the project targeted for the ROI calculation. The cost components include the following:

- Initial analysis costs

- Cost to design and develop the project

- Cost of all project materials, technology, and licenses

- Costs for consultants, experts, and support team

- Cost of the facilities for the project, if appropriate

- Travel, lodging, and meal costs for the participants and team members, if appropriate

- Participants' salaries for the time involved in the project (including employee benefits)

- Administrative and overhead costs, allocated in some convenient way

- Evaluation costs

The conservative approach is to include all these costs so that the total is fully loaded. Chapter 10 includes this step in the ROI Methodology.

CALCULATING THE RETURN ON INVESTMENT

The return on investment is calculated using the program benefits and costs. The benefit/cost ratio (BCR) is calculated as the project benefits divided by the project costs. In formula form,

$$BCR = \frac{\text{Project Benefits}}{\text{Project Costs}}$$

The return on investment is based on the net monetary benefits divided by project costs. The net monetary benefits are calculated as the project monetary benefits minus the project costs. In formula form, the ROI becomes

$$ROI\ (\%) = \frac{\text{Net Project Benefits}}{\text{Project Costs}} \times 100$$

This basic formula is used in evaluating other investments in which the ROI is traditionally reported as earnings divided by investment. Chapter 10 describes this step in more detail.

REPORTING RESULTS

The final step in the ROI process model is reporting, a critical step that is often deficient in the degree of attention and planning required to ensure its success. The reporting step involves developing appropriate information in impact studies and other brief reports. At the heart of this step are the different techniques used to communicate to a wide variety of target audiences. In most ROI studies, several audiences are interested in, and need, the information. Careful planning to match the communication method with the audience is essential to ensure that the message is understood and that appropriate actions follow.

OPERATING STANDARDS AND PHILOSOPHY

To ensure consistency and replication of impact studies, operating standards must be developed and applied as the process model is used to develop ROI studies. The results of the study must stand alone and must not vary with the individual who is conducting the study. The operating standards detail how each step and issue of the process will be handled. Table 2.1 shows the twelve guiding principles that form the basis for the operating standards.

The guiding principles serve not only to consistently address each step, but also to provide a much needed conservative approach to the analysis. A conservative approach may lower the actual ROI calculation, but it will also build credibility with the target audience.

IMPLEMENTING AND SUSTAINING THE PROCESS

A variety of environmental issues and events will influence the successful implementation of the ROI Methodology. These issues must be addressed early to ensure the success of the ROI process. Specific topics or actions include:

- A policy statement concerning results-based projects
- Procedures and guidelines for different elements and techniques of the evaluation process
- Formal meetings to develop staff skills with the ROI process
- Strategies to improve management commitment to and support for the ROI process
- Mechanisms to provide technical support for questionnaire design, data analysis, and evaluation strategy
- Specific techniques to place more attention on results

TABLE 2.1   The Twelve Guiding Principles of ROI

---

1. When conducting a higher-level evaluation, collect data at lower levels.
2. When planning a higher-level evaluation, the previous level of evaluation is not required to be comprehensive.
3. When collecting and analyzing data, use only the most credible sources.
4. When analyzing data, select the most conservative alternative for calculations.
5. Use at least one method to isolate the effects of a project.
6. If no improvement data are available for a population or from a specific source, assume that little or no improvement has occurred.
7. Adjust estimates of improvement for potential errors of estimation.
8. Avoid use of extreme data items and unsupported claims when calculating ROI.
9. Use only the first year of annual benefits in ROI analysis of short-term solutions.
10. Fully load all costs of a solution, project, or program when analyzing ROI.
11. Intangible measures are defined as measures that are purposely not converted to monetary values.
12. Communicate the results of ROI Methodology to all key stakeholders.

The ROI process can fail or succeed based on these implementation issues. In addition to implementing and sustaining ROI use, the process must undergo periodic review. An annual review is recommended to determine the extent to which the process is adding value. Chapter 12 is devoted to this important topic.

BENEFITS OF THIS APPROACH

Now for the good news: The ROI Methodology presented in this book has been used consistently and routinely by thousands of organizations in the past decade. Past successes of this method have led to defined steps with proven tools and techniques to help the organizations using it.

ALIGNING WITH BUSINESS

In healthcare, an important issue is the connection of the project to one or more impact measures such as patient revenue, patient outcomes, length of stay, or costs. The ROI Methodology ensures project alignment with the business, carried out in three steps. First, even before the project is initiated, the methodology ensures that alignment is achieved up front, at the time the project is validated as the appropriate solution. Second, by requiring specific, clearly defined objectives at the impact level, the project focuses on business impact over its course, in essence driving the business measure by its design, delivery, and implementation. Third, in the follow-up data, when the business measures may have changed or improved, a method is used to isolate the effects of the project on that data, consequently proving the connection to that business measure (i.e., showing the amount of improvement directly connected to the project and ensuring a business alignment).

VALIDATING THE VALUE PROPOSITION

In reality, most healthcare projects are undertaken to deliver value. As described in this chapter, the definition of value may, on occasion, be unclear or may not be what a project's sponsor desires. Consequently, value shifts can occur. When the value is finally determined, the value proposition is detailed. The ROI Methodology will forecast the value in advance, and if the value has been delivered, it verifies the value proposition agreed to by the appropriate parties.

IMPROVING PROCESSES

The ROI Methodology is a process improvement tool by design and by practice. It collects data to evaluate how things are—or are not—working. When things are not where they should be—as when projects are not proceeding as effectively as expected—data are available to indicate what must be changed to make the project more effective. When things are working well, data are available to show what else could be done to make them better. Thus, this process improvement system is designed to provide feedback to make changes. As a project is conducted, the results are collected, and feedback is provided to the various stakeholders for specific actions for improvement. These changes drive the project to better results, which are then measured while the process continues. This continuous feedback cycle is critical to process improvement and is inherent in the ROI Methodology approach.

ENHANCING THE IMAGE, BUILDING RESPECT

Healthcare projects are often criticized for being unable to deliver what is expected. For this reason, the image of the project team suffers. The ROI Methodology is one way to help build the respect a function or profession needs and deserves.

The ROI Methodology can make a difference in any function where projects are managed. This process connects the bottom line and the value delivered to stakeholders. It removes issues about value and a supposed lack of contribution to the organization. Consequently, this methodology is an important part of the process for changing the image of organizational functions and building needed respect.

IMPROVING SUPPORT

Securing support for healthcare projects is critical, particularly at the middle-manager level. Many projects enjoy the support of top-level executives who allocated the resources to make them viable. Unfortunately, some middle-level managers may not support certain projects because they do not see the value the projects deliver in terms the managers appreciate and understand. Having a methodology that shows how a project is connected to the manager's goals and key performance indicators can change this support level. When middle managers understand that a project helps them meet specific performance indicators or departmental goals, they will usually support the process, or will at least resist it less. In this way, the ROI Methodology may actually improve manager support.

JUSTIFYING OR ENHANCING BUDGETS

Some organizations have used the ROI Methodology to support proposed budgets. Because the methodology shows the monetary value expected or achieved with specific projects, the data can often be leveraged into budget requests. For example, one hospital used the ROI Methodology to show the value of a sleep center, enabling the director to increase its budget. When a particular function is budgeted, the amount budgeted is often in direct proportion to the value that the function adds. If little or no credible data support the contribution, the budgets are often reduced—or at least not increased.

BUILDING PARTNERSHIPS WITH KEY EXECUTIVES

Healthcare project improvement managers partner with operating executives and key managers in the organization. Unfortunately, some executives may not want to be partners. From their perspective, they may not want to waste time and effort on a relationship that does not help them succeed. They want to partner only with groups and individuals who can add value and help them in meaningful ways. Showing the projects' results will enhance the likelihood of building these partnerships, with the results providing the initial impetus for making the partnerships work.

FINAL THOUGHTS

This chapter presents the overall approach to measuring ROI. It outlines the various elements and steps in the ROI Methodology, the standards, and the concepts necessary to understand how ROI works, but without much detail. This chapter brings the methodology into focus and introduces key concepts. To be able to use the approach, the specific options, steps, and details must be absorbed. This detail will be presented throughout the rest of the book. The next chapter provides greater detail on project alignment with business needs and results.

CHAPTER 3

Achieving Business Alignment with Healthcare Initiatives

This chapter presents the first step of the process: defining the needs and corresponding objectives for a project. This step positions the project for success by aligning its intended outcomes with organizational needs. This business alignment is essential if the investment in a project is to reap a return. The term *business need* is used to reflect important outcome measures (e.g., output, quality, cost, and time) that exist in any healthcare setting, including governments, nonprofits, and nongovernmental organizations (NGOs).

OPENING STORY

Bridgeport Hospital decided to implement an employer of choice program. By doing so, the hospital would be listed among the community's preferred employers. The hospital would also be included in several national lists as an employer of choice.

To analyze the payoff of this proposed project, executives thought that if the project was successful, they would be able to sustain a positive work environment by recruiting, developing, and retaining a diverse, high-quality, engaged workforce. To begin, they needed to recruit and retain the best talent.

Next, the specific business needs were detailed. To achieve the designation of employer of choice, several specific measures must be improved. The registered nurse (RN) turnover rate had to be less than 11 percent and the overall turnover rate, less than 10 percent. The attrition rate among nursing students was to be less than 19 percent, and positive employee relations would be maintained, as evidenced by the employee satisfaction and employee engagement scores.

To meet these business needs, the performance needs were defined. The first requirement was adequate professional and support staff to care for the patients and to ensure that the staffing levels remained sufficient. Also, employees must be more engaged for organizational performance to improve. This engagement would come through increased employee participation, feedback, communication, and collaboration from the management team. Also, management development was needed to enhance customer service and focus on employee retention.

Next, the learning needs were identified in each of these categories, detailing specifically what must be learned by stakeholders to meet the performance needs. The team concluded that significant learning was necessary for each participant group.

Finally, the entire workforce, particularly the management team, must see the value and need for this program. More specifically, preference needs included the management team who should see the program as valuable, necessary, and critical to sustaining a competitive healthcare organization. All employees should see the program as motivational, satisfying, and important to their own success.

Addressing these multiple levels of needs and developing objectives ensured that the project was absolutely necessary, positioned for success, and included the proper solutions.[1]

BUSINESS ALIGNMENT ISSUES

Based on approximately 3,000 case studies, the number one cause of project failure is lack of business alignment. Projects must begin with a clear focus on desired outcomes. The end must be specified in terms of business needs and business measures so that the outcome—the actual improvement in the measures—and the corresponding ROI are clear. Clearly stated needs and measures establish the expectations throughout the analysis and project design, development, delivery, and implementation stages.

Beginning with the end in mind helps in pinning down all the details to ensure that the project is properly planned and executed according to schedule. But conducting this up-front analysis is not as simple as one might think—it requires a disciplined approach.

This standardized approach adds credibility and allows for consistent application so that the analysis can be replicated. A disciplined approach maintains process efficiency as various tools and templates are developed and used. This initial phase of project development calls for focus and thoroughness.

Not every project should be subjected to the type of comprehensive analysis described in this chapter. Some needs are obvious and require little analysis for the project. Additional analysis may be needed to confirm that the project answers the perceived need and perhaps to fine-tune the project for future application. The amount of analysis required often depends on the expected opportunity to be gained if the project is appropriate or the negative consequences anticipated if the project is inappropriate.

When analysis is proposed, individuals may react with concern or resistance. Some are concerned about the potential for "paralysis by analysis," where requests and directives lead only to additional analyses. These reactions can pose a problem for an organization because analysis is necessary to ensure that the project is appropriate. In reality, analysis need not be complicated. Simple techniques can uncover the cause of a problem or the need for a particular project.

The remainder of the chapter delves into the components of analysis that are necessary for a solid alignment between a project and the business. First, however, reviewing the model introduced in the previous chapter may be helpful. It is presented here as Figure 3.1.

Note that business alignment occurs in the beginning of the project, when it is connected to business needs (A). Also, the focus on business alignment continues throughout the project with impact objectives (B). Finally, business evaluation is validated in a follow-up evaluation (C).

DETERMINING THE POTENTIAL PAYOFF

The first step in up-front analysis is to determine the potential payoff of solving a problem or seizing an opportunity. This step begins with answers

FIGURE 3.1 Business Alignment Model

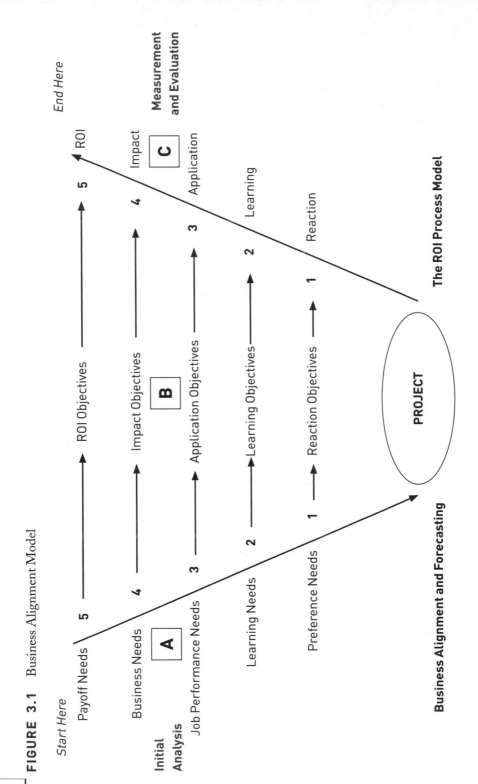

Start Here

Payoff Needs 5

Business Needs 4

Initial Analysis

Job Performance Needs 3

Learning Needs 2

Preference Needs 1

Business Alignment and Forecasting

PROJECT

5 ROI Objectives

4 Impact Objectives

B

3 Application Objectives

2 Learning Objectives

1 Reaction Objectives

1 ← Reaction

2 ← Learning

3 ← Application

C

4 ← Impact

5 ← ROI

End Here

Measurement and Evaluation

The ROI Process Model

to a few crucial questions: Is this project worth doing? Is it feasible? What is the likelihood of a positive ROI?

For projects addressing significant problems or opportunities with high potential rewards, the answers are obvious. Because life, patient outcomes, healthcare costs, and patient satisfaction are the drivers for many projects, this step may not always be necessary. The questions may take longer to answer for lower-profile projects or those for which the expected payoff is less apparent. In any case, analysis of these legitimate questions can be as simple or as comprehensive as required.

Essentially, a project will pay off in profit increases or in cost savings. Profit increases are generated by projects that drive revenue (e.g., projects that improve patient revenue), enhance market share, introduce new services, open new markets, enhance patient service, or increase patient loyalty. Other revenue-generating measures include increasing donations, obtaining grants, and generating enrollment fees from healthcare programs, all of which, after subtracting the cost of doing business, should leave a significant profit.

However, most projects drive cost savings. Cost savings can come through cost reduction or cost avoidance. Improved patient care quality, reduced cycle time, less downtime, reduced complaints, less talent turnover, and minimized delays are all examples of cost savings.

Cost avoidance projects are implemented to reduce risks, avoid problems, or prevent unwanted events. Some professionals may view cost avoidance as an inappropriate measure to use to determine monetary benefits and calculate ROI. However, if the assumptions prove correct, an avoided cost (e.g., readmission) can be more beneficial than reducing an actual cost. Preventing a problem is more cost effective than waiting for the problem to occur and then having to solve it. In the era of value-based purchasing (VBP), provider payments are linked to improved performance by healthcare providers, thus, avoiding unnecessary costs is more crucial than ever.

Determining the potential payoff is the first step in the needs analysis process. This step is closely related to the next one, determining the business need, because the potential payoff is often based on a consideration of the business. The payoff depends on two factors: the monetary value derived from the business measure's improvement and the approximate cost of the project. Identifying these monetary values in detail usually yields a more credible forecast of what can be expected from the chosen solution. However, this step may be omitted in situations where the problem (business need) must be resolved regardless of the cost, for example, if the proposed project involves a safety concern, a regulatory compliance issue, or a competitive matter, or if it becomes obvious that it is a high-payoff activity.

The target level of detail may also hinge on the need to secure project funding. If the potential funding source does not recognize the value of the project compared with the potential costs, more detail may be needed to provide a convincing case for funding.

OBVIOUS VERSUS NOT-SO-OBVIOUS PAYOFF

The potential payoff is obvious for some projects and not so obvious for others. Opportunities with obvious payoffs may include:

- Hospital operating costs 47% higher than industry average

- Patient satisfaction rating of 3.89 on a 10-point scale

- Average length of stay is 50% longer than benchmarked hospitals

- Bed occupancy rate at 40% and declining

- A cost to the city of $15,000 for healthcare annually for each homeless person

- Noncompliance fines totaling $1.2 million, up 82% from last year

- Turnover of nurses is 35% above benchmark figure

- System downtime is twice the average of last year's performance

- Very low market share in a market with little competition

- Safety record is among the worst in the industry

- Excessive patient mortality: 30% higher than previous year

- Unplanned readmission rate is the highest in the metro area

- Patient wait time is 48% more than target

- Excessive absenteeism with technicians: 12.3%, compared to 5.4% industry average

- Sexual harassment complaints per 1,000 employees are the highest in the industry

Each item appears to reflect a serious problem that needs to be addressed.

For other projects, the issues are sometimes unclear and may arise from political motives, bias, or uncertainty. Such potential opportunities are associated with payoffs that may not be so obvious. Such opportunities may include:

- Implement a physician engagement program

- Become a medical technology leader

- Become a "green" hospital

- Improve leadership competencies for all managers and directors

- Create a world-class health center

- Create a great place to work

- Conduct a healthy family expo

- Implement a new risk management system

- Implement Lean Six Sigma in each hospital

- Train all team leaders on crucial conversations

- Create a sleep center

- Provide training on sexual harassment awareness for all associates

- Develop an "open book" or transparent organization

- Implement a customer relationship management (CRM) system

- Convert to cloud computing

- Implement a transformation program involving all employees

- Implement a career advancement program

- Create a wellness and fitness center

Each of these opportunities needs more specific detail regarding the measure. For example, if the opportunity is to become a "green" hospital, one might ask: What is a green hospital? How will we know when we've reached this goal? Do we want to be *perceived* as green, do we want to *be* green, or both? Projects with not-so-obvious payoffs require greater analysis than those with clearly defined outcomes.

The potential payoff establishes the fundamental reason for pursuing new or enhanced projects. But the payoff—whether obvious or not—is not the only reason for moving forward with a project. The cost of a problem is another factor. If the cost is excessive, it should be addressed. If not, then a decision must be made as to whether the problem is worth solving.

THE COST OF A PROBLEM

Sometimes projects are undertaken to solve a problem. Problems are expensive and their solutions can result in high returns, especially when the solution is inexpensive. To determine the cost of the problem, its potential consequences must be examined and converted to monetary values. Problems may encompass time, quality, productivity, and team or patient issues. All of these factors must be converted to monetary values if the cost of the problem is to be determined. Inventory shortages are often directly associated with the cost of the inventory as well as with the cost of carrying the inventory. Time can easily be translated into money by calculating the fully loaded cost of an individual's time spent on unproductive tasks. Calculating the time for completing a project, task, or cycle involves measures that can be converted to money. Errors, mistakes, waste, delays, and bottlenecks can often be converted to money because of their consequences. Productivity problems and inefficiencies, equipment damage, and equipment underuse are other items whose conversion to monetary value is straightforward.

In examining costs, considering *all* the costs and their implications is crucial. For example, the full cost of an accident includes not only the cost of lost workdays and medical expenses, but their effects on insurance premiums, the time required for investigations, damage to equipment, and the time spent by all involved employees addressing the accident. The cost of a patient complaint includes not only the cost of the time spent resolving the complaint, but also the value of the item or service that has to be adjusted because of the complaint. The costliest consequence of a patient complaint is the price of lost goodwill from the complaining patient and from potential patients who learn of the complaint.

Placing a monetary value on a problem helps in determining whether the problem's resolutions are economically feasible. The same applies to opportunities.

The Value of an Opportunity

Sometimes projects are undertaken to pursue an opportunity. Just as the cost of a problem can be easily tabulated in most situations, the value of an opportunity can also be calculated. Examples of opportunities include implementing a new process, exploring new technology, increasing physician engagement, and upgrading the workforce to create a more competitive environment. In these situations a problem may not exist, but an opportunity to move ahead of the competition or to prevent a problem's occurrence by taking immediate action does. Assigning a proper value to this opportunity requires considering what may happen if the project is not pursued or acknowledging the windfall that might be realized if the opportunity is seized. In healthcare, the opportunity cost is not only the cost of doing the wrong thing, but also the money lost by not doing the right thing. The value is determined by following the different possible scenarios to convert specific business impact measures to money. The difficulty in this process is conducting a credible analysis. Forecasting the value of an opportunity entails many assumptions compared with calculating the value of a known outcome.

To Forecast or Not to Forecast?

The need to seek and assign value to opportunities leads to an important decision: to forecast or not to forecast ROI. If the stakes are high and support for the project is not in place, a detailed forecast may be the only way to gain the needed support and funding for the project or to inform the choice between multiple potential projects. When developing the forecast, the rigor of the analysis is an issue. In some cases, an informal forecast is sufficient, given certain assumptions about alternative outcome scenarios. In other cases, a detailed forecast is needed that uses data collected from a variety of experts, previous studies from another project, or perhaps more sophisticated analysis.

When the potential payoff, including its financial value, has been determined, the next step is to clarify the business needs.

DETERMINING BUSINESS NEEDS

Determining the business needs requires the identification of specific measures that if improved, will move the organization toward taking advantage of the payoff opportunity. Business needs refer to measures in productivity, quality, efficiency, time, and cost that can be, or need to be, improved. Improvement in these measures is important to private sector hospitals as well as in government, nonprofit, and academic healthcare organizations.

Any process, item, or perception can be measured; this measurement is critical to analysis at this level. If the project focuses on solving a problem, preventing a problem, or seizing an opportunity, business measures relevant to the opportunity are usually identifiable. These measures are normally present in a system, ready to be captured for this level of analysis. The challenge is to define the measures economically and swiftly.

Hard Data Measures

As previously presented, distinguishing between hard data and soft data may be helpful in identifying specific measures of importance. Hard data are primary measures of improvement presented in the form of rational, undisputed facts that are usually gathered within functional areas throughout an organization. These data are the most desirable type because they are easy to quantify and convert to monetary values. The fundamental criteria for gauging the effectiveness of an organization are hard data items such as revenue, productivity, and profitability, as well as measures that quantify such processes as cost control and quality assurance.

Hard data are objective and credible measures of an organization's performance. Hard data can usually be grouped in four categories, presented in Chapter 1 and repeated here as Table 3.1 for convenience. These categories—output, quality, costs, and time—are typical performance measures in any organization.

TABLE 3.1 Examples of Hard Data in Healthcare Organizations

Output	Costs
Inpatient revenue	Operating expense
Outpatient revenue	Treatment costs
Bed occupancy	Expense per discharge
Capacity	Budget variances
Clinician productivity	Unit costs
New patients	Cost by account
Forms processed	Variable costs
Discharges	Fixed costs
Screenings	Overhead cost
Inventory turnover	Operating costs
Patients served	Accident costs
ER visits	Program costs
Inpatient surgeries	Marketing expense
Tasks completed	Bad debts
Output per hour	Cost per case
Productivity	Supply chain savings
Reimbursements	
Work backlog	**Time**
Births	Length of stay
Project completions	Cycle time
	Equipment downtime
Quality	Overtime
Payment denials	On-time schedules
Nurse turnover	Time to project completion
Risk-adjusted mortality	Processing time
Risk-adjusted complications	Time to proficiency
Unplanned readmission rate	Assessment time
Medication event rate	Time to bill
Unscheduled returns	Response rate
Nosocomial infections	Patient wait times
Bloodstream infections	Efficiency
Error rates	Work stoppages
Accidents	Order response
Rework	Chart time
Shortages	Late reporting
Deviation from standard	Lost-time days
Inventory adjustments	
Incidents	
Compliance discrepancies	
Agency fines	

Hard data from a particular project involve improvements in the output of the work unit, section, department, division, or entire organization. Every healthcare organization, regardless of the type, must have basic measures of output, such as number of patients admitted, patients discharged, patients processed, and revenue generated. Because these values are monitored, changes can easily be measured by comparing "before" and "after" outputs.

Quality is an important hard data category. If quality is a major priority for the organization, processes are likely in place to measure and monitor quality. The rising prominence of quality improvement processes (such as Total Quality Management, Continuous Quality Improvement, and Six Sigma) has contributed to the tremendous recent successes in pinpointing the proper healthcare quality measures—and in assigning monetary values to them.

Cost is another important hard data category. Many projects are designed to lower, control, or eliminate the cost of a specific process or activity. Achieving cost targets has an immediate effect on the bottom line. Because of the rising cost of healthcare, and in the face of declining reimbursement, controlling costs is a critical issue. Many healthcare organizations are dedicated to lowering costs on processes and services and passing the savings along to customers.

Time is a critical measure in any organization. Some organizations gauge their performance in relation to time, such as average length of stay. Time savings translate into money savings. For example, reducing the time to process patients through MRI will increase patient revenue, decreasing the cost per patient. Sometimes, time savings may drive a classic intangible; for example, reduced patient wait time translates into increased patient satisfaction.

SOFT DATA MEASURES

Soft data are probably the most familiar measures of an organization's effectiveness, yet they can be a challenge to collect. Measures of attitude, motivation, satisfaction, and image are examples of soft data. Soft data are a substitute for hard data when hard data are not available, or they supplement hard data, providing additional information. Soft data are also more difficult to convert to monetary values. Converting soft data to money often requires using subjective techniques. They are less objective as performance measurements and are usually behavior related, yet organizations place great emphasis on them. Table 3.2 shows common examples of soft data by category presented in Chapter 1 and repeated here for convenience.

TABLE 3.2 Examples of Soft Data in Healthcare Organizations

Work Climate/Satisfaction
Grievances
Discrimination charges
Employee complaints
Employee satisfaction
Physician satisfaction
Organization commitment
Employee engagement
Nurse engagement
Physician engagement
Employee loyalty
Intent to leave
Stress

Initiative/Innovation
Creativity
Innovation
New ideas
Suggestions
New products and services
Trademarks
Copyrights and patents
Process improvements
Partnerships/alliances

Customer Service
Patient complaints
Patient satisfaction
Market share
Patient loyalty
Patient retention

Employee Development/Advancement
Promotions
Capability
Intellectual capital
Requests for transfer
Performance appraisal ratings
Readiness
Networking

Image
Brand awareness
Reputation
Leadership
Social responsibility
Environmental friendliness
Social consciousness
Diversity
External awards
Community awareness

Improvements in these measures represent important business needs, but many organizations omit them from the ROI equation because they are soft values. However, soft data can contribute to economic value to the same extent as hard data. The key is not to focus too much on the hard versus soft data distinction. A better approach is to consider data as tangible or intangible.

Tangible versus Intangible Benefits: A Better Approach

A challenge with regard to soft versus hard data is converting soft measures to monetary values. The answer to this challenge is to remember that, ultimately, all roads lead to hard data. Although creativity may be categorized as a form of soft data, a creative workplace can develop new services for patients, which leads to greater revenue—clearly a hard data measure.

Although it is possible to convert the measures listed in Table 3.2 to monetary amounts, it is often more realistic and practical to leave them in non-monetary form. This decision is based on considerations of credibility and the cost of the conversion. According to the ROI Methodology standards, Guiding Principle number 11, an intangible measure is defined as a measure that is intentionally not converted to money. If a soft data measure can be converted to a monetary value credibly using minimal resources, it is reported as a monetary value and incorporated in the ROI calculation. By converting the measure to money, it is now a tangible measure. If a data item cannot be converted to money credibly with minimal resources, it is reported as an intangible measure. Therefore, in defining business needs, the key difference between measures is not whether they represent hard or soft data, but whether they are tangible or intangible. In either case, they are important contributions toward the desired payoff and important business impact data.

BUSINESS DATA SOURCES

Sources of business data, whether tangible or intangible, are diverse. Data come from routine reporting systems in the organization. A vast array of documents, systems, databases, and reports can be used to identify specific measures to be monitored throughout the project. Impact data sources include quality reports, service records, patient tracking systems, and employee data.

Some project planners and project team members assume that corporate data sources are scarce because the data are not readily available to them. However, data can usually be located by investing a small amount of time. Rarely do new data collection systems or processes need to be developed in order to identify data representing the business needs of an organization. Table 3.3 shows a list of the sources of business data, illustrating the vast array of possibilities that exist.

In searching for the proper measures to connect to the project and to identify business needs, it is helpful to consider all possible measures that could be influenced. Sometimes, collateral measures move in harmony with the project. For example, efforts to improve safety may also improve productivity and increase job satisfaction. Weighing adverse impacts on certain

TABLE 3.3   Sources of Data

Department records	Work unit reports
Human capital databases	Payroll records
Quality reports	Marketing data
Patient care reports	Safety and health reports
Compliance reports	Patient charts
Revenue reports	Industry data from databases
Benchmarking data	Financial records
R&D status reports	Project management data
Patient satisfaction data	Employee engagement data
Cost statements	Dashboards
Scorecards	Surveys
Productivity records	Test data

measures may also help. For example, when cycle times are reduced, quality may suffer; when revenue increases, patient satisfaction may deteriorate. Finally, project team members must anticipate unintended consequences and capture them as other data items that might be connected to or influenced by the project.

In the process of settling on the precise business measures for the project, it is useful to examine various what-if scenarios. If the organization does nothing, the potential consequences of inaction should be made clear. The following questions may help in understanding the consequences of inaction:

- Will the situation deteriorate?

- Will operational problems surface?

- Will budgets be affected?

- Will we lose influence or support?

Answers to these questions can help the organization settle on a precise set of measures and can provide a hint of the extent to which the measures may change as a result of the project.

DETERMINING PERFORMANCE NEEDS

The next step in the needs analysis is to understand what led to the business need. If the proposed project addresses a problem, this step focuses on the cause of the problem. If the project makes use of an opportunity, this step focuses on what is inhibiting the organization from taking advantage of that opportunity—the performance needs.

Analysis Techniques

Uncovering the causes of the problem or the inhibitors to success requires a variety of analytical techniques. These techniques—such as problem analysis, nominal group technique, force-field analysis, and just plain brainstorming—are used to clarify job performance needs. Table 3.4 lists a few of the analysis techniques. The technique that is used will depend on the organizational setting, the apparent depth of the problem, and the budget allocated to such analysis. Multiple techniques can be used when performance may be lacking for a number of reasons.

A Sensible Approach

Analysis takes time and adds to the cost of a project. Examining records, researching databases, and observing individuals can provide important data, but a more cost-effective approach might include employing internal and/or external experts to help analyze the problem. Performance needs can vary considerably and may include ineffective behavior, a dysfunctional work climate, inadequate systems, a disconnected process flow, improper

TABLE 3.4 Analysis Techniques

Statistical process control	Diagnostic instruments
Brainstorming	Focus groups
Problem analysis	Probing interviews
Cause-and-effect diagram	Satisfaction surveys
Force-field analysis	Engagement surveys
Mind mapping	Exit interviews
Affinity diagrams	Exit surveys
Simulations	Nominal group technique

procedures, a nonsupportive culture, outdated technology, and a non-accommodating environment, to name a few. When needs vary and with many techniques from which to choose, the opportunity exists for over-analysis and excessive costs. Consequently, a sensible approach is necessary.

DETERMINING LEARNING NEEDS

The solution to performance needs uncovered in the previous step often requires a learning component—such as participants and team members learning how to perform a task differently, or learning how to use a process or system. In some cases learning is the principal solution, as in competency or capability development, major technology change, and system instal-lations. For other projects, learning is a minor aspect of the solution and may involve simply understanding the process, procedure, or policy. For example, in the implementation of a new ethics policy for an organization, the learning component requires understanding how the policy works as well as the participants' role in the policy. In short, a learning solution is not always needed, but all solutions have a learning component.

A variety of approaches are available for measuring specific learning needs. Often, multiple tasks and jobs are involved in a project and should be addressed separately. Sometimes the least effective way to identify the skills and knowledge that are needed is to ask the participants involved in implementing the project. They may not be clear on what is needed and may not know enough to provide adequate input. One of the most useful ways to determine learning needs is to ask the individuals who understand the process. They can best determine what skills and knowledge are nec-essary to address the performance issues that have been identified. This may be the appropriate time to find out the extent to which the knowledge and skills already exist.

Job and task analysis is effective when a new job is created or when an existing job description changes significantly. As jobs are redesigned and new tasks must be identified, this type of analysis offers a systematic way of detailing the job and task. Essentially, a job analysis is the collection and evaluation of work-related information. A task analysis identifies the spe-cific knowledge, skills, tools, and conditions necessary to the performance of a particular job.

Observation of current practices and procedures in an organization may be necessary as the project is implemented. This can often indicate the level of capability and help to identify the correct procedures. Observations can be used to examine work flow and interpersonal interactions, including those between management and team members.

Sometimes, the demonstration of knowledge surrounding a certain task, process, or procedure provides evidence of what capabilities exist and what is lacking. Such demonstration can be as simple as a skill practice or role play, or as complex as an extensive mechanical or electronic simulation. The point is to use it as a way to determine whether employees know how to perform a particular process. Through demonstration, specific learning needs can evolve.

Testing as a learning needs assessment process is not used as frequently as other methods, but it can be useful. Employees are tested to reveal what they know about a particular situation. This information helps to guide learning issues.

When implementing projects in organizations with existing managers or team leaders, input from a management team may be used to assess the current situation and to indicate the knowledge and skills required by the new situation. This input can be elicited through surveys, interviews, or focus groups. It can be a rich source of information about what the users of the project will need to know to make it successful.

Where learning is a minor component, learning needs are simple. Determining learning needs can be time-consuming for major projects where new procedures, technologies, and processes must be developed. As in developing job performance needs, it is important not to spend excessive time analyzing learning needs but rather to collect as much data as possible with minimal resources.

DETERMINING PREFERENCE NEEDS

Preferences drive the project requirements and provide structure for the project. These preferences define how the particular project will be implemented. If the project is a solution to a problem, this step defines how the solution will be installed. If the project makes use of an opportunity, this step outlines how the opportunity will be addressed, taking into consideration the preferences of those involved in the project.

Preference needs focus on the perceived value of the project from all stakeholders involved, particularly the participants who must make it work. Will they see it as necessary, practical, useful, and critical to patient care?

Preference needs define the parameters of the project in terms of scope, timing, location, technology, deliverables, and the degree of disruption allowed. They are developed from the input of several stakeholders rather than from one individual. The urgency of project implementation may introduce a constraint in the preferences. Those who support or own the project often impose preferences on the project in terms of timing, budget, and the use of technology. Because preferences represent a Level 1 need, the project structure and solution will relate directly to the reaction objectives and to the initial reaction to the project.

When determining the preference needs, more detail is needed. Projects often go astray and fail to reach their full potential because of misunderstandings and differences in expectations. Preference needs should be addressed before the project begins. Pertinent issues are often outlined in the project proposal or planning documentation.

DEVELOPING OBJECTIVES FOR PROJECTS

Projects are driven by objectives. Objectives position the project for success if they represent the needs of the business and include clearly defined measures of achievement. A project may be aimed at implementing a solution that addresses a particular dilemma, problem, or opportunity. In other situations, the initial project is designed to develop a range of feasible solutions, with one specific solution selected prior to implementation. Regardless of the project, multiple levels of objectives are necessary. These levels follow the five-level data categorization scheme and define precisely what will occur as a project is implemented. They correspond to the levels of needs and the levels of evaluation presented in Figure 3.1.

Reaction Objectives

For a project to be successful, the stakeholders immediately involved in the process must react favorably—or at least not negatively—to the project. Ideally, those directly involved should be satisfied with the project and see the value in it. This feedback must be obtained routinely during the project in order to make adjustments, keep the project on track, and redesign certain aspects as necessary. Unfortunately, for many projects, specific objectives at this level are not developed, nor are data collection mechanisms put in place to allow channels for feedback.

Developing reaction objectives should be straightforward and relatively easy. The objectives reflect the degree of immediate as well as long-term satisfaction and explore issues important to the success of the project. They also form the basis for evaluating the chain of impact, and they emphasize planned action when feasible and needed. Typical issues addressed in the development of reaction objectives are relevance, timeliness, usefulness, importance, appropriateness, convenience, and motivation. The following are examples of reaction objectives.

At the end of the project, participants should rate each of the following statements at least a 4 out of 5 on a 5-point scale:

- The project was organized.
- The project coordinators were effective.
- The project was valuable for my work.
- The project was important to my success.
- The project was critical for patient care.
- The project had practical content.
- The project represented an excellent use of my time.
- I will use the material from this project again.

LEARNING OBJECTIVES

Every project involves at least one learning objective, and most involve more. With projects entailing major change, the learning component is important. In situations narrower in scope, such as the implementation of a new policy, the learning component is minor but still necessary. To ensure that the various stakeholders have learned what they need to know to make the project successful, learning objectives are developed. The following are examples of learning objectives.

After the launch of the project, participants should be able to:

- Identify the six features of the new ethics policy.
- Demonstrate the use of each step of the procedure within the standard time.

- Score 75 or better on the new strategy quiz.
- Explain the value of patient satisfaction to a work group.
- Successfully complete a R402 simulation.
- Know how to properly use a catheter.

Objectives are critical to the measurement of learning because they communicate the expected outcomes from the learning component and define the competency or level of performance necessary to make the project successful. They provide a focus to allow participants to clearly identify what it is they must learn and do.

APPLICATION OBJECTIVES

Application and implementation objectives define what is expected of the project and often target the expected level of performance. Application objectives are similar to learning objectives but relate to actual performance. They provide specific milestones indicating when part or all of the process has been implemented. Typical application objectives are as follows.

When the project is implemented:
- At least 99.1% of nurses will be following the correct sequences after three weeks of use.
- Within one year, 10% of employees will submit documented suggestions for cutting costs.
- Directors will initiate three cost reduction projects within fifteen days.
- Patient service representatives will use all five interaction skills with at least half the patient within the next month.
- 95% of high-potential employees will complete individual development plans within two years.
- 80% of employees will use one or more of the three cost containment features of the healthcare plan.
- 50% of medical conference attendees follow up with at least one contact from the conference.
- The average 360° leadership assessment score will improve from 3.4 to 4.1 on a 5-point scale.

- Employees will routinely use problem-solving skills when faced with a healthcare quality problem.
- Sexual harassment activity will cease within three months after the zero-tolerance policy is implemented.
- By November, pharmaceutical sales reps will communicate adverse effects of a specific prescription drug to all physicians in their territories.

Application objectives are critical because they describe the expected outcomes in the intermediate area—between the learning of new tasks and procedures and the delivery of the impact of this learning. Application and implementation objectives describe how things should be or the desired state of the workplace once the project solution has been implemented. They provide a basis for evaluating on-the-job changes and performance.

Impact Objectives

Every major project should drive one or more business impact measures. Impact objectives indicate key business measures that should improve as the application and implementation objectives are achieved. The following are typical impact objectives.

When the project is completed:
- Incidents should decrease by 20% within the next calendar year.
- The average number of infections should decrease from 214 to 153 per month.
- The patient satisfaction index should rise by 2% during the next calendar year.
- Operating expenses should decrease by 10% in the fourth quarter.
- Readmission rates should decrease by 25% in six months.
- Overtime for shift nurses should be reduced by 20% in the third quarter of this year.
- Patient complaints should be reduced from an average of 55 per month to an average of 22 per month.

- The physician engagement index should increase by one point during the next calendar year.
- Clinician productivity should increase 10% during the next two years.
- System downtime should be reduced from three hours per month to no more than two hours per month in six months.
- Outpatient revenue should increase by 20% in one year.

Impact objectives are critical to measuring business performance because they define the ultimate expected outcome and the business unit performance that should result from the project. Above all, impact objectives emphasize achievement of the bottom-line results that key client groups expect and demand.

ROI OBJECTIVES

ROI objectives define the expected minimum payoff from investing in the project. An ROI objective is typically expressed as an acceptable ROI percentage, which is expressed as annual monetary benefits minus cost, divided by the actual cost, and multiplied by 100. A zero percent ROI indicates a breakeven project. A 50 percent ROI indicates recapture of the project cost and an additional 50 percent "earnings" (50 cents for every dollar invested).

For some projects, such as the purchase of a new company, a new building, or major equipment, the ROI objective is large relative to the ROI of other expenditures. However, the calculation is the same for both. For many organizations, the ROI objective for a project is set slightly higher than the ROI expected from other "routine investments" because of the relative newness of applying the ROI concept to the types of projects described in this book. For example, if the expected ROI from the purchase of a new hospital is 20 percent, the ROI from a new facility construction might be around 25 percent. The important point is that the ROI objective should be established up front in discussions with the project sponsor. Excluding the ROI objective leaves stakeholders questioning the economic success of a project. If a project reaps a 25 percent ROI, is it successful? Not if the objective was a 50 percent ROI.

FINAL THOUGHTS

This chapter outlines the beginning point of the ROI Methodology, showing how a project can be structured from the outset, with detailed needs identified, ultimately leading to project objectives at five levels. This level of detail ensures that the project is aligned with business needs and remains results-focused throughout the process. Without this analysis, the project runs the risk of failing to deliver the value that it should, or not being in alignment with business measures. The outputs of the analysis are objectives, which provide a focus for project designers, developers, and implementers, as well as participants and users who must make the project successful. Issues surrounding data collection are discussed in the next chapters. Collecting reaction data and perceived value data will be covered first.

Measuring Reaction
and Learning

When the initial analysis is completed and the project is positioned for success, implementation occurs. During implementation, feedback is collected from participants involved in the project. Their reactions to the project and learning connected with the project indicate its potential for success.

Participant feedback can be powerful information for making adjustments and measuring initial success. Measuring learning is also an important part of the evaluation process, especially when a project is intended to change behaviors or introduce new procedures, systems, or processes on the job. Measuring learning is particularly important in healthcare, because professionals and managers are constantly engaging in "action learning." Through the use of observation, pilot programs, clinical trials and studies, simulation centers, model units, and institutional review boards (IRBs), learning can be properly measured. Participant knowledge of what to do and how to do it is critical to a project's success. This chapter outlines the most common approaches to collecting reaction and learning data and explores ways to use the information for maximum value.

OPENING STORIES

UK PHARMACEUTICAL COMPANY

A few years ago, the IT department of a large pharmaceutical company based in the United Kingdom planned a project to place high-speed Internet connections in the homes of all of its pharmaceutical sales reps. The theory was that by having a high-speed connection, the reps would be able to download important documents and information concerning products, content, research results, symptoms for use, side effects, and marketing strategies related to each project. Having this information in hand quickly would enhance the sales effectiveness as the reps discuss issues with physicians. Also, it would save valuable time and would allow reps to see more physicians. In essence, it would increase productivity and ultimately increase sales. Before the project was implemented, the IT department contacted a group of sales reps to collect their reaction to this process. Almost all of them indicated that this information would not drive productivity or sales, it is only a minor convenience. Reps stated that they generally downloaded needed documents in the evening, when time was not an issue. Having more time and a faster Internet connection would not necessarily mean they would be able to see more physicians. Schedules and territories are set in advance, as are frequency of visits, so little value would be added. Consequently, the project was halted based on this reaction from the potential participants.

UNITED NATIONS

The United Nations (UN) has developed goals to guide different agencies. Many of these goals, called Millennium Development Goals (MDG), focus on healthcare, healthcare delivery, and the health of the citizens. Three of these goals focus directly on HIV and AIDS.[1] The first goal focuses on increasing the awareness of HIV and AIDS. To achieve this first goal, the UN must collect data about the knowledge of HIV and AIDS, what causes it, and how to prevent it. This MDG requires agencies to collect learning data in the form of a simple assessment of the knowledge that has been gained among the citizens of a particular country from the various communiqués on the topic. Essentially, it measures the learning of specific knowledge.

Memorial Health University Medical Center

In another study involving the Memorial Health University Medical Center in Savannah, Georgia, a physician portal was developed that allowed physicians to access a variety of data and important patient information. Among the measures of success were the portal usage statistics, which tracked the number of users, the number of active physicians with access, the average number of physician users per day, and the average time per physician spent using the portal. The portal also measured the reaction to the process, which included responses to questions such as "Is the portal easy to use?" "Does it save you time?" "Have you increased referrals to the medical center as a result?"

These three brief examples show the importance of measuring reaction and learning, which are the beginning points of any project and, if ignored, can cause the project to suffer and be unsuccessful.

THE IMPORTANCE OF REACTION

It is difficult to imagine that a project can be successful when those involved in the project react adversely. Collecting reaction is critical to understanding how well a project serves those involved with it and the potential of the project to meet the identified business needs.

Stakeholder Satisfaction

Reaction and perceived value are customer satisfaction measures for the participants involved in the project. Without sustained, favorable reactions, the project may not succeed. The participants who have a direct role in the project are immediately affected by it and often must change processes or procedures or make other job adjustments to make the project successful. Participant feedback on preferences is critical to making adjustments and changes in the project as it unfolds. For example, in a project involving new procedures to reduce infections in the ICU, the participants are the nurses and physicians who must make the project work.

The feedback of project supporters is also important because this group is in a position to influence the project's continuation and development. Supporters include managers of participants, individuals who support the participants and the groups who are interested in the outcomes of the project.

The sponsors, who approve budgets, allocate resources, and ultimately live with the project's success or failure, must be completely satisfied with the project—and their overall satisfaction must be measured early and often.

Immediate Adjustments

A project can quickly go astray if it is mismatched to the solution from the beginning, so securing feedback early in the process is necessary to allow for immediate adjustments. Feedback can help prevent misunderstandings, miscommunications, and, more importantly, misappropriations. Collecting and using reaction data promptly can enable an improperly designed project to be altered before more serious problems arise.

Predictive Capability

Reaction data can be used to predict application of a project using analytical techniques. In a follow-up, project participants provide input on effectiveness of the project's application, and the data are compared to the reaction data. A significant correlation between the two indicates a causal chain, and the reaction data become a forecast. Figure 4.1 demonstrates

FIGURE 4.1   Correlations Between Reaction and Application

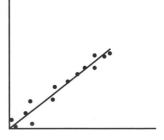

the correlation between reactive feedback and application data. Countless studies have been conducted to verify this correlation and causation.

For example, the reaction measures are taken as the project is introduced, and the success of the implementation is later judged using the same scale (e.g., a 1 to 5 rating). When significant positive correlations are present, reaction measures can have predictive capability. Some reaction measures shown to have predictive capability include the following:

- The project is relevant to my work.
- The project is necessary.
- The project is important to my success.
- The project is important to the success of this organization.
- I intend to make this project successful.
- I would recommend this project to others.

These measures and others like them consistently lead to strong positive correlations and consequently represent more powerful feedback than typical measures of satisfaction with the project. Some organizations collect these data (or at least some of the measures) for every project or program initiated.

THE IMPORTANCE OF LEARNING

A project will not be successful if those involved do not learn what they need to know to make it successful. Obviously, new medical procedures, new equipment, new technology, or new processes will fail if participants do not have the knowledge or skills to make them successful. Several key principles illustrate the importance of measuring learning during the project. Each in itself is sufficient to justify the measurement of learning; collectively, they provide an indication of the range of benefits that result from measuring the changes in skills and knowledge needed for a project.

THE IMPORTANCE OF INTELLECTUAL CAPITAL

Intellectual capital has become an important concept as organizations have progressed from agricultural to industrial to knowledge-based systems.

FIGURE 4.2 Intellectual Capital

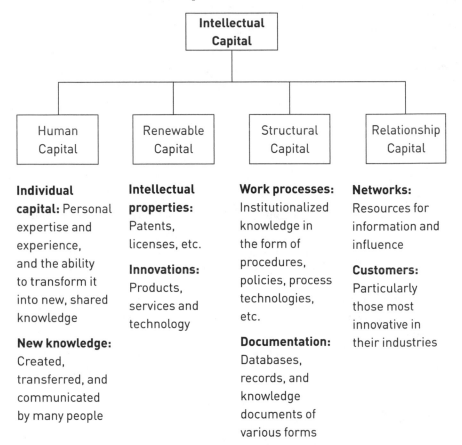

Intellectual capital is what the organization knows, and it can be classified in a variety of ways for measurement purposes. Figure 4.2 illustrates one categorization of intellectual capital, showing intellectual capital as a combination of human capital, renewable capital, structural capital, and relationship capital.[2] As projects are implemented, they focus on increasing one or more of these major elements of intellectual capital.

THE LEARNING ORGANIZATION

In the past two decades, organizations in the healthcare field have experienced a rapid transformation of competitive markets as a result of economic changes. These organizations must learn new ways to serve patients and use innovations and technology to enhance their efficiency and restructure, reorganize, and execute their functions. In response to this need for a change in strategy, the concept of the learning organization evolved. This concept requires organizations to use learning proactively in an integrated way and to support growth for individuals, teams, and entire organizations.

With the new focus on creating learning organizations—where countless activities and processes are in place to promote continuous learning—measurement has become an even more important issue.

THE COMPLIANCE ISSUE

Healthcare organizations face an increasing number of regulations with which they must routinely comply. These regulations involve all aspects of operations and are considered essential by governing bodies to protect patients, investors, and the environment. Employees must have a certain amount of knowledge about the regulations to maintain compliance. Consequently, an organization must measure the extent of employee learning and understanding with regard to regulations to ensure that compliance is not a problem. Ensuring compliance is routinely accomplished in healthcare organizations through the use of institutional review boards (IRBs).

Some projects are compliance driven. For example, one hospital chain had to implement a project to reduce sexual harassment complaints. This project was precipitated by the hospital's continuing failure to comply with the regulations. The problem appeared to be a lack of knowledge of the law and what constitutes sexual harassment. As the project was initiated, learning was measured on a pretest, with a follow-up posttest conducted.

THE USE AND DEVELOPMENT OF COMPETENCIES

A competency model describes a particular combination of knowledge, skills, and characteristics necessary to perform a role in an organization. The use of competencies and competency models has dramatically increased in recent years in the healthcare area. In the struggle for competitive advantage, many healthcare firms have focused on people as the key to success. Competency models are used to ensure that employees do the right things, clarifying and articulating what is required for effective performance. Competency models help organizations align behavior and skills with the strategic direction of the company.

The Role of Learning in Projects

When projects involve new equipment, processes, and technology, the human factor is critical to project success. Whether a healthcare organization is restructuring or adding new systems, employees must learn how to work in the new environment, which requires the development of new knowledge and skills. Complex environments, procedures, and tools must be used in an intelligent way to reap the desired benefits for the organization. Employees must learn in different ways—not just in a formal classroom environment, but through technology-based learning and on-the-job practice, such as in simulations and pilot programs. Administrators and managers serve as coaches or mentors in some projects. In a few cases, learning coaches or on-the-job trainers are used with projects to ensure that learning is transferred to the job and is implemented as planned.

Project participants don't always fully understand what they must do. Although the chain of impact can be broken at any level, a common place for such a break is at Level 2, Learning. Employees simply may not know what to do or how to do it properly. When the application and implementation do not go smoothly, learning deficiency is often the problem. By addressing learning throughout project implementation and measuring the level of learning that occurs, project managers increase the chances that participants will perform as they should.

SOURCES OF DATA

Collecting the first two levels of outcome data begins with selecting the source. Several sources of reaction and learning data are readily available and accessible for any level of evaluation. Even though six distinct categories of sources are possible, the challenge is to use the most credible source.

Project Participants

The most widely used data source for project evaluation is the participants, those directly involved in the project. These "users" must take the skills and knowledge they acquired in the project and apply them in their work. They also may be asked to explain the potential impact of that application. Participants are a rich source of data for almost every aspect of a project. They are usually the most credible source of reaction and learning data.

Participant Managers

Another key source of data is the individuals who directly lead the participants. These individuals have a vested interest in the project and are often in a position to observe the participants as they attempt to use the knowledge and skills acquired in the project. Consequently, they can report on the successes associated with the project as well as the difficulties and problems. Although managerial input is usually most valuable as a source of reaction and learning data, it is also useful for other levels of evaluation.

Support Team

When teams are involved in the implementation of the project, those who support the team can provide useful information about the perceived changes prompted by the project. Input from this group is pertinent only to issues directly related to their work. Although data from this group can be helpful and instructive, they are sometimes not collected because of the potential for introducing inaccuracies to the feedback process. Data collection should be restricted to those team members capable of providing meaningful insight into the value of the project.

Internal or External Customers

The internal customers of the project are another source of data. In some situations, internal customers provide input on perceived changes linked to the project. This source of data is more appropriate for projects directly affecting the internal customers. For example, an IT project involves a new system to process and use data. The various departments that are affected by the system are the internal customers for the project. They report on how the project has influenced (or will influence) their work or the service they receive. Although this group may be somewhat limited in their knowledge of the scope of a project, their perceptions can be a source of valuable data that may indicate a direction for change in the project. Sometimes a project directly affects the external customers, the patients. For example, a project to reduce patient wait time in an outpatient facility may require input directly from patients.

PROJECT LEADERS AND CONSULTANTS

The project leader and project team may also provide input on the success of the project. This input may be based on on-the-job observations during the implementation of the project and after its completion. For example, several consultants (with a project leader) are working with collaborative work teams to reduce the average length of stay. Data are also collected from the consultants. Data from this source have limited utility because project leaders often have a vested interest in the outcome of the evaluation, and thus may lack objectivity.

SPONSORS AND SENIOR MANAGERS

One of the most useful data sources is the sponsor or client group, usually a senior management team. The perception of the sponsor, whether an individual or a group, is critical to project success. Sponsors can provide input on all types of issues and are usually available and willing to offer feedback. This is a preferred source for reaction data, because these data usually indicate what is necessary to make adjustments and to measure success.

TOPICS FOR REACTION MEASURES

When capturing reaction data, it is important to focus on the content of the project. Too often, feedback data reflect aesthetic (or experience) issues that may not be relevant to the substance of the project.

Many topics are critical targets for feedback. Table 4.1 presents some examples of topics explored for reaction feedback. Feedback is needed in connection with almost every major issue, step, or process to make sure things are advancing properly. Stakeholders will provide reaction input on the appropriateness of the project planning schedule and objectives, and the progress made with the planning tools. If the project is perceived as irrelevant or unnecessary to the participants, more than likely it will not succeed in the workplace. Support for the project—including resources—represents an important area of feedback.

TABLE 4.1 Topics for Reaction Input

Readiness	Patient centered	Valuable
Timely	Importance	Powerful
Relevance	Motivational	Leading edge
Intent to use	Rewarding	Project leadership
Useful	Execution	Just for me
Necessary	New information	Efficient
Recommend to others	Facilities/environment	Easy/Difficult
Appropriate	Practical	User friendly

Participants must be assured that the project has the necessary commitment and is adding appropriate value. Issues important to project management and sponsors include readiness of participants, motivation to make the project successful, and intent to use the project content, materials, and tools. Perceived value of the project is often a critical parameter. Major funding decisions are made based on perceived value when stronger evidence of value is unavailable.

TOPICS FOR LEARNING MEASURES

Measuring learning focuses on knowledge, skills, and attitudes as well as the individual's confidence in applying or implementing the project. Typical measures collected at this level are:

- Skills
- Knowledge
- Awareness
- Understanding
- Contacts
- Attitudes
- Capacity
- Readiness
- Confidence

The concept of knowledge is quite general and often includes the assimilation of facts, figures, and ideas. Instead of knowledge, terms such as awareness, understanding, and information may be used to denote specific categories. Sometimes, perceptions or attitudes are changed based on what a participant has learned. For example, participants' perceptions about a diverse work group are often changed with the implementation of a major diversity program. In some cases, the issue is developing a reservoir of knowledge and related skills for improving capability, capacity, or readiness. Networking is sometimes a part of a project, and developing contacts that may be valuable later is important. This networking may occur within or externally to an organization. For example, within the organization, a leadership development project may include different functional parts of the organization, and an expected outcome from a learning perspective is knowing who to contact at particular times in the future. For projects that involve prospective patients, such as a marketing event, new contacts that result from the event can be important and ultimately pay off in terms of patient revenue growth.

DATA COLLECTION TIMING

The timing of data collection centers on particular events connected with the project. Capturing reaction and learning data during the early stages of implementation is critical. Ideally, this feedback validates the decision to go forward with the project and confirms that alignment with business needs exists. Problems identified by initial feedback mean that adjustments can be made early in its implementation. In practice, however, many organizations omit this early feedback, waiting until significant parts of the project have been implemented, at which point feedback may be more meaningful.

For longer projects, feedback may be needed at multiple points in time. Measures can be taken at the beginning of the project and then at routine intervals when the project is under way.

THE CHALLENGES AND BENEFITS OF MEASURING LEARNING

Measuring learning involves major challenges that may inhibit a comprehensive approach to the process. However, besides being an essential part of the ROI Methodology, this measurement provides many other benefits that help ensure a project's success.

CHALLENGES

The greatest challenge in measuring learning is to maintain objectivity without crossing ethical or legal lines while keeping costs low. A common method of measuring learning is testing, but this approach generates additional challenges.

The concern about testing is the "fear" factor. Few people enjoy being tested. Many are offended by it and feel that their professional prowess is being questioned. Another concern with tests is the legal and ethical repercussions of basing decisions involving employee status on test scores.

Because of these concerns, organizations use other techniques to measure learning, such as surveys, questionnaires, and simulations. The challenge with these methods, however, is the potential for inaccurate measures and the financial burden they impose. Consequently, organizations need to be aware of the constant trade-off between additional resources and the accuracy of the learning measurement process.

THE BENEFITS OF MEASURING LEARNING

The benefits of measuring learning are reflected in the reasons for learning measurement described earlier. First, measurement at this level checks the progress of the project against the objectives. Objectives are critical to a project and should be established at each level. Fundamentally, the measurement of learning reveals the extent of knowledge and skill acquisition in relation to the project. This critical element is particularly important for knowledge-based projects, new technology applications, and projects designed to build competencies.

In addition to assessing improvement in skills or knowledge, measurement at this level provides feedback to the individuals delivering the skills or knowledge so that adjustments can be made. If project participants are not learning, a problem with the way the learning is being delivered indicates a need for modification. A learning measure can identify strengths and weaknesses in the method of project presentation or execution and may point out flaws in the design or delivery. Thus, measuring learning can pinpoint mismatches among various aspects of a project and thereby lead to changes or improvement.

Another important benefit is that, in many cases, learning measures enhance participant performance. Verification and feedback concerning the knowledge and skills acquired can encourage participants to improve in certain areas. When employees excel, feedback motivates them to enhance their performance even further. In short, positive feedback on learning builds confidence and the desire to continue improving. Without such measurement, participants will never know their potential to perform.

Finally, measuring learning helps to maintain accountability. Because projects are aimed at making organizations better—whether new procedures are being implemented, competencies are being improved, or systems and processes are being enhanced—learning is an important part of any project and its measurement is vital in confirming that improvement has in fact occurred.

DATA COLLECTION METHODS

A variety of methods can be used to collect reaction and learning data. Instruments range from simple surveys to comprehensive interviews. The appropriate instrument depends on the type of data needed (quantitative versus qualitative), the convenience of the method to potential respondents, the culture of the organization, and the cost of a particular instrument.

QUESTIONNAIRES AND SURVEYS

The questionnaire or survey is the most common method of collecting reaction and learning data. Questionnaires and surveys come in all sizes, ranging from short forms to detailed multiple-page instruments. They can be used to obtain subjective data about participants' reactions and learning, as well as to document responses for future use in a projected ROI analysis. Proper design of questionnaires and surveys is important to ensure versatility.

Several basic types of questions are used when measuring reaction and learning. The dichotomous question (yes/no) and the numerical scale (e.g., 1 to 5) are typical reaction measurement formats. Essentially, the individual is indicating the extent of his or her agreement with a particular statement or is giving an opinion of varying conviction on an issue. Surveys are a type of questionnaire but focus on attitudinal elements. Surveys have many applications in the measurement of reaction and learning for projects designed to improve work. Depending on the purpose of the evaluation, the questionnaire or survey may contain one or more question types. The key is to select the question or statement that is most appropriate for the information sought. However, open-ended questions can sometimes be used, particularly in asking about specific problem areas. Checklists, multiple-choice questions, and ranking scales are more appropriate for measuring application, which is described in later chapters.

For most reaction and learning evaluations, questionnaires and surveys are used. When a follow-up evaluation is planned, a wide range of issues will be covered in a detailed questionnaire. Asking for too much detail in either the reaction questionnaire or the follow-up questionnaire can reduce the response rate. The objective, therefore, of questionnaire and survey design and administration is to maximize response. Table 4.2 lists actions that can help ensure adequate response rates for questionnaires and surveys.

TABLE 4.2   Maximizing Response Rates for Questionnaires and Surveys

- Provide advance communication.
- Communicate the purpose.
- Identify who will see the results.
- Describe the data integration process.
- Let the target audience know that they are part of a sample.
- Add emotional appeal.
- Design for simplicity.
- Make it look professional and attractive.
- Use the local manager support.
- Build on earlier data.
- Pilot test the questionnaire.
- Recognize the expertise of participants.
- Consider the use of incentives.
- Have an executive sign the introductory letter.
- Report the use of results.
- Provide an update to create pressure to respond.
- Present previous responses.
- Introduce the questionnaire at the beginning of the project.
- Use follow-up reminders.
- Consider a captive audience.
- Consider the appropriate medium for easy response.
- Estimate the necessary time to complete the questionnaire.
- Show the timing of the planned steps.
- Personalize the process.
- Collect data anonymously or confidentially.
- Send a copy of the results to the participants.

INTERVIEWS

Interviews, although not used as frequently as questionnaires to capture reaction and learning data, may be conducted by the project team, an internal staff group, or a third party to secure data that are difficult to obtain through written responses. Interviews can uncover success stories that may help to communicate early achievements of the project. Respondents may be reluctant to describe their experiences using a questionnaire but may volunteer the information to a skillful interviewer using probing techniques. The interview is versatile and is appropriate for soliciting reaction and learning data as well as application and implementation data. A major disadvantage of the interview is that it consumes time, which increases the cost of data collection. It also requires interviewer preparation to ensure that the process is consistent.

FOCUS GROUPS

Focus groups are particularly useful when in-depth feedback is needed. The focus group format involves a small-group discussion conducted by an experienced facilitator. It is designed to solicit qualitative judgments on a selected topic or issue. All group members are required to provide input, with individual input building on group input.

The focus group approach has several advantages. The basic premise behind the use of focus groups is that when quality judgments are subjective, several individual judgments are better than one. The group process, where participants often motivate one another, is an effective method for generating and clarifying ideas and hypotheses. It is inexpensive and can be quickly planned and conducted. Its flexibility allows exploration of a project's unexpected outcomes or applications.

PERFORMANCE TESTS

Performance testing allows participants to exhibit the skills (and occasionally knowledge or attitudes) that have been learned in a project. A skill can be manual, verbal, or analytical, or a combination of the three. Performance testing is used frequently in task-related projects; here the participants are allowed to demonstrate what they have learned and to show how they would use the skill on the job, such as demonstrating CPR or demonstrating a new medical procedure. This method is common in healthcare. In other situations, performance testing may involve skill practice or role-playing such as participants demonstrating a discussion or problem-solving skills that they have acquired.

In a particular situation, technicians were participating in a quality improvement project. As part of the project, participants were given the assignment of designing and testing a quality system. A project team manager observed participants as they checked out the system; then the manager completed the same design and compared his results with those of the participants. These comparisons and the performance of the designs provided an evaluation of the project and represented an adequate reflection of the skills learned in the project.

TECHNOLOGY AND TASK SIMULATIONS

Another technique for measuring learning is simulation. This method involves the construction and application of a procedure or task that simulates or models the work involved in the project or program. The simulation is designed to represent, as closely as possible, the actual job situation. Participants try out the simulated activity and their performance is evaluated based on how well they accomplish the task. Simulations offer several advantages. They permit a job or part of a job to be reproduced in a manner almost identical to the real setting. Through careful planning and design, the simulation can have all the central characteristics of the real situation. Even complex jobs can be simulated adequately. Some hospitals use a simulated OR where physicians and staff can practice skills in real-time environment.

Although the initial development can be expensive, simulations can be cost-effective in the long run, particularly for large projects or situations where a project may be repeated. Another advantage of using simulations is safety. Safety considerations for many jobs require participants to be trained in simulated conditions. For example, emergency medical technicians risk injury and even death if they do not learn the needed techniques prior to encountering a real-life emergency. Most hospitals have a disaster plan in place, which is rehearsed periodically to ensure employees react appropriately should the event actually occur.

Although a variety of simulation techniques are used to evaluate learning during a project, two of the most common techniques are technology and task simulation. A technology simulation uses a combination of electronic and mechanical devices to reproduce real-life situations. These simulations are used in conjunction with programs to develop operational and diagnostic skills. A comprehensive example is a simulated "patient." Less-expensive devices have been developed to simulate equipment operation.

A task simulation involves a participant's performance in a specific activity. For example, a charge nurse must demonstrate the task of creating a new medical chart. This task simulation serves as the evaluation.

DATA USE

Unfortunately, reaction and learning data are sometimes collected and then disregarded. Too many project evaluators use the information to feed their egos and then allow it to quietly disappear into their files, forgetting the original purpose behind its collection. In an effective evaluation, the information collected must be used to make adjustments or verify success; otherwise, the exercise is a waste of time.

Because this input is the principal measure supplied by key stakeholders, it provides an indication of their reaction to, and satisfaction with, the project. More important, these data provide evidence relating to the potential success of the project. Reaction data should be used to:

- Identify the strengths and weaknesses of the project and make adjustments.

- Evaluate project team members.

- Evaluate the quality and content of planned improvements.

- Develop norms and standards.

- Link with follow-up data.

- Market future projects based on the positive reaction.

Learning data are used to:

- Provide individual feedback to build confidence.

- Validate that learning has been acquired.

- Improve the project.

- Evaluate project leaders/facilitators.

- Build a database for project comparisons

FINAL THOUGHTS

This chapter discussed data collection at the first two levels of evaluation—reaction and learning. Measuring reaction and learning is a component of every study and is a critical factor in a project's success. The data are collected using a variety of techniques, although surveys and questionnaires are most often used because of their cost-effectiveness and convenience. The data are important in allowing immediate adjustments to be made on the project.

Reaction data are important, but importance to executives increases as the evaluation moves up the chain of impact. Data collection at the second level, learning, is usually more important. The next chapter focuses on Level 3, measuring application and implementation.

CHAPTER 5

Measuring Application and Implementation

M any projects fail because of breakdowns in implementation. In those situations, project participants just don't do what they should, when they should, at the frequency they should. Measuring at this level (Level 3) is critical to understanding the success of the implementation of new processes, procedures, systems, or equipment. Without successful implementation, positive business impact will not occur—and no positive ROI will be achieved. This chapter explores the most common ways to evaluate the application and implementation of healthcare projects.

OPENING STORIES

REGIONAL HEALTHCARE

A regional healthcare firm has implemented a new enterprise resource management system. The implementation focuses on the healthcare organization's current procurement, inventory control processes, financial management system, payroll system, discount structures, and specific benchmarks. In addition, cost accounting and capital allocation systems were pinpointed to align with payroll and productivity systems such as scheduling and forecasting. To make this system work properly as it is installed, the users of the system must:

- Manage hospital assets and resources effectively.

- Integrate suppliers.

- Standardize supplies, devices, and equipment across departments and physicians.

- Develop an allocation process.

- Identify areas where the firm is paying too much for specific items.

- Employ more self-service procurement technology.

- Decentralize the inventory management process.

- Employ handheld technology.

- Complete the implementation on schedule.

Although this system will have tremendous payoffs in cost savings, time savings, reductions in unnecessary orders, and overpayments, these benefits will not occur unless the new system is implemented properly and all users are following correct application and use.

VA HEALTHCARE

When implementing a leadership program within the Veterans Administration Healthcare Centers, leadership skills identified as inadequate were targeted for change to improve the VA medical center system. As participants entered the program, they were asked to change behaviors, approaches, and processes as they worked to improve the medical centers. After implementation, a follow-up evaluation showed evidence that participants:

- Applied the 11-step goal-setting process.

- Used a 12-step leadership planning process.

- Used 10 ways to create higher levels of employee loyalty and satisfaction.

- Applied the concept for adjustment in at least 5 scenarios.

- Used a creative problem solving process in 80% of problems identified.

- Implemented at least 5 of the 7 ways to build positive relationships.

- Used a 4-step process to address mistakes.

- Used at least 5 ways to improve communications.

These specific improvements showed change in leadership behavior. In light of the important consequences for these behaviors and significant impact on the medical centers, the initial data provides evidence that the skills transferred to the job.

These opening stories illustrate that application and implementation are necessary for business impact and a positive ROI. A project will typically break down at this level if it is not addressed properly, measured correctly, and adjusted accordingly.

THE IMPORTANCE OF APPLICATION AND IMPLEMENTATION

Measuring application and implementation is absolutely necessary. For some projects, it provides the most critical data set because it delivers information on the degree to which successful project implementation occurs, and of the barriers and enablers that influence success.

VALUE OF INFORMATION

The value of information increases as progress is made through the chain of impact, from Reaction (Level 1) to ROI (Level 5). Information concerning Application and Implementation (Level 3) is more valuable to the project sponsor than are Reaction and Learning data, which is not to discount the importance of the first two levels, but rather to emphasize the importance of moving up the chain of impact. Measuring the extent to which a project is implemented provides critical data about its success and about factors that lead to success in the future.

Reaction and learning measurements occur during a project's early stages, when more attention and direct focus are placed on the participants' involvement in the project. Measuring application and implementation occurs after the project has been implemented and captures the success of moving the project forward through participants' use of knowledge, skills, technology, and procedures connected to the project. Essentially, this measure reflects the degree to which the project is implemented by those who are charged with its success as the first step in transitioning to a new state, behavior, or process.

PROJECT FOCUS

Because many projects and programs focus directly on implementation and application or new behaviors and processes, a project sponsor often speaks in these terms and has concerns about these measures of success. The sponsor of a major project designed to transform an organization will be greatly concerned with implementation and application, and will want to know the extent to which key stakeholders adjust to and implement the desired new behaviors, processes, and procedures.

Sometimes this data set is misrepresented as the ultimate outcome. Unfortunately, in many measurement processes, the healthcare organization will focus on this level. For example, in 2010, in the 78 measures of the Healthcare Effectiveness Data and Information Set (HEDIS), the most widely used quality measurement system, all but 5 were application measures.[1] Compliance with evidence-based guidelines is often seen as sufficient without the need to measure outcomes. Compliance with a guideline is sometimes used as a basis for pay-for-performance systems, rather than patient results.

The focus on application and implementation is not necessarily surprising. These activities are easy to track, and they are sometimes built into the organization. They represent a tempting shortcut to the ultimate outcomes. They are often easy to control, and connecting application and implementation to a project can be accomplished easily, which is especially important when multiple projects are aimed at the same application. In short, while the application and implementation outcomes are popular and are the focus of many projects, they should not be regarded as the ultimate outcomes, at least for those projects that are critical to healthcare and designed to add value.[2]

Problems and Opportunities

If the chain of impact breaks at this level, little or no corresponding improvement in impact data will be available. Without impact, a positive ROI does not happen. This breakdown most often occurs because participants encounter barriers, inhibitors, and obstacles (covered later) that deter implementation. Frustration arises when reactions to the project are favorable and participants learn what is needed for success, but they fail to overcome the barriers and accomplish what's necessary for application.

When a project goes astray, the first question usually asked is, "What happened?" More importantly, when a project appears to add no value, the first question ought to be, "What can we do to change its direction?" In either scenario, it is important to identify the barriers to success, the problems in implementation, and the obstacles to application. At Level 3, measuring implementation and application, these problems are identified and addressed. In many cases, the stakeholders directly involved in the process can provide important recommendations for making changes for using a different approach in the future.

When project implementation is successful, the obvious question is, "How can we repeat this success or even improve it in the future?" The answer to this question is also found at this level of measurement. Identifying the factors that contribute directly to the success of the project is important. The same items can be used to replicate the process and produce enhanced results in the future. Using the enablers properly provides an important case history of what is necessary for success.

Reward Effectiveness

Measuring application and implementation allows the sponsor and project manager to reward those who do the best job of applying the information and implementing the project. Measures taken at this level provide clear evidence of success and achievement, and provide an excellent basis for performance reviews. Rewards often have a reinforcing value, helping to keep employees on track and communicating a strong message for future improvement.

CHALLENGES

Collecting application and implementation data brings into focus some key challenges that must be addressed for success at this level. These challenges often inhibit an otherwise successful evaluation.

LINKING WITH LEARNING

Application data should be linked closely with learning data. Essentially, this level of evaluation captures what has been accomplished and what activities have been implemented, based on what the individuals learned in the early stages of the project. This level measures the extent to which participants accurately took what they learned and applied it properly.

BUILDING DATA COLLECTION INTO THE PROJECT

Application data are collected after the project's implementation. Because of the time between project implementation and data collection, it is sometimes difficult to secure the appropriate quality and quantity of data. Consequently, one of the most effective ways to ensure that data are collected is to build data collection into the project from the beginning. Data collection tools positioned as application tools must be included as part of the project design. For example, many software applications contain overlay software that shows a user performance profile. Essentially, the overlay software tracks the user invisibly, capturing the steps, pace, and difficulties encountered while using the software. When the process is complete, a credible data set has been captured, simply because project leaders built it into the process at the beginning.

In healthcare organizations, many processes that occur at the application and implementation level are actually recorded in the system through checklists, charts, and procedures. When the people involved know in advance that these things must be included, the organization should encounter less resistance to tracking and reporting the data at this level than in nonhealthcare organizations.

Ensuring a Sufficient Amount of Data

When collecting data by questionnaire or through action plans, interviews, or focus groups, inadequate response rates are a problem in most organizations. Having individuals participate in the data collection process is a challenge. To ensure that adequate amounts of high-quality data are available, a serious effort is needed to improve response rates.

Because many projects are planned on the basis of the ROI Methodology, it is expected that project managers will collect impact data, convert them to monetary values, and calculate the actual ROI. This need to "show the money" sometimes results in less emphasis being placed on measuring application and implementation. In many cases, it may be omitted or slighted in the analysis; but it is through focused effort on process and behavior change that business impact will occur. Therefore, emphasis must be placed on collecting data in the application and implementation categories. Although a positive ROI is the goal, attention must be given to changing processes, procedures, and tasks, and on removing barriers. Doing things differently can result in substantial benefits, but knowing the degree to which things are done differently is essential to guaranteeing those benefits.

MEASUREMENT ISSUES

When measuring the application and implementation of projects and programs, several key issues should be addressed, which are largely similar to those encountered when measuring reaction and learning. A few issues may differ slightly because of the later time frame for collecting this type of data.

METHODS

A variety of methods are available for collecting data at Level 3, including traditional survey and questionnaire methods, as well as methods based on observation, interviews, and focus groups. Sometimes, the data are available in records when medical procedures are implemented or new technology is used. Implementation data may be contained in systems, charts, and checklists. In these situations, the data collection method is performance monitoring. Other powerful methods include action planning, where individuals plan their parts of the implementation, and performance contracting.

Objectives

As with the other levels, the starting point for data collection is the objectives set for project application and implementation. Without these clear objectives, collecting data will be difficult. Application and implementation represent activity, and objectives define what activity is expected.

Areas of Coverage

To a certain extent, the areas of coverage for this process parallel the areas identified in Chapter 4. The later time frame for data collection changes the measurement to a postproject measure rather than a predictive measure. The key point is that this level focuses on activity or action, not on the ability to act (Level 2) and not on the consequences (Level 4). The sheer number of activities to measure can be mind-boggling. Table 5.1 shows examples of coverage areas for application, which will vary from project to project.

Data Sources

The sources of data mirror those identified in Chapter 4. Essentially, all key stakeholders are potential sources of data. Perhaps the most important sources of data are the users of the project (i.e., project participants), those directly involved in the application and implementation of the project or program. Good sources may also be the managers of the participants who are charged with the implementation. In some cases, the source may be the organizational records or system.

Timing

The timing of data collection can vary significantly. Because it constitutes a follow-up after the project launch, the key issue is determining the best time for a postimplementation evaluation. The challenge is to analyze the nature and scope of the application and to determine the earliest time that a pattern will evolve, which occurs when the application of skills becomes routine and the implementation is making significant progress. The timing is a judgment call and will require input from knowledgeable sources.

TABLE 5.1 Examples of Coverage Areas for Application

Action	Explanation	Example
Eliminate	Stopping a particular task or activity	Eliminate the formal follow-up meeting, and replace it with a virtual meeting
Maintain	Keeping the same level of activity for a particular process	Continue to monitor the process with the same schedule previously used
Create	Designing or implementing a new procedure, process, or activity	Create a procedure for clarifying physician orders in crucial situations
Use	Using a particular process, procedure, skill, or activity	Use the new skill in situations for which it was designed
Perform	Carrying out a particular task, process, or procedure	Conduct a post-audit review at the end of each activity
Participate	Becoming involved in various activities, projects, or programs	Submit a suggestion for reducing costs
Enroll	Signing up for a particular process, program, or project	Enroll in a fitness program
Respond	Reacting to groups, individuals, or systems	Respond to patient inquiries within 15 minutes
Network	Facilitating relationships with others who are involved in or have been affected by the project	Continue networking with contacts on (at minimum) a quarterly basis
Increase	Increasing a particular activity or action	Increase the frequency of use of the physician portal
Decrease	Decreasing a particular activity or action	Decrease the number of times a particular process must be checked

Going in as early as possible is important so that potential adjustments can still be made. At the same time, you must wait long enough so that behavior changes are allowed to occur and so that the implementation can be observed and measured. In projects spanning a considerable length of time, several measures may be taken at three- to six-month intervals, for example. Using effective measures at well-timed intervals will provide successive input on implementation progress, and clearly show the extent and sustainability of improvement.

Convenience and constraints also influence the timing of data collection. A meeting at which participants are gathering to observe a milestone or special event would be an excellent opportunity to collect data. Sometimes, however, constraints are placed on data collection. Consider, for example, the time constraint that sponsors may impose. If they are eager to have the data to make project decisions, they may order the data collection moved to an earlier time than ideal. A word of caution is in order here. If the collection is too early, the data will clearly show it and a later collection will be necessary.

RESPONSIBILITIES

Measuring application and implementation may involve the responsibility and work of others. With data collection occurring later than Levels 1 and 2, an important issue may surface in terms of who is responsible for this follow-up. Many possibilities exist, ranging from project staff, support staff, and sponsors to external independent consultants. Sometimes finance and accounting team members are available to assist with data collection. This matter should be addressed in the planning stages so that no misunderstanding arises as to the distribution of responsibilities. More importantly, those who are responsible should fully understand the nature and scope of their accountabilities and what is needed to collect the data.

DATA COLLECTION METHODS

Some of the techniques previously mentioned are appropriate to collect application and implementation data. They are easy to administer and provide quality data. Other techniques are more robust, providing greater detail about success but raising more challenges in administration.

PERFORMANCE MONITORING

The easiest approach to collecting data is to go to the records. In the systems and processes, the many sources of data include checklists, procedures, charts, databases, and monitoring systems. Excellent examples for collecting data using systems are the Electronic Health Record (EHR) or the Ambulatory Electronic Health Record (AEHR). The most credible and perhaps easiest way to collect data is to monitor the records directly.

USING QUESTIONNAIRES TO MEASURE APPLICATION AND IMPLEMENTATION

Questionnaires have become a popular data collection tool for measuring application and implementation because of their flexibility, low cost, and ease of administration. One of the most difficult tasks is determining the specific issues to address in a follow-up questionnaire. Figure 5.1 presents content items necessary for capturing application, implementation, and impact information (Level 3 and Level 4 data).

USING INTERVIEWS, FOCUS GROUPS, AND OBSERVATION

Interviews and focus groups can be used during implementation or on a follow-up basis to collect data on implementation and application. However, the steps needed to design and administer these instruments are the same as for measuring reaction and learning in Chapter 4.

For this level of data collection, observing participants on the job and recording any changes in behavior and specific actions taken are sometimes used. Even though observation is used in collecting learning data, a fundamental difference is that participants should not necessarily know they are being observed when observation is used to collect application data. When observation is known, the behavior often changes to reflect what is desired, not what is typical. If observation cannot be invisible, it should be unnoticeable.

The observer may be a member of the project staff, the participant's manager, a member of a peer group, or an external resource such as a mystery visitor or caller. The most common observer, and probably the most practical one, is a member of the project staff. Technology also lends itself as a tool to assist with observations. Recorders, video cameras, and computers play an important role in capturing application data.

The use of technology is not uncommon in healthcare organizations. Sometimes video recording of processes and procedures from operating rooms to patient floors ensures that the proper procedures are followed as

FIGURE 5.1   Questionnaire Content Checklist

[ ] Progress with objectives
[ ] Action plan implementation
[ ] Use of procedures
[ ] Use of checklist
[ ] Use of materials
[ ] Use of technology
[ ] Use of knowledge/skills
[ ] Changes with work/actions
[ ] Barriers
[ ] Enablers
[ ] Improvement/accomplishments
[ ] Definition of measure
[ ] Amount of change
[ ] Unit value
[ ] Basis   Optional unless business impact
[ ] Total impact   and ROI analysis are pursued
[ ] Other factors that caused change
[ ] Percent linked with project
[ ] Confidence estimate (0–100%)
[ ] Linkage with intangible measures
[ ] Management support
[ ] Other benefits
[ ] Other solutions needed
[ ] Recommendations for others
[ ] Suggestions for improvement
[ ] Other comments

service is delivered. These technological observations become unnoticeable. They are not invisible because the staff, physicians, and nurses know they are there, but they become unnoticed and can be important for capturing what is actually occurring. On the downside, this approach is sometimes resisted, particularly in certain areas as an invasion of privacy and freedom. The unions have resisted this type of monitoring, but in the long run, it usually wins out for delivering great patient care.

Using Action Plans

In some cases, an action plan can be used to measure application. Typical action planning requires participants to meet a goal or complete a task or project by a set date. A summary of the results of the completed tasks or actions provides further evidence of the project's success. With this approach, participants are required to develop action plans as part of the project. Action plans contain the detailed steps necessary to accomplish specific objectives related to the project. The process is one of the most effective ways to enhance project support and build the sense of ownership needed for successful project implementation.

The action plan typically shows what is to be accomplished by whom, and by what date. The action plan approach is a straightforward, easy-to-use method for determining how participants will apply the project on the job and achieve success with project implementation. The approach produces data that answer questions such as:

- What specific actions have been taken since the project was implemented?

- Are these actions routine?

- What may have prevented participants from accomplishing specific action items?

- What helped participants to accomplish specific outcomes?

- What on-the-job improvements have been realized?

- What other factors could have caused this improvement?

- How many and how much of the improvements are linked to the project?

Collectively, these data can be used to assess the success of project implementation and to make decisions regarding changes to improve it. Figure 5.2 shows an example of an action plan for a performance improvement project for nurse managers.

In this specific example, Nadia Farley, a nurse manager, is improving the unplanned absenteeism rate for shift nurses. The form captures application data (Level 3) and impact data (Level 4). Unplanned absenteeism,

136

FIGURE 5.2 Example of an Action Plan

Name: *Nadia Farley*   Project Leader: _____   Follow-up Date: *1 May*

Objective: *Reduce Unplanned Absenteeism for Shift Nurses*   Evaluation Period: *January to April*

Improvement Measure: *Unplanned Absenteeism Rate*   Current Performance: *8.7%*   Target Performance: *3.2%*

Action Steps		Analysis
1. Meet with nurses to discuss reasons for absenteeism—using problem-solving skills	9 Jan. ✓	A. What is the unit of measure? *One Unplanned Absence*
2. Review absenteeism records for each nurse—to search for trends and patterns.	18 Jan. ✓	B. What is the value (cost) of one unit? *$135.00*
3. Counsel with "problem employees" to correct habits and explore opportunities for improvement.	As needed ✓	C. How did you arrive at this value? *Value from HR Rep*
4. Conduct a brief "performance discussion" with a nurse returning to work after an unplanned absence.	As needed ✓	D. How much did the measure change during the evaluation period? (monthly value) *4.3% (8.7 – 4.4%)*
5. Provide recognition to all nurses who have perfect attendance.	22 Feb. ✓	E. What other factors could have caused the improvement? *An HR Campaign on Perfect Attendance*
6. Follow-up with each discussion and discuss improvement or lack of improvement and plan other action.	As needed ✓	F. What percent of this change was actually caused by this program? *70%*
7. Monitor improvement and provide recognition when appropriate.	As needed ✓	G. What level of confidence do you place on the preceding estimate? (100% = Certainty; 0% = No Confidence) *80%*
Barriers: *Time to do this, some resistance from nurses*		Enablers: *Support of HR and my director*
Intangible Benefits: *Less stress, greater job satisfaction for me*		

the impact, is disruptive and costly to manage for delivering quality patient care. An unplanned absence occurs when a nurse calls at the beginning of the shift to let the nurse manager know that he or she will not be present that day. Although some of this type of absenteeism cannot be prevented, part of it can. This nurse manager aims to improve it using the skills and knowledge from a performance management training program. Each participant in this program selects two performance measures to improve as the action plan is built into the program.

To gain maximum effectiveness from the evaluation data collected from action plans, the action plan process should be an integral part of the project and not necessarily an add-on or optional activity. Ideally, the action planning process should be implemented using the steps in Figure 5.3.

PERFORMANCE CONTRACTING

The action plan can be slightly modified to develop a performance contract. This adjustment can be extremely powerful. The change brings in the concept of making a commitment. For example, the participant in a project would make a commitment with his or her immediate supervisor to meet certain levels of improvement. In the action plan from Nadia Farley (Figure 5.2), if she had negotiated with her manager the actual measures and the amount of improvement of those measures, she would have essentially been entering into a performance contract with her director. The process can be enhanced by bringing in the facilitator or project leader. By having the facilitator or leader sign and agree to the same improvement, the contract then provides a three-way understanding among the project leader, the participant, and the manager of the participant. Such awareness and agreement are powerful because in this example, Nadia not only has the use of the project content, tools, and processes contained in it, but also the support of her immediate manager and the extra support of the project leader, who are all committed to improving this performance. These factors can provide tremendous motivation in performance. The downside is that to some participants, this process resembles a performance evaluation and may be resented (i.e., participation in the particular project becomes performance review for them). Such resistance may be more likely in public sector organizations and organizations where unions are involved. However, if important measures can benefit from improvement, this technique is powerful in achieving success.

FIGURE 5.3 Action Planning Checklist

Before Project	[ ]	Communicate the action plan requirement early
	[ ]	Have participants select one or more measures to improve
During Project	[ ]	Describe the action planning process at the beginning of the project
	[ ]	Teach the action planning process during the project
	[ ]	Allow time to develop action the plan
	[ ]	Secure the project leader's approval of the action plan
	[ ]	Require participants to assign a monetary value to each improvement
	[ ]	Assist participants with these monetary values
	[ ]	Have participants present the plans to the group
	[ ]	Explain the follow-up process
Follow-Up After Project	[ ]	Have participants report the improvement on the measure
	[ ]	Ask participants to identify the other factors that could have caused the improvement
	[ ]	Have participants indicate the amount of improvement related to the project
	[ ]	Ask participants to provide a confidence estimate on the amount of allocation
	[ ]	Collect action plans at the predetermined follow-up time
	[ ]	Summarize the data

BARRIERS AND ENABLERS TO APPLICATION

One of the important reasons for collecting application and implementation data is to uncover barriers and enablers to the improvement. Although both groups are important, barriers can kill a project quickly.

Barriers

Barriers are a serious problem that exists in every project. They must be identified and actions must be taken to minimize or remove them. In most projects, the number one barrier is lack of support. When barriers are identified, they become important reference points for change and improvement. The top 15 barriers that will stifle the success of projects are:

1. My immediate supervisor/manager does not support the project.

2. This project is not needed here.

3. Resources are not available to implement the project.

4. The culture in our team does not support the project.

5. We had no opportunity to use the information, knowledge, or skills.

6. We had no time to implement the project.

7. Tools and templates were not available to use.

8. Technology was not available for the project.

9. Our systems and processes did not support the project.

10. Other priorities got in the way.

11. We didn't see a value for this project.

12. My job changed and this project no longer applies to me.

13. This project is not appropriate for our work.

14. Our funding ran out.

15. We lost interest.

The important point is to identify any barriers and to use the data in meaningful ways to make the barriers less of a problem.

Enablers

Complementary to the barriers are the enablers. These factors, when present, enhance success. When a participant has achieved success, the reasons behind that success sometimes extend beyond participant motivation and responsibility. When such factors can be identified, they offer important process improvement opportunities. It is important to understand these behaviors so they can be enhanced, added, improved, and required for other projects. Sometimes the enablers actually mirror the barriers. For example, in most projects, the number one barrier is lack of support from the immediate manager. At the same time, the number one enabler is the support of the immediate manager. If lack of resources is a barrier, having resources available is often an enabler. Although they won't always mirror each other, sometimes unexpected and unintended enablers can be seen alongside the barriers. These enablers should be detailed and used for process improvement.

USE OF APPLICATION DATA

Data become meaningless if they are not used properly. As you move up the chain of impact for data collection, the data become more valuable in the minds of sponsors, key executives, top administrators, and others who have a strong interest in the project. Although data can be used in dozens of ways, the following are the principal uses for this level of data:

- To report and review results with various stakeholders (funding, support)
- To identify and remove barriers (improvement)
- To identify and enhance enablers (improvement)
- To adjust project design and implementation (improvement)
- To recognize individuals who have contributed to project success (commitment)
- To reinforce in current and future project participants the value of desired actions (support)
- To improve management support for projects (support, relationships)
- To market future projects (funding)

The ultimate goals of the use of data are in parentheses. Improvement, support, relationships, commitment, and funding are the key reasons for almost every evaluation.

FINAL THOUGHTS

Measuring application and implementation is critical in determining the success of a project or program. This essential measure not only determines the success achieved, but also identifies areas where improvement is needed and where success can be replicated in the future. This chapter presents a variety of techniques to collect application data, ranging from observation to use of questionnaires and action plans. The method chosen must match the scope of the project. Understanding success with application is important in providing evidence that business needs should be met, but it is only through measurement at Level 4, Impact, and its consequences that a direct link between the project and business impact can be made. The next chapter focuses on the impact measurement.

CHAPTER 6

Measuring
Business Impact

M ost healthcare project sponsors regard business impact
data as the most important data type because of its
connection to business success. Patient outcomes, patient revenue, patient
safety, operational efficiency, length of stay, and patient satisfaction are
some of the most important impact data found in the healthcare industry.
Top executives rate impact data as their number one category for data
from performance improvement projects. For many projects, inadequate
performance in business measures (the business need) is usually what
initiated a particular project. For example, adverse patient outcomes drive
a healthcare improvement project to improve outcomes. Improvement
is needed to either meet existing needs, or to improve the anticipated
future state. Business impact data taken from a follow-up after the
project is implemented to close the loop by showing a project's success in
meeting the business needs. This chapter examines a variety of business
impact measures and the specific method to collect the measures within a
project.

OPENING STORY

Birmingham Heart Clinic is a nine-provider cardiology practice established in 1994. Specializing in adult coronary, peripheral artery disease (PAD), and carotid diseases, the practice offers electrophysiology for invasive and noninvasive cardiac arrhythmia. Birmingham Heart Clinic also features an on-site accredited diagnostic facility for echocardiograms, EKGs, nuclear stress testing, and CT scans.

With a decentralized operation and continued growth, Birmingham Heart Clinic crucially needed to coordinate patient care away from paper charts, reconcile administrative tasks, and ensure that each patient was receiving optimal continuums of care as overall patient population increased.

In addition, Birmingham Heart sought to modernize technology to address public and private quality reporting initiatives such as Physician Quality Reporting, meaningful use, and anticipated accountable care, in part due to the proximity and association with St. Vincent's Hospital, part of the Catholic network Ascension Health.

Birmingham Heart Clinic selected Greenway's electronic health record (EHR) practice management and interoperability solution PrimeSUITE to accomplish its clinical, operational, and financial goals.

Following a 12-month implementation period, Birmingham Heart realized substantial outcome measures compared to predeployment baseline data. For example:

- Total charges increased by nearly 3% per month through enhanced charge capture.

- Total receipts were greatly impacted, increasing by more than 10% per month.

- Total physician clinics increased by 300 per month.

- Overall practice income reflected a 3% annual increase.

- Transcription costs decreased 9%.

- Chart supply and storage costs decreased by almost 100%.

In addition, Birmingham Heart received $70,000 in PQRS funds, minus a $4,500 investment, because of the new system. These direct cost savings and additional income of funds shows the impact of this EHR practice management solution.[1]

THE IMPORTANCE OF BUSINESS IMPACT

In addition to executive interest, several rationales support the collection and analysis of business impact data related to a project. Clearly, it is the most important data set.

The Chain of Impact

Following the assumption that higher-level data create more value for project sponsors (from the chain of impact presented in Chapter 2), business impact measures offer more valuable data. Impact data are the consequence of the application and implementation of a project. They represent the bottom-line measures positively influenced when a project is successful. For some stakeholders, these data are the most valuable.

The chain of impact can be broken at this level (Level 4), and it happens in many projects. If the project does not drive business impact data—or drives too little data—the ROI is usually negative. In extreme cases, the project can have success at the lower levels but fail completely at the impact level. In this case participants may react positively to the project, learn successfully to implement the project, and follow the correct implementation steps or use the skills needed to implement the project. However, when the business impact measure (which is anticipated to be influenced by the project) does not change or improve, the project does not add value.

What could cause failure at the impact level? The first of two possibilities is that the business alignment for the project may not have been completed properly during the initial analysis, which would keep it from being the right solution. The second possibility is that other factors are influencing the business measure. Although the project may be connected to the measure, other factors may be affecting it in a direction opposite of that desired by project planners. For example, a collaborative work team may be assembled to tackle excessive length of stay, and at the same time, the health status of new patients has deteriorated, increasing the length of stay. At first glance, it may appear that the project has no value, but in reality it could. This scenario brings into focus the importance of isolating the effects of a project. The business data may be disappointing, but even more disappointing without the project. Isolating the effects of the project is presented in Chapter 7.

A BUSINESS DRIVER FOR PROJECTS

For most projects, business impact data (business needs) represent the initial drivers for the project. Avoiding waste, adverse patient outcomes, excessive wait times, high readmission rates, excessive turnover of critical care nurses, and low clinician productivity are examples of business needs. The problem of deteriorating (or less than expected) performance or the opportunity for improvement of a business measure usually leads to a project. If the business needs are the drivers for a project, then the key measure for evaluating the project is the business measure. The extent to which these measures have changed is the principal determinant of project success.

"THE MONEY" FOR SPONSORS

From the perspective of the sponsor, business impact data reflect key payoff measures. They are the measures often desired by the sponsor for change or improvement and often represent hard, indisputable facts that reflect performance critical to operating units of the organization. Business impact leads to "the money," which is so important to understand the costs, efficiency, profits, and value. Without credible business impact data linked directly to the project, it would be impossible to establish a credible monetary value for the project. This need for credible monetary value makes this level of data the most critical category for project sponsors.

EASY TO MEASURE

One unique feature of business impact data is that they are often easy to measure. Hard and soft data measures at this level often reflect key measures found in plentiful numbers throughout a healthcare organization. It is not unusual for a hospital to have hundreds (if not thousands) of measures reflecting specific business impact items. The challenge is to connect the project to the appropriate business measures. The impact measures (from business needs) become the impact objectives for the project, which is more easily accomplished at the beginning of the project, as described in Chapter 3.

COLLECTING IMPACT MEASURES

Data can be collected in a variety of categories and must be directly connected to the project. First, specific measures linked to the project must be identified in the beginning. Then, the measures are tracked in a follow-up evaluation, using one or more methods.

DATA CATEGORIES

Chapter 3 defined four data categories (hard, soft, tangible, and intangible). In addition to being classified as hard or soft and tangible or intangible, data can be categorized at several different levels, as shown in Figure 6.1. The figure illustrates that some data are considered strategic and are linked to the corporate level of an organization. Other data are more operational and are linked to the business unit or hospital level. Still others are considered more tactical in nature and scope and are used at the operating or department level of an organization.

Examples of data categorized at the strategic level include financial, people-oriented, and internal versus external data. At the business unit level, classifications such as output, quality, time, cost, job satisfaction, and

FIGURE 6.1 Measures at Different Levels

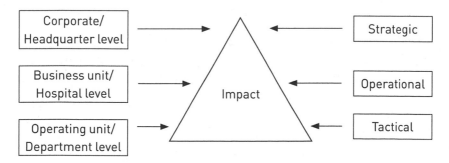

customer satisfaction are critical categories. At the tactical level, the categories are more plentiful and include productivity, efficiency, cost control, quality, time, attitudes, and individual and team performance. The importance is not in the classification of data itself but in the awareness of the vast array of data available. Regardless of their categories, these data are consequence measures (Level 4) of project success. The challenge is to find the data items connected directly to the project.

METRIC FUNDAMENTALS

When determining the type of measures to use, reviewing metric fundamentals can be helpful. The first important issue is identifying what makes an effective measure. Table 6.1 shows some of the criteria of an effective measure. These issues should be addressed when examining any type of measure.

These criteria serve as a screening checklist as measures are considered, developed, and ultimately added to the list of possibilities. In addition to meeting criteria, the factual basis of the measure should be stressed. In essence, the measure should be subjected to a fact-based analysis, a level of analysis never before applied to decisions about many projects, even when these decisions have involved huge sums of money. Distinguishing between the various "types" of facts is beneficial. The basis for facts ranges from common sense, to what employees "say," to factual data.

- *No facts.* Common sense tells us that employees will be more satisfied with their employer if they are allowed to have a flexible work arrangement.

- *Unreliable facts.* Nurses say they are more likely to stay with the hospital if they are offered a pay-for-performance plan.

- *Irrelevant facts.* We have benchmarked three world-class companies using cloud computing: a bank, a hotel chain, and a defense contractor. All reported good results.

- *Fact-based.* A new procedure in the intensive care unit is reducing infections and operational costs.[2]

TABLE 6.1 Criteria for Effective Measures

Criteria: Effective Measures Are	Definition: The Extent to Which a Measure
Important	Connects to strategically important business objectives rather than to what is easy to measure
Complete	Adequately tracks the entire phenomenon rather than only part of the phenomenon
Timely	Tracks at the right time rather than being held to an arbitrary date
Visible	Is visible, public, openly known, and tracked by those affected by it, rather than being collected privately for management's eyes only
Controllable	Tracks outcomes created by those affected by it who have a clear line of sight from the measure to results
Cost-effective	Is efficient to track using existing data or data that are easy to monitor without requiring new procedures
Interpretable	Creates data that are easy to make sense of and that translate into employee action
Simplicity	Simple to understand from each stakeholder's perspective
Specific	Is clearly defined so that people quickly understand and relate to the measure
Collectible	Can be collected with no more effort than is proportional to the usefulness that results
Team-based	Will have value in the judgment of a team of individuals, not in the judgment of just one individual
Credible	Provides information that is valid and credible in the eyes of management

Source: Steve Kerr, "On the Folly of Rewarding A, While Hoping for B," *Academy of Management Journal*, 18 (1995): 769–783; and Andrew Mayo, *Measuring Human Capital* (London: The Institute of Chartered Accountants, June 2003).

SCORECARDS

In recent years, interest has increased in developing documents that reflect appropriate measures in an organization. Scorecards provide a variety of measures for top executives. In their book *The Balanced Scorecard*, Robert Kaplan and David Norton explore the concept of the scorecard for use by organizations.[3] Kaplan and Norton suggest that data can be organized in the four categories of process, operational, financial, and growth.

What exactly is a scorecard? The *American Heritage Dictionary* defines a scorecard from two perspectives:

1. A printed program or card enabling a spectator to identify players and record the progress of a game or competition.

2. A small card used to record one's own performance in sports.

Scorecards vary in type, ranging from Kaplan and Norton's balanced scorecard to the scored set in the U.S. president's management agenda that uses an "eye chart" such as a traffic-light grading system (green for success, yellow for mixed results, red for unsatisfactory). Top executives place great emphasis on scorecards, regardless of type. In some organizations, the scorecard concept has filtered down to various functional business units, and each unit of the business has been required to develop a scorecard. A growing number of executives in different functions have developed scorecards to reflect their segments of the business.

The scorecard approach is appealing because it provides a quick comparison of key business impact measures and examines the status of the organization. As a management tool, scorecards are directional in nature and can be important in shaping and improving or maintaining the performance of the organization through the implementation of preventive projects. Scorecard measures often link to particular healthcare improvement projects. In many situations, it was a scorecard deficiency measure that initially prompted the project. Although scorecards can be helpful, it is important to dig deeper for additional data sources.

IDENTIFYING SPECIFIC MEASURES LINKED TO PROJECTS

An important issue that often surfaces when considering ROI applications is the understanding of specific measures that are often driven by common types of projects. Although no standard answers are available, Table 6.2 represents a summary of typical impact measures for specific types of projects. The measures are quite broad for some projects. For example, a reward systems project can pay off in a variety of measures, as in improved patient outcomes and safety, improved productivity, enhanced patient revenues, improved quality, cycle-time reduction, increased patient satisfaction, and even direct cost savings. Essentially, the project should drive the measure that the reward is designed to influence. In other projects, the influenced measures are quite narrow. For example, in labor-management cooperation projects, the payoffs are typically in reduced grievances, reduced absenteeism, fewer work stoppages, increased patient revenue, and improved employee satisfaction. Orientation projects typically pay off in measures of early turnover (turnover in the first 90 days of employment), job satisfaction, training time, and productivity. The measures that are influenced depend on the objectives and the design of the project.

Table 6.2 illustrates the immense number of opportunities for measuring ROI and the even larger set of measures that can be driven or influenced. In most of these situations, assigning monetary values to these measures (as the monetary benefits of a given project are compared to the costs) and developing the ROI become reasonable tasks.

A word of caution: presenting specific measures linked to a typical healthcare project may give the impression that these are the only measures influenced. In practice, a given project can have many outcomes. The good news is that most projects are driving business measures. The monetary values are based on what is being improved in the various departments and business units, clinics, hospitals, divisions, regions, and individual workplaces. These measures are the ones that matter to senior executives. The difficulty often comes in ensuring that the connection to the project exists. Making this connection is accomplished through a variety of techniques that isolate the effects of the project on the particular business measures.

MONITORING BUSINESS PERFORMANCE DATA

Data are available in every healthcare organization to measure business impact. Monitoring or recording impact data enables management to measure performance in terms of output, quality, costs, time, job satisfaction, patient satisfaction, and other measures. When determining the source of data for collection, the first consideration should be existing

TABLE 6.2 ROI Applications

Project	Key Impact Measurements
Absenteeism control/reduction	Absenteeism, patient satisfaction, job satisfaction, stress
Advertising	Patient revenue, market share, patient loyalty, new patients, patient satisfaction, brand awareness
Branding projects	Brand awareness, image, patient loyalty, new patients, market share
Business coaching	Productivity, patient outcomes, physician engagement, quality, time savings, efficiency, costs, employee satisfaction, patient satisfaction
Business development	Revenue, patient loyalty, new patients, patient satisfaction
Career development/Career management	Turnover, internal promotions, recruiting expenses, job satisfaction, nurse engagement
Cloud computing	Costs, response time, down time, reliability
Communications	Medical errors, stress, conflicts, productivity, job satisfaction, patient complaints
Compensation	Patient outcomes, costs, productivity, quality, job satisfaction, patient satisfaction
Compliance	Discrepancies, penalties/fines, charges, settlements, losses
Diversity/Inclusion	Turnover, absenteeism, complaints, charges, settlements, losses, productivity, patient outcomes, innovation
e-Learning/Mobile learning	Compliance discrepancies, cost savings, productivity improvement, patient outcomes, quality improvement, cycle times, error reductions, job satisfaction
Employee benefits projects	Costs, time savings, job satisfaction
Employee relations	Complaints, turnover, absenteeism, job satisfaction, engagement
Engagement initiatives	Patient outcomes productivity, quality, turnover, absenteeism, cycle time
Flexible work systems	Productivity, turnover, office space costs, sick leave, absenteeism
Gainsharing plans	Operating costs, productivity, turnover
Job satisfaction projects	Turnover, absenteeism, stress

TABLE 6.2 ROI Applications *(continued)*

Project	Key Impact Measurements
Labor-management cooperation projects	Work stoppages, employee grievances, absenteeism, patient revenue, job satisfaction
Leadership development	Productivity, output, patient outcomes, patient safety, quality, efficiency, time savings, operating costs, employee satisfaction, physician engagement, patient satisfaction
Lean Six Sigma	Patient outcomes, cost savings, productivity improvement, response times, quality measures, wait times, patient safety, cycle times, error reductions, job satisfaction, patient satisfaction
Marketing	Patient revenue, market share, patient loyalty, new patients, patient satisfaction, brand awareness
Medical meetings/events	Revenue, productivity, output, patient outcomes, quality, time savings, job satisfaction, patient satisfaction
Medical procedures	Medical errors, patient safety, patient outcomes, wait times, cycle time, operating costs, efficiency, patient satisfaction, patient complaints, legal claims
Motivational programs	Patient outcomes, patient safety, patient satisfaction, patient revenues, productivity, patient revenue, quality, cycle time, costs
Nurse engagement	Patient outcomes, patient safety, patient satisfaction, nurse turnover, operating costs, efficiency, time savings
Orientation, on-boarding	Early turnover, training time, productivity, job satisfaction
Outsourcing initiatives	Operating costs, productivity, quality, cycle times, patient revenue
Physician engagement	Operating costs, patient outcomes, quality, productivity, cycle times, wait times, patient satisfaction
Personal productivity/time management	Time savings, productivity, stress reduction, job satisfaction, job engagement
Procurement	Operating costs, time savings, quality, stability, schedule
Project management	Time savings, quality improvement, budgets, stress, job satisfaction

(continued)

TABLE 6.2 ROI Applications *(continued)*

Project	Key Impact Measurements
Public policy projects	Patient outcomes, patient safety, patient satisfaction, time savings, cost savings, quality, satisfaction, image
Public relations	Image, brand awareness, patient satisfaction, new patients, investor satisfaction, reputation
Quality improvements	Patient outcomes, cost savings, productivity improvement, response times, quality measures, wait times, patient safety, cycle times, error reductions, job satisfaction, patient satisfaction
Recruiting source (new)	Costs, yield, early turnover, job satisfaction
Retention management	Turnover, job engagement, job satisfaction
Rewards systems	Patient outcomes, patient safety, patient satisfaction, patient revenues, productivity, patient revenue, quality, cycle time, costs
Risk management	Fines, penalties, legal claims, losses, downtime, stress
Safety programs	Incidents, accident frequency rates, accident severity rates, first aid treatments, lost time accidents
Selection process	Early turnover, training time, productivity, job satisfaction
Self-directed teams	Productivity, output, patient outcomes, quality, patient safety, patient satisfaction, operating costs, turnover, absenteeism, job satisfaction
Sexual harassment prevention	Complaints, turnover, absenteeism, job satisfaction, charges, legal claims
Six Sigma	Patient outcomes, quality, waste, patient safety, wait times, downtime, response time, rework, operating costs
Skill-based pay	Labor costs, productivity, turnover, absenteeism, job engagement
Strategy/Policy	Patient revenue, productivity, output, market share, patient outcomes, safety, quality/service levels, cycle times, operating costs, job satisfaction, patient satisfaction
Stress management	Medical costs, turnover, absenteeism, job satisfaction

TABLE 6.2 ROI Applications *(continued)*

Project	Key Impact Measurements
Systems and software	Patient outcomes, cycle times, error rates, productivity, efficiency, patient satisfaction, job satisfaction
Talent management	Productivity, output, patient outcomes, quality, efficiency, cost/time savings, employee satisfaction
Technical training	Productivity, errors, quality, times savings, operating costs, patient outcomes, patient quality, patient satisfaction
Technology implementation	Process times, cycle times, response rates, error rates, productivity, efficiency, patient satisfaction, job satisfaction.
Wellness/Fitness	Turnover, medical costs, accidents, sick leave, absenteeism, job satisfaction, productivity
Workforce management systems	Staffing levels, costs, overtime, patient satisfaction

databases, operating reports, key performance indicators, scorecards, and the data sources listed in Chapter 3. In most organizations, impact data will be available that are suitable for measuring improvement resulting from a project. If data are not available, additional record-keeping systems will have to be developed for measurement and analysis. The question of economics surfaces at this point. Is it economical to develop the record-keeping systems necessary to evaluate a project? If the costs will be greater than the expected benefits, developing those systems is pointless.

IDENTIFY APPROPRIATE MEASURES

Existing performance measures should be thoroughly researched to identify those related to the proposed objectives of the project. Often, several performance measures are related to the same item. For example, the patient outcomes can be measured in several ways, including the following:

- Patient complaints
- Medical errors

- Medication errors

- Patient incidents

- Infections

- Readmissions

- Mortality

- Length of stay

- Patient satisfaction

Each of these in its own way has an adverse impact on patients. All related measures should be reviewed to determine those most relevant to the project.

CONVERT CURRENT MEASURES TO USABLE ONES

Occasionally, existing performance measures will become integrated with other data. Keeping existing performance measures isolated from unrelated data may be difficult. In these situations, all existing related measures should be extracted and retabulated to make them more appropriate for comparison in the evaluation. At times, it may be necessary to develop conversion factors. For example, employee turnover (the number of employees leaving in a month divided by the average employment for the month) is usually calculated monthly and annualized. A 1 percent monthly turnover represents a 12 percent annual rate. When evaluating a new on-boarding program, the early turnover is needed (the percentage of new employees leaving in the first 60 days). A new calculation is often needed.

DEVELOP NEW MEASURES

In some cases, data needed to measure the effectiveness of a project are not available, and new data are needed. The project staff must work with the sponsor to develop record-keeping systems, if economically feasible. In one organization, patient care staff delays in responding to patient complaints were an issue. This issue was discovered from patient feedback. The feedback data prompted a project to improve the response time. By implementing rounding practices, nurses began making more frequent rounds to reduce the use of call lights. To help ensure the success of the project, several measures were planned, including measuring the actual time to respond to a patient complaint. Initially, this measure was not available. As the project was implemented, new software was used to measure the time that elapsed in responding to patient complaints.

OTHER DATA COLLECTION METHODS

For many projects, business data are readily available to be monitored. However, at times, data won't be easily accessible to the project team or to the evaluator. Sometimes data are maintained at the individual, work unit, or department level and may not be known to anyone outside that area. Tracking all those data sets may be too expensive and time-consuming. In such cases, other data collection methods may be used to capture data sets and make them available for the evaluator. Three other options described in this chapter are the use of action plans, performance contracts, and questionnaires.

USE ACTION PLANS TO DEVELOP BUSINESS IMPACT DATA

Action plans can capture application and implementation data. They can also be a useful tool for capturing business impact data. For business impact data, the action plan is more focused and credible than using a questionnaire. The basic design principles and the issues involved in developing and administering action plans are the same for business impact data as for application and implementation data. However, a few issues are unique to business impact and ROI, and are presented here. The following steps are recommended when an action plan is developed and implemented to capture business impact data and to convert the data to monetary values. Figure 6.2 presents an example of an action plan for a workplace safety project.

SET GOALS AND TARGETS

An action plan can be developed with a direct focus on business impact data. Participants develop an overall objective for the plan, which is

FIGURE 6.2 Action Plan Example

Safe Workplace Action Plan

Name: *Ellie Hightower*   Facilitator Signature: _____   Follow-up Date: *1 June*

Objective: *Improve workplace safety*   Evaluation Period: *December to May*

Improvement Measure: *Monthly slips and falls*   Current Performance: *11/six months*   Target Performance: *2/six months*

Action Steps		Analysis
1. *Meet with team to discuss reasons for slips and falls*	2 Dec.	A. What is the unit of measure? *1 slip and fall*
2. *Review slip and fall records for each incident with safety—look for trends and patterns.*	18 Dec.	B. What is the value (cost) of one unit? *$1,750*
3. *Make adjustments based on reasons for slips and falls.*	22 Dec.	C. How did you arrive at this value? *Safety and Health—Frank M.*
4. *Counsel with housekeeping and explore opportunities for improvement.*	5 Jan.	D. How much did the measure change during the evaluation period? (monthly value) *8 (11 – 3)*
5. *Have safety conduct a brief meeting with team members.*	11 Jan.	E. What other factors could have caused the improvement? *A new campaign from safety and health.*
6. *Provide recognition to team members who have made extra efforts for reducing slips and falls.*	As needed	F. What percent of this change was actually caused by this program? *70%*
7. *Follow-up with each incident and discuss improvement or lack of improvement and plan other action.*	As needed	G. What level of confidence do you place on this information? (100% = Certainty; 0% = No Confidence) *80%*
8. *Monitor improvement and provide adjustment when appropriate.*	As needed	
Intangible Benefits: *Image, risk reduction*		

usually the primary objective of the project. In some cases, a project may have more than one objective, which requires additional action plans. In addition to the objective, the improvement measure and the current levels of performance are identified. In Figure 6.2, the objective is to improve workplace safety. The measure is slips and falls by patients or employees. These types of claims are called "indemnity claims" and come at a cost of $95,000 each in the state of California. The cost is determined by adding the cost of medical treatment, lost time, reserves, and processing. The current level is 11 for six months. The target level is 2. This information requires the participant to anticipate the application and implementation of the project and to set goals for specific performances that can be realized.

The action plan is completed during project implementation, often with the input, assistance, and facilitation of the project team. The evaluator or project leader actually approves the plan, indicating that it meets the requirements of being specific, motivational, achievable, realistic, and time-based (SMART). The plan can be developed in a one- to two-hour time frame and often begins with action steps related to the implementation of the project. These action steps are Level 3 activities that detail the application and implementation. All these steps build support for and are linked to business impact measures.

DEFINE THE UNIT OF MEASURE

The next important issue is to define the actual unit of measure. In some cases, more than one measure may be used, which will subsequently be contained in additional action plans. The unit of measure is necessary to break down the process into the simplest steps so that its ultimate value can be determined. The unit may be output data, such as one more patient through the MRI department or one new patient admitted. In terms of quality, the unit can be one error or one mistake, such as one less bloodstream infection or readmission. Time-based units are usually measured in minutes, hours, days, or weeks, reflecting data such as length of stay or time to process a lab test. Other units are specific to their particular type of data, such as one incident, one complaint, one absence, or one less employee leaving the hospital. The important point is to break down impact data into the simplest terms possible. In Figure 6.2, the unit of measure is one slip and fall (s/f).

PLACE A MONETARY VALUE ON EACH IMPROVEMENT

During project implementation, participants are asked to locate, calculate, or estimate the monetary value of each improvement outlined in their plans. The unit value is determined using a variety of methods, including standard values, expert input, external databases, and estimates. The process used in arriving at the value is described in the instructions for the action plan. When the actual improvement occurs, participants use these values to capture the annual monetary benefits of the plan. For this step to be effective, it is helpful to understand the ways values can be assigned to the data.

In the worst-case scenario, participants are asked to calculate the values themselves, although use of standard values and consultation with an expert are better courses of action. When it is necessary for participants to make the calculations themselves, they must explain the basis of those calculations. In Figure 6.2, the monetary value of one unit ($1,750) is an expert input from the safety and health department.

IMPLEMENT THE ACTION PLAN

Participants implement the action plan during project implementation, which often lasts for weeks or months following the launch of the project. The participants follow action plan steps, and the subsequent business impact results are achieved. In Figure 6.2, the evaluation period is set for six months.

PROVIDE SPECIFIC IMPROVEMENTS

At the end of the specified follow-up period—usually three months or six months—the participants indicate the specific improvements made, usually expressed as a daily, weekly, or monthly amount based on the actual amount of change observed, measured, or recorded. Participants must understand the need for accuracy as data are recorded. In most cases, only the changes are recorded, as these amounts are needed to calculate the monetary value of the project. In other cases, before-and-after data may be recorded, allowing the evaluator to calculate the difference. In Figure 6.2, the participants report improvement in six months. In total,

3 slips and falls were reported during those six months (December through June), compared to 11 in the previous six months. The improvement is 8 (11 − 3).

ISOLATE THE EFFECTS OF THE PROJECT

Although the action plan is initiated because of the project, the actual improvements reported on the action plan may be influenced by other factors. Consequently, the action plan process should not be given full credit for the improvement. For example, an action plan to implement a new system in a hospital could only be given partial credit for an improvement in operating costs because other variables may have affected the impact measures. Although several ways are available to isolate the effects of a project, participant estimation is usually most appropriate in the action planning process. Consequently, participants are asked to estimate the percentage of the improvement actually related to a particular project. This question can be asked on the action plan form or in a follow-up questionnaire. Sometimes it is beneficial to precede this question with a request to identify the entire list of factors that could have influenced the results. This process allows participants to think through the relationships before actually allocating a portion to this particular project. In Figure 6.2, the participant allocated 70 percent to the safety project, giving the remaining 30 percent to a new campaign (with posters and articles) from safety and health.

PROVIDE A CONFIDENCE LEVEL FOR ESTIMATES

When an estimate is used to isolate the amount of the improvement that is related to the project, it is not usually precise. To improve the credibility, participants are asked to indicate their level of confidence in their estimates. Using a scale of 0 to 100 percent—where 0 indicates no confidence and 100 percent indicates absolute certainty—participants have a way to express their uncertainty related to their estimates. This confidence estimate is used as an adjustment. In Figure 6.2, the participant is 80 percent confident in the allocation (20% error).

COLLECT ACTION PLANS AT SPECIFIED TIME INTERVALS

Because having a high response rate is essential, several steps may be necessary to ensure the action plans are completed and returned. Participants usually see the importance of the process and develop their plans in detail at the beginning of the project. Some organizations send follow-up reminders by mail or e-mail; others phone participants to check their progress. Others offer assistance in developing the final plan. These steps may require additional resources, which must be weighed against the importance of having more data.

SUMMARIZE THE DATA AND CALCULATE THE ROI

If developed properly, each action plan should have annualized monetary values associated with improvements. Also, each individual should have indicated the percentage of the improvement directly related to the project. Finally, participants should have provided a confidence percentage to reflect their uncertainty with the process and the subjective nature of some of the data that may be provided.

Because this process involves estimates, it may appear to be inaccurate, although certain adjustments during analysis can make the process credible and more accurate. These adjustments reflect the guiding principles that form the basis of the ROI Methodology. The adjustments are made in five steps as follows:

> **Step 1:** If participants provide no data, assume they had no improvement to report. (This approach is a conservative one.)

> **Step 2:** Check each value for realism, usability, and feasibility. Discard extreme values and omit them from analysis.

> **Step 3:** Because the improvement is annualized, assume the project had no improvement after the first year (for short-term projects). In Figure 6.2, the annual improvement is 8 s/f × $1,750 × 2 = $28,000. Because the data are reported for six months, the factor of two annualizes the data for a one year value. (Chapter 8 discusses projects that add value after two or more years.)

Step 4: Adjust the new values by the percentage of the improvement related directly to the project, using multiplication to isolate the effects of the project. In Figure 6.2, 70% is allocated to the safety project, resulting in an improvement of $19,600 ($28,000 × 70%).

Step 5: Finally, adjust the improvement calculated in Step 4, using the confidence level multiplied by the confidence percentage. The confidence level is actually a percentage of error suggested by the participants. For example, in Figure 6.2, the participant indicating 80% confidence with the process is reflecting a possibility of 20% error ($3,920). In a $19,600 value with an 80% confidence factor, the participant is suggesting a value in the range of $15,680 to $23,520 (i.e., a range between 20% less and 20% more). To be conservative, use the lower number. This calculation is the same as multiplying the confidence factor by the value of the improvement ($19,600 × 80% = $15,680).

The monetary values determined in these five steps are totaled for all the participants to arrive at the final project monetary benefits. Because these values are already annualized, the total of these benefits becomes the annual benefits for the project. This value is placed in the numerator of the ROI formula to calculate the ROI.

$$\text{ROI} = \frac{\text{Benefits} - \text{Costs}}{\text{Costs}} \times 100$$

USING PERFORMANCE CONTRACTS TO MEASURE BUSINESS IMPACT

Another technique for collecting business impact data is the performance contract. The performance contract is essentially a slight variation of the action plan. Based on the principle of mutual goal setting, a performance contract is a written agreement between a participant and the participant's manager. The participant agrees to improve performance in an area of mutual concern related to the project. The agreement is in the form of a goal to accomplish during the project or after the project's completion. The agreement details what is to be accomplished, at what time, and with what results.

Although the steps can vary according to the organization and the specific kind of contract, a common sequence of events follows:

1. The employee (participant) becomes involved in project implementation.

2. The participant and his or her immediate manager agree on a measure or measures for improvement related to the project (What's in it for me?).

3. Specific, measurable goals for improvement are set, following the SMART requirements discussed earlier. The participant and manager sign the document.

4. The project coordinator (or facilitator) concurs with the measure and improvement goal and signs the document.

5. In the early stages of the project, the performance contract is discussed and plans are developed to accomplish the goals.

6. During project implementation, the participant works to meet the deadline set in the contract.

7. The participant reports the results and discusses them with his or her manager.

8. The manager and participant document the results and forward a copy, with appropriate comments, to the evaluation team.

The action plan in Figure 6.2 can be converted to a performance contract by having Ellie Hightower discuss this measure with her manager and secure her approval.

The process of selecting the area for improvement is similar to the process used in an action plan. The topic can cover one or more of the following areas:

- Routine performance related to the project, including specific improvement in measures such as patient outcomes, patient safety, quality, efficiency, and error rates

- Problem solving, focused on such problems as an unexpected increase in readmission rates, a decrease in patient satisfaction, or a loss of morale

- Innovative or creative applications arising from the project, which could include the initiation of improvements in work practices, new systems, and physician engagement techniques and processes

- Personal development connected to the project, such as leadership development, coaching, or executive education

The topic of the performance contract should be stated in terms of one or more objectives that are

- Written

- Understandable by all involved

- Challenging (requiring an unusual effort to achieve)

- Achievable (something that can be accomplished)

- Largely under the control of the participant

- Measurable and dated

The performance contract objectives are accomplished by following the guidelines for action plans presented earlier, and the methods for analyzing data and reporting progress are essentially the same as those used to analyze action plan data.

USING QUESTIONNAIRES TO COLLECT BUSINESS IMPACT MEASURES

As described in the previous chapters, the questionnaire is one of the most versatile data collection tools and can be appropriate for Levels 1, 2, 3, and 4 data. Essentially, the design principles and content issues are the same as at other levels, except that questionnaires developed for a business impact evaluation will include additional questions to capture those data specific to business impact.

The use of questionnaires for impact data collection brings both good news and bad news. The good news is that questionnaires are convenient, easy to implement, and low cost. Data analysis is efficient, and the time required to provide the data is often minimal, making questionnaires among the least disruptive of data collection methods. The bad news is that the data can be distorted and inaccurate and are sometimes missing. The challenge is to take all the steps necessary to ensure that questionnaires are complete, accurate, and clear, and that they are returned on a timely basis.

Even though questionnaires can be among the weakest methods of data collection, they are the most commonly used because of their advantages. Of the first 200 case studies published on the ROI Methodology, roughly 50 percent used questionnaires as a method of data collection. The challenge is to improve them, make them as credible as possible, and have participants provide accurate and complete data, with return rates in the 70 to 80 percent range.

The reason return rates must be high is explained in Guiding Principle 6 of the ROI Methodology. If an individual provides no improvement data, it is assumed that the person had no improvement to report. "No data, no improvement" is a conservative principle but necessary for the credibility of the results. Consequently, using questionnaires will require effort, discipline, and personal attention to ensure proper response rates. Chapter 4 presented suggestions for ensuring high response rates for Level 1 and Level 2 data collection. The same techniques should be considered here. Table 6.3 repeats some of the suggestions in the form of a checklist. These steps are powerful when at least a dozen techniques are used in a project. These steps are also useful for obtaining high response rates for action plans and performance contracts. They are derived from a significant research base.[4]

SELECTING THE APPROPRIATE METHOD FOR EACH LEVEL

The data collection methods presented in this and earlier chapters offer a wide range of opportunities for collecting data in a variety of situations. The following eight issues about data collection should be considered when deciding on the most appropriate collection method.

TABLE 6.3 Techniques to Increase Response Rates

Increasing Response Rates	
1. Provide advance communication.	[ ]
2. Communicate the purpose.	[ ]
3. Identify who will see the results.	[ ]
4. Describe the data integration process.	[ ]
5. Let the target audience know that they are part of a sample.	[ ]
6. Add emotional appeal.	[ ]
7. Design for simplicity.	[ ]
8. Make it look professional and attractive.	[ ]
9. Use the local manager support.	[ ]
10. Build on earlier data.	[ ]
11. Pilot test the questionnaire.	[ ]
12. Recognize the expertise of participants.	[ ]
13. Consider the use of incentives.	[ ]
14. Have an executive sign the introductory letter.	[ ]
15. Send a copy of the results to the participants.	[ ]
16. Report the use of results.	[ ]
17. Provide an update to create pressure to respond.	[ ]
18. Present previous responses.	[ ]
19. Introduce the questionnaire during the program.	[ ]
20. Use follow-up reminders.	[ ]
21. Consider a captive audience.	[ ]
22. Consider the appropriate medium for easy response.	[ ]
23. Estimate the necessary time to complete the questionnaire.	[ ]
24. Show the timing of the planned steps.	[ ]
25. Personalize the process.	[ ]
26. Collect data anonymously or confidentially.	[ ]

Source: Adapted from Patricia Pulliam Phillips. *Survey Basics: A Guide to Developing Surveys and Questionnaires* (Alexandria, VA: ASTD Press, 2013).

FIGURE 6.3 Usual Collection Methods for Types of Data

Method	Level 1	2	3	4
Surveys	✓	✓	✓	
Questionnaires	✓	✓	✓	✓
Observation		✓	✓	
Interviews			✓	
Focus groups			✓	
Tests/Quizzes		✓		
Demonstrations		✓		
Simulations		✓		
Action planning/ Improvement plans				✓
Performance contracting				✓
Performance monitoring			✓	✓

Type of Data

One of the most important issues to consider when selecting the method is the type of data to be collected. Some methods are more appropriate for business impact. Follow-up surveys, observations, interviews, and focus groups are best suited for application data (Level 3). Performance monitoring, action planning, performance contracting, and questionnaires can easily capture business impact data. Figure 6.3 shows specific data collection methods for the types of data.

Investment of Participants' Time

Another important factor when selecting the data collection method is the amount of time participants must spend with data collection and evaluation systems. Time requirements should always be minimized, and the method should be positioned so that it is a value-added activity. Participants must understand that data collection is a valuable undertaking, and not an activity to be resisted. Sampling can be helpful in keeping total participant time to a minimum. Methods such as observations and performance monitoring require no participant time, whereas others, such as conducting interviews and focus groups, require a significant investment in time. Questionnaires and surveys usually require minimal amounts of time.

INVESTMENT OF MANAGERS' TIME

The time that a participant's manager must allocate to data collection is another issue in method selection. This time requirement should always be minimized. Methods, such as performance contracting, require involvement from the manager before and after project implementation, whereas other methods, such as participants' completion of a questionnaire, may not require any manager time.

COST OF METHOD

Cost is always a consideration when selecting the method. Some data collection methods are more expensive than others. For example, interviews and observations are expensive, whereas surveys, questionnaires, and performance monitoring are usually inexpensive.

DISRUPTION OF NORMAL WORK ACTIVITIES

The issue that generates perhaps the greatest concern among managers and directors is the degree of work disruption that data collection will create. Routine work processes should be disrupted as little as possible. Data collection techniques such as performance monitoring require little time and little or no distraction from normal activities. Observation entails no disruption. Questionnaires generally do not disrupt the work environment and can often be completed in just a few minutes, perhaps even after usual work hours. At the other extreme, techniques, such as the focus group and interview, may disrupt the normal flow of work.

ACCURACY OF METHOD

The accuracy of the technique is another factor to consider when selecting the method. Some data collection methods are more accurate than others. For example, performance monitoring is usually accurate because data come from the organization's records, whereas questionnaires are vulnerable to subjective distortion and may be unreliable. If on-the-job behavior must be captured, observation is clearly one of the most accurate methods, but only when the observation is invisible or unnoticeable. Often a trade-off between the accuracy and costs of a method needs to be considered.

UTILITY OF AN ADDITIONAL METHOD

Because many different methods to collect data exist, using too many methods is tempting. Multiple data collection methods add time and cost to the evaluation and may result in little added value. Utility refers to the value added by each additional data collection method. When more than one method is used, this question should always be addressed: Does the value obtained from the additional data warrant the extra time and expense of the method? If the answer is no, the additional method should not be implemented. The same issue must be addressed when considering multiple sources and time frames.

CULTURAL BIAS OF DATA COLLECTION METHOD

The culture or philosophy of the organization can dictate which data collection methods are best to use. For example, if a healthcare organization or audience is accustomed to using questionnaires, they may work well within the culture of that organization. Some organizations will not use observation because their culture will not support the potential invasion of privacy. Still others prefer interviews while some may not.

MEASURING THE HARD TO MEASURE

The focus of this chapter is on capturing the measures that are easy to collect and easy to measure. They consist of the classic definitions of hard data and soft data—or tangible data and intangible data. Much attention today is focused on the hard-to-measure aspects—the classic soft items that are even softer than patient satisfaction and job engagement. Although this subject is discussed at length in Chapter 9, Measuring the Intangibles, a few comments are appropriate here.

EVERYTHING CAN BE MEASURED

Contrary to the thinking of some professionals, everything can be measured. Any item, issue, or phenomenon that is important to an organization can be measured. Even images, perceptions, and ideas in a person's mind can be measured. The tricky issue is usually in identifying the best way and the best resources to do the measuring. Although the image of an issue can be measured accurately, doing so takes time and money.

A case in point is the project launched by a government health services organization in North America. Having employees take a few shots a year should keep them from being sick and the patients from catching the flu from employees. What better way to set an example for the public? Top executives were concerned as to why only 35 percent of employees were getting flu shots. Their concern came at a time when several campaigns with employees had failed to improve the rate of participation. A sample of employees was surveyed to uncover the reasons for the lack of success. The results were impressive and demonstrated several misconceptions about flu shots. By properly addressing them, and measuring success at lower levels, the participation rates improved.

THE IMPORTANCE OF PERCEPTIONS

Some soft, or intangible, items are not based on perceptions, but others are. For example, consider innovation. An important component of innovation in a healthcare organization is image or perception. Also, some clear measures determine how innovative the organization is able to be in its processes, products, and services (e.g., number of new patents, number of new services). However, concepts such as brand awareness are based strictly on perception (i.e., on what a person knows or perceives about an item, product, or service). In the past, perceptions were not considered especially valuable, but today many decisions are based on perceptions.

FINAL THOUGHTS

Business impact data are critical to address an organization's business needs. These data lead the evaluation to the "money." Although perceived as difficult to find, business impact data are readily available and credible. After describing the types of data that reflect business impact, this chapter provides an overview of several data collection approaches that can be used to capture business data. Some methods are gaining greater acceptance for use in capturing impact data. Performance monitoring, follow-up questionnaires, action plans, and performance contracts are used regularly to collect data for an impact analysis. This chapter focuses on methods to collect data on project impact and consequences. Linking these consequences directly to the project requires the important step of isolating the effects of the project, a topic discussed in the next chapter.

Isolation of Project Impact: Addressing the Attribution Issue

Reporting improvement in impact measures is an important step in a healthcare project evaluation that leads to the money. The question comes up (as it should): How much of this improvement was the result of the project? Unfortunately, the answer is rarely provided with any degree of accuracy and confidence. Although the change in performance may, in fact, be linked to the project, other, non-project-related factors may have contributed to the improvement as well. If this issue is not addressed, the results reported will lack credibility. This chapter explores useful methods for isolating the effects of the project, sometimes labeled attribution. These methods have been used in some of the most successful organizations as they attempt to measure the ROI from projects.

OPENING STORIES

ALBERTA HEALTH SERVICES

Alberta Health Services (AHS) is Canada's largest healthcare organization, serving the entire province of Alberta, including the two large metropolitan areas of Calgary and Edmonton. AHS offers programs and services at 400 facilities throughout the province, including hospitals, clinics, continuing care facilities, mental health facilities, and community health sites.[1] With almost 100,000 employees, AHS faces a serious shortage of nurses. Each year, AHS recruits about 5,000 nurses and projections for the future show an impending acute shortage. Because of this serious issue, AHS has created a variety of programs to attract students and other professionals to the healthcare industry, particularly in the field of nursing. One program is a cooperative education program where students alternate work and school. This program is attractive to students because it provides a way for students to fund their education, while gaining valuable work experience in the process.

For several years, the cooperative education program has been producing a steady stream of nurse talent. Now, the executives at AHS would like to understand the full value of this program. To conduct a study, the human resources team tracked a group of co-op students to study the success on the job and the retention rates among them. In order to compare the success and retention of this group of students (experimental group) with the non–co-op students (control group), a comparison group was selected. The comparison group was matched carefully with the co-op students for the study using criteria of age, gender, type of degree, and tenure with AHS. Essentially, the study had a matched group of non–co-op students to compare with the success of the co-op students. This classic experimental versus control group arrangement provided AHS with a way to sort out the effect of this particular program and show the contribution directly attributed to it.

VA HEALTH SYSTEM

The Veterans Health Administration, one of the largest healthcare providers in the United States, operates under the Department of Veterans Affairs. The Veterans Health Administration is home to the United States' largest integrated healthcare system consisting of 152 medical centers, nearly 1,400 community-based outpatient clinics, community living centers, Vet Centers, and domiciliaries. Together these healthcare facilities and the more than 53,000 independent licensed healthcare practitioners who work within them provide comprehensive care to more than 8.3 million veterans each year.[2] One of the important challenges for improvement in the VA is the length of stay for veterans who are receiving treatment in a hospital. Of the many veterans in the United States, those who are older typically have longer lengths of stay. To reduce the length of stay would not only help the VA be more efficient, but also allow them to serve the growing needs of additional veterans, including those injured or disabled from the recent Iraq and Afghanistan wars.

Several programs are in place to reduce length of stay, but a particularly important project consisted of a group of collaborative teams at each facility to address this important topic. The teams explored the reasons behind length of stay, particularly in areas where it seemed to be excessive. Working through action plans, these teams tackled this issue and success followed. Because several other factors were in play, it was important to show the value of the collaborative teams process, and VA leadership wanted to see the actual ROI. The cost of the collaborative teams process was compared to the monetary benefits derived from a shorter length of stay. To isolate the effects of the collaborative teams process, a group of experts who were familiar with all the factors was assembled to provide input.

Prior to meeting with the team in a focus group format, the factors that contributed to the actual reduction in length of stay (the facts) were detailed. The focus group discussed the cause-and-effect relationship, linking each of the factors that influenced the measure to the success that was achieved. In a carefully controlled focus group format, each individual discussed the perceived linkage from each of the influences. Each person in the meeting had no ownership in any of the other factors; they were neutral, as was the focus group facilitator. At the end of the meeting, the individuals allocated the reduction in length of stay to different factors in a pie chart. To adjust for the error in the allocations, each participant indicated their confidence in the allocation on a scale of 0 to 100 percent, where 0 represented no confidence, and 100 percent represented absolute certainty. This confidence adjustment served as an error margin and adjusted the allocations downward. For example, if an individual gave 30 percent improvement to collaborative work teams and was 80 percent confident in their allocation, the group would allocate 24 percent of improvement to this process (30% × 80%).

This particular attribution method was used because the classic experimental group versus control group was impossible, and no other analytical methods could be developed to determine these influences. However, executives felt that this method was effective because the sources were the individuals who understood length of stay (most credible source), the data were collected in a nonthreatening and unbiased way (no names were attached to comments or data), and the resulting allocations were adjusted for the error from the estimators.

These two stories illustrate an important trend that is sweeping organizations today: the discipline to always isolate the effects of the particular healthcare project from other influences. Without this attribution, the healthcare improvement project that drives the measure may be inconclusive unless a method is used to isolate the program from other influences.

THE IMPORTANCE OF THIS ISSUE

In almost every healthcare improvement project, multiple factors influence the targeted business measures. Imagine a project designated to reduce readmission rates. When an improvement occurs, several factors will usually be involved because this issue is an important one. Determining the effect of each factor attributed to the project is crucial. Without this isolation, the project's success cannot be confirmed, rendering it invalid and inconclusive. Moreover, the effects of the project will usually be overstated if the change in the business impact measure is attributed entirely to the project, which places pressure on evaluators and project leaders to demonstrate the actual effects of their projects on business improvement as opposed to other possible factors.

REALITY OF ATTRIBUTION

Isolating the effects of projects on business measures leads to some important conclusions. First, other influences are almost always present. In almost every situation, multiple factors generate impact results. The rest of the world does not stand still while a project is being implemented. Also, if the measure is one that matters, other processes are also operating to improve the same metrics targeted by several projects and initiatives.

Next, if the project effect is not isolated, no business link can be established. Without steps taken to document the project's contribution, proof that the project actually influenced the measures is missing. The evidence will show only that the project *might* have made a difference. Results have improved, but other factors may have influenced the data.

Also, the other factors and influences have their own protective owners. These owners will insist that their processes made the difference. Some of them will probably be certain that the results are due entirely to their efforts. They may present a compelling case to management, stressing their achievements.

Finally, isolating the effects of the project on impact data is a challenging task. For complex projects in particular, the process is not easy, especially when strong-willed owners of other processes are involved. Fortunately, a variety of approaches are available to facilitate the procedure.

MYTHS ABOUT ATTRIBUTION

The myths surrounding the attribution create confusion and frustration with the process. Some researchers, professionals, and consultants go so far as to suggest that isolation is not necessary. Here are the most common myths:

1. **Our project is complementary to other processes; therefore, we should not attempt to isolate the effects of the project.** A project often complements other factors at play, all of which, together, drive results. If the sponsor of a project needs to understand its relative contribution, the isolation process is the only way to do it. If accomplished properly, it will reveal how the complementary factors interact to drive improvements.

2. **Other evaluators do not address this issue.** While some project leaders do not grapple with the isolation problem because they wish to make a convincing case that all of the improvement is directly related to their own processes, others are addressing the topic. More professional managers are tackling this important issue.

3. **If we cannot use a research-based experiment-versus-control group, we should not attempt this procedure.** Although an experimental research design using randomly selected control and experimental groups is the most reliable approach to identifying effects and causes, it is not feasible in the majority of real situations. Consequently, other methods must be used to isolate the effects of a project. The challenge is to find a method that

is effective and whose results are reproducible, even if it is not as credible as the group comparison method.

4. Stakeholders will understand the link to business impact measures; therefore, we do not need to attempt to isolate the effects of the project. Unfortunately, stakeholders try to understand only what is presented to them. The absence of information about attribution makes it difficult for them to understand the business links, particularly when others are claiming full credit for the improvement.

5. Estimates of improvement provide no value. It may be necessary to tackle the isolation process using estimates from those who understand the process best. Although this approach should be pursued only as a last alternative, it can provide value and credibility, particularly when the estimates have been adjusted for error in order to reduce subjectivity.

6. If I ignore the issue, maybe the others won't think about it. Unfortunately, audiences are becoming more sophisticated on this topic, and they are aware of the presence of multiple influences. If no attempt is made to isolate the effects of the project, the audience will assume that the other factors have had a major effect, perhaps the only effect. A project's credibility can deteriorate quickly. The literature is laced with explanations as to why isolating project effects is so important.

These myths emphasize the importance of tackling this issue. The emphasis on isolation is not meant to suggest that a project is implemented independently and exclusively of other processes. Obviously, all groups should be working as a team to produce the desired results. However, when funding is parceled among different functions or organizations—with different owners—the struggle becomes one of showing and attempting to understand the connection between activities and their results. If you do not undertake this process, others will—leaving your project with reduced budgets, resources, and respect.

PRELIMINARY ISSUES

The challenge is to develop one or more specific methods to isolate the effects of the project early in the process, usually as part of an evaluation plan conducted before the project begins. Up-front attention ensures that appropriate techniques will be used with minimal cost and time commitments. Two important issues in isolating the effects of a project are covered next, followed by specific methods.

CHAIN OF IMPACT

Before presentation of the methods, examining the chain of impact implicit in the different levels of evaluation will be helpful. Measurable results from a project should be derived from the application of the project (Level 3 data). Successful application of the project should stem from project participants learning to do something different, something necessary to implement the project (Level 2 data). Successful learning will usually occur when project participants react favorably to the project's content and objectives (Level 1 data). Without this preliminary evidence, isolating the effects of a project is difficult.

To be sure, in the event of an adverse reaction, no learning, or no application, it is difficult to conclude that any business impact improvements were caused by the project. From a practical standpoint, data collection at four levels for an ROI calculation (Guiding Principle 1 in Table 2.1) is necessary. Although this requirement is a prerequisite to isolating the effects of a project, it does not establish a direct connection, nor does it pinpoint the extent of the improvement caused by the project. It does show, however, that without improvements at previous levels, making a connection between the ultimate outcome and the project is difficult or impossible.

IDENTIFYING OTHER FACTORS: A FIRST STEP

As a first step in isolating a project's impact on performance, key factors that may have contributed to the performance improvement should be identified. This step communicates to interested parties that other factors may have influenced the results, underscoring that the project is not the sole source of improvement. Consequently, the credit for improvement is shared among several possible variables and sources—an approach that is likely to garner the respect of the client. Several potential sources are available for identifying major influencing variables:

- Subject matter experts

- The sponsor

- Experts on the environment where the project is implemented

- The project support team

- The immediate managers of participants

- Project manager

- Auditors

- Other process owners

- Experts on external issues

- Other managers and administrators

The importance of identifying all of the factors is underscored by an example. A large hospital chain has a sophisticated system for identifying the reasons patients make decisions about healthcare products and services. At the point of purchase decision, patient care personnel record the reason(s) for the purchase: Was it the price, the product or service design, the advertising, the medical research, or the referral from a satisfied patient? This system, owned by the marketing department, is designed to isolate the factors underlying the success of various marketing projects. However, it omits factors outside marketing ownership. In essence, it assumes that 100 percent of the purchase decision can be attributed to some marketing influence. It ignores the effect of the economy, competition, information technology, reward systems, learning, process improvement, job design, and other factors that could have had an important influence. Without identifying all the factors, the credibility of the analysis will suffer. Thus, competing factions within that organization reassessed and changed the system so that other factors would be considered in the analysis.

ANALYTICAL ISOLATION METHODS

Just as many data collection methods are available for collecting data at different levels, a variety of methods are also available to isolate the effects of a project. The possibilities range from research methods to approaches involving estimates.

CONTROL GROUPS

The most accurate approach for isolating the impact of a project is an experimental design with control groups. This approach involves the use of an experimental group that goes through the implementation of the project and a control group that does not. The two groups should be as similar in composition as possible and, if feasible, participants for each group should be randomly selected. Once the groups are selected and are subjected to the same environmental influences, differences in performance between the two groups can be attributed to the project, with a reasonable degree of certainty.

As illustrated in Figure 7.1, the control group and experimental group do not necessarily require preproject measurements. Measurements can be taken during the project and after the project has been implemented, with the difference in performance between the two groups indicating the amount of improvement that is directly related to the project.

One caution should be observed: The use of control groups may create the impression that the project leaders are reproducing a laboratory setting, which can cause a problem for some healthcare executives and administrators. To avoid this perception, some organizations conduct a pilot project using participants as the experimental group. A similarly constituted

FIGURE 7.1   Use of Control Groups

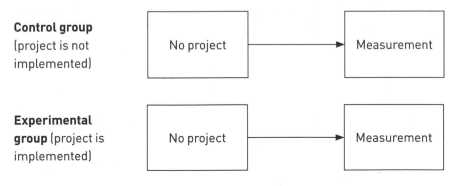

nonparticipant comparison group is selected but does not receive any communication about the project. The terms *pilot project* and *comparison group* are a little less threatening to executives than *experimental group* and *control group*.

The control group approach has some inherent challenges that can make it difficult to apply in practice. The first major challenge is the selection of the groups. From a theoretical perspective, having identical control and experimental groups is next to impossible. Dozens of factors can affect performance, some individual and others contextual. On a practical basis, it is best to select the four to six variables that will have the greatest influence on performance. Essentially then, it means following the Pareto principle (the 80–20 rule), which works from the most important factor down to the least important factor in order to cover perhaps four or five issues that capture the vast majority (80 percent) of the factors having influence.

Another major challenge is that the control group process is not suited to many situations. For some types of projects, withholding the program from one particular group while implementing it with another may not be appropriate, particularly where critical solutions are needed immediately. Management is typically not willing to withhold a solution from one area to see how it works in another. For example, if an adverse patient outcome is the focus of a new procedure designed to prevent it, an experiment involving a pilot group, while withholding the procedure from another comparable group, may not be appropriate. This limitation keeps control group analyses from being implemented in many situations.

In practice, opportunities do surface for a natural control group to develop, even in situations where a solution is implemented throughout an organization. If it takes several months for the solution to encompass everyone in the organization, enough time may be available for a parallel comparison between the first group and the last group to be affected. In these cases, ensuring that the groups are matched as closely as possible is critical. This naturally occurring control group arrangement can often be feasible in situations where major enterprise-wide project implementations occur in large healthcare organizations. The challenge is to address this possibility early enough to influence the implementation schedule to ensure that similar groups are used in the comparison.

Another challenge is contamination, which can develop when participants involved in the project group (experimental group) communicate with people in the control group. Members of the control group may model the behavior or use the procedures of the experimental group. The experiment becomes contaminated as the influence of the project is carried over to the control group. This hazard can be minimized by ensuring that the control and project groups are at different locations, on different shifts, or occupy different floors of the same building. When this level of separation is not possible, it should be explained to both groups that one group will be involved in the project now and the other will be involved at a later date. Appealing to participants' sense of responsibility and asking them not to share information with others may help prevent problems.

A closely related issue involves the passage of time. The longer an experimental-versus-control group comparison operates, the greater the likelihood that other influences will affect the results. More variables will enter into the situation, potentially contaminating the results. On the other end of the scale, enough time must pass to allow a clear pattern to emerge distinguishing the two groups. Thus, the timing of control group comparisons must strike a delicate balance between waiting long enough for performance differences to show, but not so long that the results become contaminated.

Still another problem occurs when the different groups function under different environmental influences, usually when groups are at different locations. For example, two nursing units are being observed (one is the experimental group and the other is the control group). The experimental group has a new manager during the evaluation period. The results could be contaminated with that change. Sometimes this issue can be avoided by using more groups than necessary and discarding those groups that show some environmental differences.

A final issue is that the use of control and experimental groups may appear too research oriented for some business organizations. For example, management may not want to take the time to experiment before proceeding with a project, in addition to the selective withholding problem discussed earlier. Because of these concerns, some project managers will not entertain the idea of using control groups.

Because the use of control groups is an effective approach for isolating impact, it should be considered when a major ROI impact study is planned. In these situations, isolating the project impact with accuracy is essential, and the primary advantage of the control group process is

FIGURE 7.2 Experimental versus Control Group Comparison for Overtime Reduction

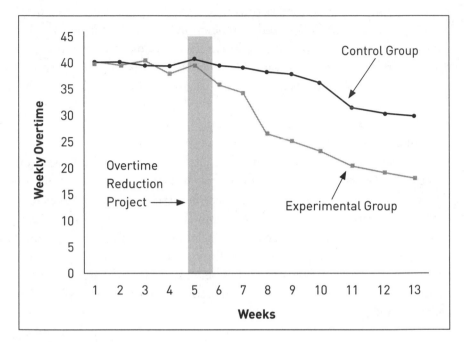

accuracy. Figure 7.2 shows an experimental-and-control group comparison. Both groups are experiencing about 40 hours per week overtime, too much for these two nursing units. An overtime reduction project involving nurse managers was implemented with the experimental group. The control group was not involved. The criteria used to select the two groups included current performance on overtime, staffing levels, type of care, and sick time use. The control group experienced a reduction from 40 hours to 28 hours. The experimental group moved from 40 hours to 18 hours. The improvement, connected to the overtime reduction project, is 10 (28 – 18) hours per week.

TREND LINE ANALYSIS

Another useful technique for approximating the impact of a project is trend line analysis. In this approach, a trend line is drawn to project the future, using previous performance as a base. When the project is fully implemented, actual performance is compared with the trend line projection. Any improvement in performance beyond what the trend line predicted can be reasonably attributed to project implementation. Even though this process is not a precise one, it can provide a credible estimate of the project's impact.

Figure 7.3 shows a trend line analysis from a medium-sized hospital. The vertical axis reflects the rate of disabling injury. The horizontal axis represents time in months. Data reflect conditions before and after the safe operations practice (SOP) project was implemented in May. As shown in the figure, an upward trend for the data existed prior to project implementation. However, the project apparently had an effect on the disabling frequency rate (DFR) as the trend line is much greater than the actual. Project leaders may have been tempted to measure the improvement by comparing the one-year average for the DFR prior to the project to the one-year average after the project. However, this approach understates the improvement because the measure in question is moving in the wrong direction and the SOP turns the DFR in the right direction.

A more accurate comparison is actual value after the project impact has occurred (the last month or two) versus the trend line value for the

FIGURE 7.3 Trend Line Example

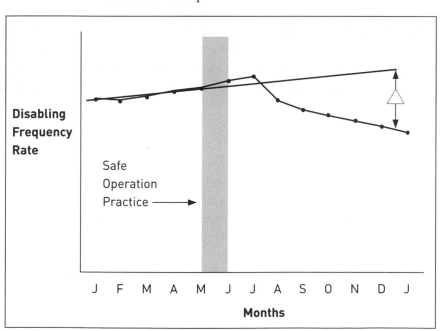

same period. Using this measure increases the accuracy and credibility of the process in terms of isolating the project's impact.

To use this technique, two conditions must be met:

- It can be assumed that the trend that developed prior to the project would have continued if the project had not been implemented to alter it. In other words, had the project not been implemented, this trend would have continued on the same path. The process owner(s) should be able to provide input to confirm this assumption. If the assumption does not hold, trend line analysis cannot be used. If the assumption is a valid one, the second condition is considered.

- No other new variables or influences entered the process during project implementation and evaluation period. The key word here is *new*; the understanding is that the trend has been established from the influences already in place, and no additional influences have entered the process beyond the project. If this is not the case, another method will have to be used. Otherwise, the trend line analysis presents a reasonable estimate of the impact of this project.

For this technique to be used, preproject data must be available and the data should show a reasonable degree of stability. If the variance of the data is high, the stability of the trend line will be an issue. If the stability cannot be assessed from a direct plot of the data, more detailed statistical analyses can be used to determine whether the data are stable enough to allow a projection. The trend line can be projected directly from historical data using a simple routine that is available in many calculators and software packages, such as Microsoft Excel.

A primary disadvantage of the trend line approach is that it is not always possible to use it. This approach assumes that the events that influenced the performance variable prior to project implementation are still in place, except for the effects of the implementation (i.e., the trends established prior to the project will continue in the same relative direction). Also, it assumes that no new influences entered the situation during the course of the project, which may not be the case.

The primary advantage of this approach is that it is simple and inexpensive. If historical data are available, a trend line can quickly be drawn and the differences estimated. Although not exact, it does provide a quick general assessment of project impact.

FORECASTING METHODS

A more analytical approach to trend line analysis is the use of forecasting methods that predict a change in performance variables. This approach represents a mathematical interpretation of the trend line analysis when other variables enter the situation at the time of implementation. With this approach, the output measure targeted by the project is forecast based on the influence of variables that have changed during the implementation or evaluation period for the project. The actual value of the measure is compared with the forecast value, and the difference reflects the contribution of the project.

An example will help illustrate the effect of the forecasting. One healthcare organization was focusing on decreasing length of stay. In July, a new project involved changing several procedures that made the diagnosis, treatment, and healing process faster, with various ways to recognize improvement quickly and make decisions and adjustments accordingly. All of these procedures were aimed at reducing the average length of stay. Figure 7.4 shows that the length of stay prior to the change in medical procedures and the actual data shows a significant downward improvement in the 10 months since the program was implemented. However, two important changes occurred about the same time as the new project was implemented. A major provider reissued a maximum length of stay that they would reimburse for illnesses. This influence has a tendency to cause organizations to focus more intensely on getting patients discharged as quickly as possible. At the same time, the severity of the influx of patients had slightly decreased. The types of illnesses dramatically affect the length of stay. The analysts in the business process improvement department developed a forecast showing the effects of the provider reimbursement process and the change in the illnesses of the patients upon admission. They were able to develop a multiple variable analysis to forecast the LOS, as shown in the figure. The data from March show the difference in the forecasted value and the actual value. That difference represents the impact of the new medical procedures, because they were not included in the forecasted value.

FIGURE 7.4 Forecasting Sample

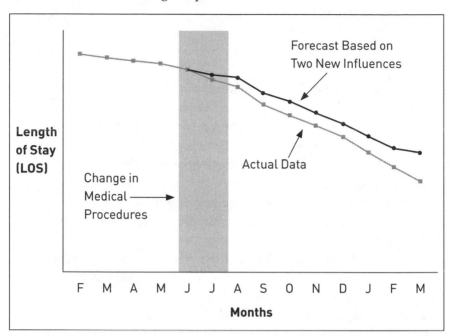

A major disadvantage emerges when several variables enter the process. The complexity multiplies, and the use of sophisticated statistical packages designed for multiple variable analyses is necessary. Even with this assistance, however, a good fit of the data to the model may not be possible.

The good news is that some healthcare organizations have developed mathematical relationships for output variables as a function of one or more inputs, making forecasting possible. The use of business analytics has entered the healthcare industry, bringing a variety of tools for complex analysis.

CALCULATING THE IMPACT OF OTHER FACTORS

It is sometimes possible, although not appropriate in all cases, to calculate the impact of factors (other than the project) that account for part of the improvement and then credit the project with the remaining part. That is, the project assumes credit for improvement that cannot be attributed to other factors.

Although this process may not be applicable to all situations, it can sometimes be a helpful tool. One clinic changed a scheduling process for the MRI department. The new process was designed to implement more efficient scheduling of patients so the profit from the MRI technology could be maximized. The data were tracked before the new scheduling process was implemented and then compared to a post period. However, near the same time, new MRI equipment was installed and the manufacturer suggested that MRIs administered from this equipment would increase 20 percent over the previous equipment. When the study was completed, it showed 35 percent improvement in MRIs. With 20 percent being attributed to the new equipment, the remaining percentage (15 percent) was attributed to the new scheduling process.

This method is appropriate when the other factors can be easily identified and the appropriate mechanisms are in place to calculate their impact on the improvement. In some cases, estimating the impact of other factors is just as difficult as estimating the impact of the project, limiting this approach's applicability. However, the results can be reliable if the procedure used to isolate the impact of other factors is sound.

ISOLATION WITH ESTIMATES

The most common method of isolating the effects of a project is to use estimates from some group of individuals. Although it is the weakest method, it is practical in many situations and it can enhance the credibility of the analysis if adequate precautions are taken. When using this method, the beginning point is to ensure that the estimates are provided by the most credible source, which is often the participant in a project—not a higher-level manager or executive removed from the process. The individual who provides this information must understand the different factors and, particularly, the influence of the project on those factors. Essentially, four categories of input are used. In addition to the participants directly involved in the project, patients and other customers may provide credible estimates in the particular situations where they are involved. External experts may be helpful, and managers are another possible source. These input sources are all described next.

PARTICIPANTS' ESTIMATE OF IMPACT

An easily implemented method of isolating the impact of a project is to obtain information directly from participants during project implementation. The participants are the individuals who are charged with making a project work. The usefulness of this approach rests on the assumption that participants are capable of determining or estimating how much of a performance improvement is related to the project implementation. Because their actions have led to the improvement, participants may provide highly accurate data. Although an estimate, the estimate they provide is likely to carry considerable weight with management because they know that these participants are at the center of the change or improvement. The estimate is obtained by defining the improvement, identifying the factors that cause it (if possible), and then asking participants the series of questions in Table 7.1.

Participants who do not provide answers to the questions listed in Table 7.1 are excluded from the analysis. Erroneous, incomplete, and extreme information should also be discarded before the analysis. This is Guiding Principle 8 (from Table 2.1). To obtain a conservative estimate, the confidence percentage is factored into the estimates. The confidence percentage is a reflection of the error in the estimate. Thus, an 80 percent confidence level equates to a potential error range of plus or minus 20 percent.

TABLE 7.1 Questions for Participant Estimation

What other factors have contributed to this improvement in performance?

What is the link between these factors and the improvement?

What percentage of this improvement can be attributed to the implementation of this project?

How much confidence do you have in this estimate, expressed as a percentage? (0% = no confidence; 100% = complete confidence)

What other individuals or groups could provide a reliable estimate of this percentage to determine the amount of improvement contributed by this project?

In this approach, the estimate is multiplied by the level of confidence to obtain the low side of the error range (Guiding Principle 7).

An example will help describe the situation. Nurse turnover in a community hospital had been a persistent problem because of the shortage of nurses, particularly in the critical care area. In an effort to decrease nurse turnover, the community hospital implemented three new approaches to correct it. One approach was to offer a career pathways program to allow for a faster way to progress in the organization. A second approach was to implement a pay-for-performance program for nurse managers to link patient satisfaction more directly to pay. A third solution was to provide leadership development to first-level managers in the nursing areas. This program was designed to shape critical skills needed to engage nurses, motivate them, treat them with respect, and create a great place to work. With these three programs in place, nurse turnover decreased from 23 percent to 11 percent in one year. Turnover is reported monthly with annualized numbers (i.e., a 1percent monthly turnover is 12 percent annually).

With these programs implemented, it was important to understand the effects of each of these processes. In a focus group, a sample of nurse managers were asked to allocate the percentage that each of these services averted turnovers. It was concluded that the nurse managers were the most credible inputs to sort out the individual effects. They were involved in the pay-for-performance and career pathways projects. Also, they were participants in the leadership program. After reviewing the purpose of the meeting and the ground rules of the focus group, managers were asked to indicate whether other factors could have caused the decrease in addition to the three processes. The managers mentioned only a few other processes. Table 7.2 shows one manager's response. In the example, the manager allocates 30 percent of the improvement to the leadership development program and has a level of confidence in the estimate of 80 percent.

The confidence percentage is multiplied by the estimate to produce a usable project value of 24 percent. This adjusted percentage is then multiplied by the actual amount of the improvement in turnover volume ($12\% \times 620$ nurses $\times 24\%$) to isolate the portion attributed to leadership development. In this case, 18 nurse turnovers would be attributed to the leadership development program. The adjusted improvement is now ready for conversion to monetary value and, ultimately, use in the ROI calculation.

TABLE 7.2 Example of One Participant's Estimation

Fact: Nurse turnover has reduced from 23% to 11% = 12% Target Audience: 620 nurses			
Factor That Influenced Improvement	Percentage of Improvement Caused by	Confidence Expressed as a Percentage	Adjusted Percentage of Improvement Caused by
Leadership development	30%	80%	24%
Career pathways	20	70	14
Pay-for-performance	30	90	27
Other	5	60	3
Total	100%		

Although the reported contribution is an estimate, this approach has considerable accuracy and credibility. Five adjustments are effectively applied to the participant estimate to produce a conservative value:

1. Managers (the participants) who do not provide usable data are assumed to have achieved no improvements.

2. Extreme data values and unsupported claims are omitted from the analysis, although they may be included in the "other benefits" category.

3. For short-term projects, it is assumed that no benefits are realized from the project after the first year of full implementation. For long-term projects, several years of benefits may be used in the analysis.

4. The amount of improvement is adjusted by the portion directly related to the project, expressed as a percentage.

5. The improvement value is multiplied by the confidence level, expressed as a percentage, to reduce the amount of the improvement in order to reflect the potential error.

As an enhancement of this method, the level of management above the participants may be asked to review and approve the participant estimates.

When using participants' estimates to measure impact, several assumptions are made:

1. The project encompasses a variety of different activities, practices, and tasks all focused on improving the performance of one or more business measures.

2. One or more business measures were identified prior to the project and have been monitored since the implementation process. Data monitoring has revealed an improvement in the business measure.

3. Associating the project with a specific amount of performance improvement and determining the monetary impact of the improvement are necessary. This information forms the basis for calculating the actual ROI.

4. The individuals sorting out the influences (the participants) are the most credible ones to provide the data.

Given these assumptions, the participants can specify the results linked to the project and provide data necessary to develop the ROI. This task can be accomplished using a focus group, interview, action plan, or questionnaire.

USING INTERVIEWS

In this example, a focus group was used to collect the participant data. Sometimes, focus groups are unavailable or are considered unacceptable for the use of data collection. Participants may be unavailable for a group meeting or the focus groups may become too expensive. In these situations, collecting similar information with an interview can be beneficial. Participants must address the same elements as those addressed in the focus group, but with a series of probing questions in a face-to-face interview. The interview may focus solely on isolating the effects of the project or serve as a part of collecting other data sets. A telephone or web interview (e.g., on Skype) may also be used.

USING ACTION PLANS

As described in the previous chapter, the action planning process is an important way for participants to drive improvements. The action plan provides a way to indicate what specific steps are taken, when they are taken, and the impact that the actions have on the organization. When the planning process is complete and the impact has occurred, improvement is the result. This improvement is reported on the action plan itself. With this process in mind, three questions are needed in the action plan to isolate the effects of the project on that data:

1. What other factors could have caused this improvement?

2. What percentage of this improvement is directly related to this project?

3. What is your confidence in this allocation, on a scale of zero to 100 percent, where zero is no confidence and 100 percent is complete confidence?

Isolation is usually an easy task for these types of projects, because participants have taken a variety of steps to cause the business impact. Thus, they have a good understanding of how they influence this particular project. When these three questions are followed, accuracy can be credible.

Some may suggest that if an action plan is developed for a particular project, all the improvement should go to the project with no steps needed for the isolation process. Not so! Some of these projects or actions would be initiated anyway. Also, other factors often cause the measures to change. Isolation is absolutely critical to make sure that only the amount of increase driven by the action plans is reported.

USING QUESTIONNAIRES

Sometimes indicators of improvement in a particular project are collected by questionnaire, where success with application and impact is detailed in literally dozens of questions. Based on these data, the results need to be isolated to the program. To accomplish this isolation, ask the same three questions as were asked about action plans (see the previous section).

This process is credible, because the results as reported in the questionnaire have been achieved by the responding participant, who will usually have some appropriate level of understanding of the connection. The error adjustments can often take care of the uncertainties in this process. This approach does have the inherent weaknesses that parallel the use of the questionnaire when compared to other methods. Individuals can ignore it or provide inaccurate or perhaps even biased data. To limit the effects of any weaknesses, apply the techniques described in the previous chapter to assure a great response rate.

Manager's Estimate of Impact

In lieu of, or in addition to, participant estimates, the participants' manager may be asked to provide input concerning the project's role in improving performance. In some settings, managers may be more familiar with the other factors influencing performance and therefore may be better equipped to provide estimates of impact. The questions to ask managers, after identifying the improvement ascribed to the project, are similar to those asked of the participants.

Managers' estimates should be analyzed in the same manner as the participants' estimates, and they may also be adjusted by the confidence percentage. When participants' and managers' estimates have both been collected, the decision of which estimate to use becomes an issue. Given a reason to believe that one estimate is more credible than the other, then that estimate should be used. If they are equally credible, then the most conservative approach is to use the lowest value and include an appropriate explanation. These two steps are Guiding Principles 3 and 4.

In some cases, upper management may provide an estimate of the percentage of improvement attributable to a project. After considering other factors that could contribute to the improvement—such as technology, procedures, and process changes—they apply a subjective factor to represent the portion of the results that should be attributed to the project. Despite its subjective nature, this input by upper management is usually accepted by the individuals who provide or approve funding for the project. Sometimes their comfort level with the processes used is the most important consideration.

Patients'/Customers' Estimate of Project Impact

An approach that is useful in some narrowly focused project situations is to solicit input on the impact of a project directly from patients or other customers. Patients are asked why they chose a particular service or are asked to explain how their reaction to a project or service has been influenced by individuals or systems involved in the project. This technique often focuses directly on what the project is designed to improve. For example, after the implementation of a patient care project involving patient care representative (PCRs), patients were asked to indicate the extent to which their patient satisfaction increased because of the way PCRs handled their situation. This approach connected impact (patient satisfaction) to the patient care project.

Routine patient surveys provide an excellent opportunity to collect input directly from patients concerning their reactions to new or improved services, processes, or procedures. Preproject and postproject data can pinpoint the improvements spurred by a new project.

Ideally, patient input should be secured using current data collection methods; the creation of new surveys or feedback mechanisms should be avoided. This measurement process should not add to the data collection systems in use. Patient input may constitute the most powerful and convincing data if it is complete, accurate, and valid.

Experts' Estimate of Impact

External or internal experts can sometimes estimate the portion of results that can be attributed to a project. With this technique, experts must be carefully selected based on their knowledge of the process, project, and situation. For example, an expert in wellness might be able to provide estimates of how much change in medical costs can be attributed to a wellness project.

This approach has its drawbacks, however. It can yield inaccurate data unless the project and the setting in which the estimate is made are quite similar to a project with which the expert is familiar. Also, this approach may lack credibility if the estimates come from external sources and do not involve those close to the process.

This process has the advantage of being a quick and easy form of input from a reputable expert or consultant. Sometimes top management has more confidence in such external experts than in its own staff.

Estimate Credibility: The Wisdom of Crowds

The following story is a sample of the tremendous amount of research showing the power of input from average individuals. It is taken from James Surowiecki's best-selling book, *The Wisdom of Crowds*.[3]

One day in the fall of 1906, British scientist Francis Galton left his home in the town of Plymouth and headed for a country fair. Galton was 85 years old and was beginning to feel his age, but he was still brimming with the curiosity that had won him renown—and notoriety—for his work on statistics and the science of heredity. On that particular day, Galton's curiosity turned to livestock.

Galton's destination was the annual West of England Fat Stock and Poultry Exhibition, a regional fair where the local farmers and townspeople gathered to appraise the quality of each other's cattle, sheep, chickens, horses, and pigs. Wandering through rows of stalls examining workhorses and prize hogs may seem like a strange way for a scientist to spend an afternoon, but there was certain logic to it. Galton was a man obsessed with two things: the measurement of physical and mental qualities and breeding. And what, after all, is a livestock show but a large showcase for the effects of good and bad breeding?

Breeding mattered to Galton because he believed that only a few people had the characteristics necessary to keep societies healthy. He had devoted much of his career to measuring those characteristics, in fact, in an effort to prove that the vast majority of people did not possess them. His experiments left him with little confidence in the intelligence of the average person, "[T]he stupidity and wrong-headedness of many men and women being so great as to be scarcely credible," Galton believed. "Only if power and control stayed in the hands of the select, well-bred few, could a society remain healthy and strong."

As he walked through the exhibition that day, Galton came across a weight judging competition. A fat ox had been selected and put on display, and many people were lining up to place wagers on what the weight of the ox would be *after* it was slaughtered and dressed. For sixpence, an individual could buy a stamped and numbered ticket and fill in his or her name, occupation, address, and estimate. The best guesses would earn prizes.

Eight hundred people tried their luck. They were a diverse lot. Many of them were butchers and farmers, who were presumably expert at judging the weight of livestock, but there were also quite a few people who had no insider knowledge of cattle. "Many non-experts competed," Galton wrote later in the scientific journal *Nature*. "The average competitor was probably as well fitted for making a just estimate of the dressed weight of the ox, as an average voter is of judging the merits of most political issues on which he votes."

Galton was interested in figuring out what the "average voter" was capable of because he wanted to prove that the average voter was capable of very little. So he turned the competition into an impromptu experiment. When the contest was over and the prizes had been awarded, Galton borrowed the tickets from the organizers and ran a series of statistical tests on them. Galton arranged the guesses (totaling 787; 13 were discarded because they were illegible) in order from highest to lowest and plotted them to see if they would form a bell curve. Then, among other things, he added up all of the contestants' estimates and calculated the mean. That number represented, you could say, the collective wisdom of the Plymouth crowd. If the crowd were viewed as a single person, that would be the person's guess as to the ox's weight.

Galton had no doubt that the average guess of the group would be way off the mark. After all, mix a few very smart people with some mediocre people and a lot of dumb people, and it seems likely that you would end up with a dumb answer. But Galton was wrong. The crowd had guessed that the slaughtered and dressed ox would weigh 1,197 pounds. In fact, after it was slaughtered and dressed, the ox weighed 1,198 pounds. In other words, the crowd's judgment was essentially perfect. The "experts" were not even close. Perhaps breeding didn't mean so much after all. Galton wrote later: "The result seems more creditable to the trustworthiness of a democratic judgment than it might have been expected." That was something of an understatement.

What Francis Galton stumbled on that day in Plymouth was a simple but powerful truth: Under the right circumstances, groups are remarkably intelligent, and are often smarter than the smartest people in them. Groups do not need to be dominated by exceptionally intelligent people in order to be smart. Even if most of the people within a group are not especially informed or rational, collectively they can reach a wise decision.

METHOD SELECTION

With all of these methods available to isolate the impact of a project, selecting the most appropriate ones for a specific project can be difficult. Some methods are simple and inexpensive; others are time-consuming and costly. When choosing among them, the following factors should be considered:

- Feasibility of the method

- Accuracy associated with the method

- Credibility of the method with the target audience

- Specific cost to implement the method

- Amount of disruption in normal work activities resulting from the method's implementation

- Participant, staff, and management time required for the method

The use of multiple methods should be considered because two sources are usually better than one. When multiple methods are used, the most credible method should be used in the analysis. If both methods are credible, the most conservative one should be used in the analysis. The most conservative one is the method that generates the lowest ROI. The reason is that a conservative approach builds acceptance. The target audience should always be provided with an explanation of the process and the subjective factors involved. Multiple sources allow an organization to experiment with different strategies and build confidence in the use of a particular method. For example, if management is concerned about the accuracy of participants' estimates, the combination of a control group arrangement and participant estimates could be useful for checking the accuracy of the estimation process.

It is not unusual for the ROI of a project to be extremely large. Even when a portion of the improvement is allocated to other factors, the magnitude can still be impressive in many situations. The audience should understand that even though every effort has been made to isolate the project's impact, it remains an imprecise figure that is subject to error. It represents the best estimate of the impact given the constraints, conditions, and resources available. Chances are it is more accurate than other types of analysis regularly used in other functions within the organization.

FINAL THOUGHTS

Isolating the effects of a project is an important step in answering the question of how much of the improvement in an impact measure was caused by the project. The methods presented in this chapter are the most effective approaches available to answer this question and are used by some of the most progressive organizations. Too often, results are reported and linked to a project with no attempt to isolate the exact portion of the outcome associated with the project. This practice leads to an invalid report trumpeting project success. If healthcare professionals are committed to meeting their responsibility to obtain results, the need for isolation must be addressed early in the process for all major projects. When this important step is completed, the impact data are converted to monetary values, a process that is detailed in the next chapter.

CHAPTER 8

Converting Data to Money

With the current focus on ROI and cost avoidance, "Show me the money" is a typical request these days. To show the real money, the improvement in business measures attributable to the project must be converted to monetary values. To develop the ROI, the monetary value is then compared to the project costs. ROI represents the ultimate level in the five-level evaluation framework presented in Chapter 2. This chapter explains how healthcare improvement projects include a step to develop the monetary values used in the ROI calculation.

The Healthcare Financial Management Association has conducted several studies on the status of healthcare, including a 2011 critical project report, "Value in Healthcare; Current State and Future Directions."[1] This landmark study sheds light on the efforts to convert quality improvements to monetary values. The study indicated that many providers, while recognizing the significance between quality improvements and cost reduction efforts, are just now starting to measure the cost impact of poor quality and waste in their organizations. They are just beginning to move beyond the traditional methods of cost accounting. Almost one third of respondents believe no, or limited, dependency exists between quality improvement and cost reduction efforts. Only one half believe in some dependency, and the link is increasing. Less than one quarter believes the mutual dependency between quality improvement and cost reduction efforts is extensive. These statistics are critical because most research clearly shows that when quality improvements are converted to cost savings or cost avoidance, not only can a direct link be shown, but the results can be staggering.

This same study showed that 43 percent of the studied organizations do not measure the cost of adverse events. Another 37 percent measure the impact but do not manage the metrics. Only 20 percent actually measure the cost of adverse events and manage the metrics to reduce the cost or improve margins. Finally, the study showed that 50 percent of participants are not measuring the cost of waste in care processes, such as duplicate/ unnecessary tasks or procedures. Another 29 percent measure them but do not manage the metrics. Only 21 percent actually measure and manage these metrics to reduce the cost or improve margins. The results clearly show that a critical issue in healthcare is to determine the actual cost of unwanted events or processes. It is a vital way to manage the costs and have more efficient healthcare processes.

OPENING STORY

A southeast-based, religiously affiliated hospital chain had an excessive number of sexual harassment complaints throughout its network of 8,000 employees. The complaints were formally filed with the human resource director, which triggered an investigation to determine whether the complaints had merit and, if so, steps were taken to resolve the issue. Most of the complaints were based on lack of knowledge of the organization's sexual harassment policy and what actually constitutes sexual harassment activity. The HR executives took action to set up a sexual harassment prevention process, which involved all 8,000 employees, including managers, administrators, and directors.

To show the value of these types of efforts, the HR director asked for the actual ROI calculation. To do so, the HR director needed to know the actual cost of a sexual harassment complaint. In addition, as the number of complaints dramatically improved, the level of voluntary employee turnover was reduced as well. The study showed that some individuals were leaving because of the unfriendly workplace created by the sexual harassment activity.

To calculate the cost of the sexual harassment complaints, the HR director examined the total cost of sexual harassment prevention, litigation, and defense for the previous year. Charges and lawsuits that were either settled or resulted in losses for the organization were considered in the total. Other costs were added, which included the time of everyone involved in the process. Both direct and indirect costs were added and divided by the number of sexual harassment complaints that were reduced and attributed to this project, which yielded an average of $24,000 per complaint.

The employee turnover value was derived from studies that had been conducted by other organizations and published in a variety of journals located in a research database called ERIC.[2] The numbers showed that the cost of the voluntary turnover in the healthcare arena averaged about 1.25 times the annual salary. Using this average as a value, the HR director calculated the ROI of the sexual harassment prevention project.[3]

THE IMPORTANCE OF CONVERTING DATA TO MONEY

The need to convert data to monetary amounts is not always clearly understood by healthcare managers. The success of a project can be demonstrated just by connecting the impact data showing the amount of change directly attributable to the project. For example, a change in nurse turnover, patient outcomes, patient safety, or wait time could represent a significant improvement linked directly to a project. For some projects, these calculations may be sufficient. However, many sponsors require the actual monetary value, detailing the cost savings or cost avoidance of these improvements. More healthcare managers are taking this extra step of converting data to monetary values.

VALUE EQUALS MONEY

For some stakeholders, the most important value is money. Chapter 2 described several different types of value. However, monetary value is becoming one of the primary criteria of success as the economic benefits of healthcare projects are pursued. Executives, sponsors, clients, administrators, politicians, and other leaders are concerned with the amount of allocation of funds and want to see evidence of the contribution of a project in terms of monetary value. To them, value is money; any other outcome for these key stakeholders would be unsatisfactory.

USING MONETARY VALUES TO UNDERSTAND PROBLEMS

In any business, particularly in healthcare, costs are essential to understanding the magnitude of a problem. Consider, for example, the cost of nurse turnover. Traditional records and even those available through activity-based costing will not indicate the full cost of the problem. A variety of estimates and expert inputs may be necessary to supplement cost statements to arrive at a definite value. The good news is that organizations have developed a number of standard procedures for identifying undesirable costs. For example, when hospital employees are injured at work, the cost can be substantial. The fully loaded cost of a disabling injury includes direct medical costs, lost time of the injured, time for investigating and managing the accident, time of others, and other related costs. These cost figures are usually already developed to show the magnitude of the problem.

MAKING IMPACT MORE UNDERSTANDABLE

For some projects, the impact is more understandable when stated in terms of monetary value. Consider, for example, the impact of a physician leadership program. When physicians change their leader behavior and become more engaged, the impacts can vary, depending on where they are located. Physicians are in all parts of the organization, across all departments, functions, units, hospitals, and clinics. The impact may include patient outcomes, quality, efficiency, and time savings, among others. Essentially, any of the measures listed in Tables 3.1 and 3.2 could be influenced. The only way to understand the value of this type of program is to convert the individual, specific impacts into monetary values. Totaling the monetary values of all the improvements would provide some sense of the value of the physician leadership development program.

Consider the impact of a lean project designed for healthcare. As part of the project, the managers (participants) are asked to select at least two important measures that need improvement. Using lean principles, the participants make improvements in each measure. In total, the measures could number in the dozens, if not hundreds. When the project's impact is evaluated, a large number of small improvements are identified. Converting them to monetary values allowed the improvements to be expressed in the same terms, enabling the outcomes to be more clearly reported.

SIMILARITIES TO BUDGETING

Healthcare professionals and administrators are familiar with budgets and are expected to develop project budgets with an acceptable degree of accuracy. They are also comfortable with cost issues. When it comes to benefits, however, many are not comfortable, although some of the same techniques used in developing budgets are used to determine monetary benefits. Most of the benefits of the project will take the form of cost savings, cost reductions, or cost avoidance, which can make identification of the costs or value easier for some projects. The monetary benefits resulting from a project is a natural extension of the development of a budget.

IMPORTANCE TO ORGANIZATIONAL OPERATIONS

With competitiveness and the drive to improve the efficiency of operations, awareness of the costs related to particular processes and activities is essential. In the 1990s, this emphasis gave rise to activity-based costing (ABC) and activity-based management. ABC is not a replacement for traditional, general ledger accounting. Rather, it is a bridge between cost accumulations in the general ledger and the end users who must apply cost data in decision making. The problem lies in the typical cost statements, where the actual cost of a process or problem is not readily discernible. ABC converts inert cost data to relevant, actionable information. ABC has become increasingly useful for identifying improvement opportunities and measuring the benefits realized from performance initiatives on an after-the-fact basis. More than 85 percent of the ROI studies conducted show projects benefiting the organization through cost savings (cost reductions or cost avoidance). Consequently, understanding the cost of a problem and the payoff of the corresponding solution is essential to proper management of the business.

KEY STEPS IN CONVERTING DATA TO MONEY

Converting data to monetary values involves five steps for each data item:

1. **Focus on a unit of measure.** First, a unit of measure must be defined. For output data, the unit of measure is one new patient, one additional patient through the X-ray department, or one more patient served. Time measures could include the time to complete a project, cycle time, patient wait time; these units are usually expressed in terms of minutes, hours, or days. Quality is another common measure, with a unit defined as one medical error, one adverse patient outcome, one incident, or one unplanned absence. Soft data measures vary, with a unit of improvement expressed in terms of one patient complaint, one stress change, or a one–unit change in the patient satisfaction index. Specific examples of units of measure are shown in Table 8.1.

2. **Determine the value of the unit.** Now comes the challenge: placing a value (V) on the unit identified in step 1. For measures of output, quality, cost, and time, the process is relatively easy. Most healthcare organizations maintain records or reports that can pinpoint the cost of one unit of output or one mistake. Soft data are more difficult to convert to money. For example, the monetary value of one patient complaint or a one-point change in physician engagement may be difficult to determine. The techniques described in this chapter provide an array of approaches for making this conversion. When more than one value is available, the most credible or lowest value is used in the calculation.

3. **Calculate the change in performance data.** The change in output data is calculated after the effects of the project have been isolated from other influences. This change (Δ) is the performance improvement that is directly attributable to the project, represented as the (Level 4) impact measure. The value may represent the performance improvement for an individual, a team, a group of participants, or several groups of participants.

4. **Determine the annual amount of change.** The Δ value is annualized to develop a value for the total change in the performance

TABLE 8.1   Examples of Units of Measure

• One patient served	• One student intern
• One voluntary turnover	• One FTE employee
• One patient billing error	• One unplanned absence
• One unit of waste	• One bloodstream infection
• One disabling injury	• One minute of system downtime
• One hour of overtime	• One minute of wait time
• One patient complaint	• One person removed from workers
• One less day in the hospital	compensation
• One grievance	• One malpractice claim

data for one year (ΔP). Using annual figures is a standard approach for organizations seeking to capture the benefits of a particular project, although the benefits may not remain constant throughout the year. For a short-term project, first-year benefits are used even when the project produces benefits beyond one year. For long-term projects, multiple years are used. This approach is considered conservative and will be discussed later in the chapter.

5. **Calculate the annual value of the improvement.** The total value of improvement is calculated by multiplying the annual performance change (ΔP) by the unit value (V) of the impact measure(s) for the group in question. For example, if one group of participants is involved in the project being evaluated, the total value will include the total improvement for all participants providing data in the group. This value for annual project benefits is then compared with the costs of the project to calculate the BCR, ROI, or payback period.

A simple example will demonstrate these five steps. Suppose a large hospital chain pilots an effort to replace all traditional lighting with energy-efficient LED bulbs as part of their efforts to become a green hospital. Prior to project implementation, the 90,000-square-foot hospital where the pilot program occurs uses approximately 14 kilowatt-hours (kWh) per square foot annually for a total of 1,260,000 kWh per year, which averages

TABLE 8.2   Converting Kilowatt-Hours to Monetary Values

Becoming a Green Hospital
Setting: Hospital chain is piloting replacement of traditional lighting to LED lighting.
Step 1: Define the unit of measure. The unit of measure is defined as one kilowatt hour (kWh).
Step 2: Determine the value (V) of each unit. According to standard data (i.e., the cost per kWh paid per month), the cost is 10 cents per kWh (V = 10 cents).
Step 3: Calculate the change (Δ) in performance data. Six months after the project was completed, electricity usage decreased an average of 31,500 kWh per month. The isolation technique used was a control group (see Chapter 7).
Step 4: Determine an annual amount of the change (ΔP). Using the six-month average of 31,500 kWh per month yields an annual improvement of 378,000 (ΔP = 31,500 × 12 = 378,000).
Step 5: Calculate the annual monetary value of the improvement. (ΔP × V) = 378,000 × .10 = $37,800 cost savings

105,000 kWh per month. After implementing the project, the hospital monitors electricity usage for six months, showing a new average monthly usage of 73,500 kWh, a decrease of 31,500 kWh per month. By comparing this hospital's usage to that of another hospital with comparable characteristics, the 31,500 reduction is attributed to the change in bulbs. Given a monthly change in performance, the annual change is 378,000 kWh. The value of a kWh is approximately 10 cents per kWh. The total annual savings to the hospital is $37,800. Table 8.2 shows the example using the five steps.

STANDARD MONETARY VALUES

Most hard data items (output, quality, cost, and time) have standard values. A standard value is a monetary value assigned to a unit of measurement that is accepted by executives and is known to the individuals involved in the project (e.g., the participants). Standard values have been developed because they are often the measures that matter to the organization. They reflect problems and opportunities, and their conversion to monetary values shows their impact on the operational and financial well-being of the healthcare organization.

Recently, quality implementations in healthcare have focused on the cost of inadequate quality. Quality professionals have been obsessed with placing a monetary value on mistakes or the payoff from avoiding these mistakes. This assigned value—the standard cost of quality—is an important outgrowth of the quality management movement. In addition, a variety of process improvement initiatives—such as reengineering, reinventing, transformation, and continuous process improvement—have included a component where the cost of a particular measure is determined. Also, the development of a variety of cost control, cost containment, and cost management systems—such as activity-based costing—have forced hospitals, clinics, and departments to place costs on activities and, in some cases, relate those costs directly to the patient revenues (or profits) of the organization. The following section describes how measures of output, quality, and time have been converted to standard values.

CONVERTING OUTPUT DATA TO MONEY

When a project results in a change in output, the value of the increased output can usually be determined from activity-based accounting or operating records. For healthcare organizations operating on a profit basis, this value is typically the marginal profit contribution of an additional unit of service provided. For example, a southeast-based hospital created a sleep center to treat patients with serious sleep disorders. The patient revenue minus operating expenses provided a profit margin associated with this service. This organization is performance driven rather than profit driven, so this value is usually reflected as net patient revenue. Within the organization, output value is realized when an additional unit of output is realized for the same input. For example, in the X-ray department, one additional patient served at no additional employee cost translates into a cost savings roughly equal to the unit cost of processing a patient.

The formulas used to calculate this contribution depend on the type of organization and the nature of its record keeping. Most organizations have standard values readily available for performance monitoring and goal setting. Managers (and accountants) often use marginal cost statements and sensitivity analyses to pinpoint values associated with changes in output. If the data are not available, the project team must initiate or coordinate the development of appropriate values.

The benefit of converting output data to money using standard values is that these calculations are already available for the most important data items. One area that has much experience with standard values is the patient revenue area. Table 8.3 shows a sampling of the patient revenue and marketing measures that are sometimes calculated and reported as standard values.[4]

CALCULATING THE COST OF QUALITY

Quality and the cost of quality are critical issues in healthcare organizations. Because many projects are designed to improve quality, the project team may have to place a value on the improvement of certain quality measures. For some quality measures, the task is easy. For example, if quality is measured in terms of having to repeat a process or procedure, the value of the improvement is the cost to provide the procedure again. The readmission rate is one of the most important measures in this category.

The most obvious cost of unacceptable quality is the amount of waste generated by mistakes. Defective products, spoiled materials, improper schedules, and discarded supplies all reflect inadequate quality. Waste translates directly into a monetary value. The annual waste in healthcare is estimated to be $765 billion.[5] (See Figure 8.1 on page 214.)

In the healthcare environment, the cost of a defective service is the cost incurred up to the point at which the deficiency is identified, plus the cost to correct the problem, the cost to make the patient satisfied, the loss of patient loyalty, and any legal costs. Mistakes and errors can be expensive. The costliest form of mistakes occurs when a service is delivered to a patient that causes an adverse outcome that must be treated, corrected, and properly addressed. In the worst case, patient mortality is the outcome. In some organizations, the cost of mistakes and errors can constitute as much as 30 percent of operating expenses. The classic comment, "The most unsafe place to be is in a hospital," is true for some facilities.

TABLE 8.3   Examples of Standard Values from Patient Revenue and Marketing

Metric	Definition	Notes
Patient revenue	The patient revenue for the service recorded in a variety of different ways by service, treatment, time period, or patient	The data must be converted to monetary value by applying the profit margin for a particular revenue category
Profit margin	$\dfrac{\text{Revenue} - \text{Cost}}{\text{Cost}} \times 100$ For the service, patient, or time period	Convert patient revenue to monetary value-added to the organization
Unit margin	Unit revenue less unit cost	Shows the value of incremental revenue, which helps to price the services
Retention rate	The ratio of patients retained to the number of patients at risk of leaving	Value of the money not spent to acquire a replacement patient, which is important in competitive markets
Net patient revenue	The difference between the revenues earned from and the cost associated with the patient relationship during the specified period	The monetary value-added or profit (or net revenue) obtained from patients, which all goes toward the bottom line and shows which patients are costing the most money
Patient value, lifetime	The present value of the future cash flows attributed to the patient relationship	Bottom line; patient value increases add directly to the profits (or revenue); also, as a patient is added, the incremental value is the patient lifetime average

(continued)

TABLE 8.3 Examples of Standard Values from Patient Revenue and Marketing *(continued)*

Metric	Definition	Notes
Cannibal-ization rate	The percentage of new patient revenue taken from existing locations	Represents an adverse effect on existing revenues and is to be minimized because value added comes from preventing the loss of profits (or net revenue) due to the revenue loss; this measure is important as hospitals build new facilities to reach growing markets
Market share	Patient revenue as a percentage of total market revenue	Conversion of actual revenues to money through the profit margins (net revenues); a measure of competitiveness that is important for many healthcare firms, particularly in large markets
Loyalty	The length of time the patient is served by the organization, the willingness to pay a premium for services	Calculated as the additional profit (net revenue) from the revenue or profit (net revenue) on the premium, which is helpful for upscale services such as executive physicals
Case mix	The average patient case adjusted for the acuity of illness of the patient (1.0 equals the average patient)	Calculated to reflect the severity of illness and impact on costs or revenue of an average patient
Cost per discharge	The dollar value of total costs per patient day in the hospital with the number of patient days adjusted for outpatient activity	Calculated as the total cost for a patient day; used to control costs

TABLE 8.3 Examples of Standard Values from Patient Revenue and Marketing *(continued)*

Metric	Definition	Notes
Revenue per discharge	The dollar value of total patient revenue per day in the hospital with the number of patient days adjusted for outpatient activity	Analyzed to understand the amount of revenue expected from a patient
Cost per adjusted discharge	The dollar value of total costs for all activity for a patient per each patient discharge regardless of length of stay in the hospital	Analyzed to understand the average cost to care for a patient
Revenue per adjusted discharge	The dollar value of total revenue per patient day in the hospital with the number of patient days adjusted for outpatient activity	Analyzed to understand the total amount of revenue per patient regardless of length of stay

Quality costs can be grouped into several major categories:

1. *Internal failure* represents costs associated with problems detected prior to service delivery. Typical costs in this category are reworking and retesting.

2. *Prevention costs* involve efforts undertaken to prevent the delivery of unacceptable service quality. These efforts include service quality administration, inspections, process studies, and process improvements.

3. *Penalty costs* are fines or penalties incurred as a result of unacceptable quality.

4. *External failure* refers to problems detected after service delivery. Typical items here are technical support, complaint investigation, and fixes.

FIGURE 8.1 The Cost of Healthcare: How Much Is Waste?

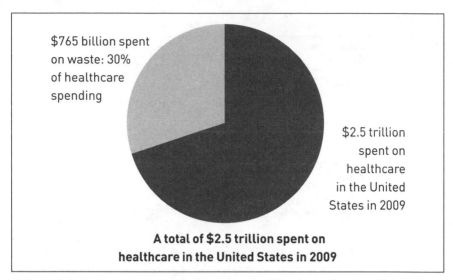

$765 billion spent
on waste: 30%
of healthcare
spending

$2.5 trillion
spent on
healthcare
in the United
States in 2009

**A total of $2.5 trillion spent on
healthcare in the United States in 2009**

Source: *Value in Healthcare: Current State and Future Directions* (Westchester: Healthcare Financial
Management Association, June 2011). Accessed http://www.hfma.org/HFMA-Initiatives/Value-Project
/Value-in-Health-Care--Current-State-and-Future-Directions/ (February 16, 2012).

5. *Appraisal costs* are the expenses involved in determining the magnitude of adverse outcomes. Typical costs involve investigation,
research, problem solving, data analysis, and related activities.

6. *Legal defense, losses, and settlements related to mistakes and errors*
are significant in healthcare. They include internal and external
legal expenses, litigation expenses, losses, and settlements. If the
organization is fully insured, these costs will appear in insurance
premiums.

7. *Patient dissatisfaction* is perhaps the costliest element of inadequate
quality. In some cases, serious mistakes result in lost business.
Patient dissatisfaction is difficult to quantify, and arriving at
a monetary value may be difficult using direct methods. The
judgment and expertise of risk management, marketing, or quality
managers are usually the best resources to draw upon in measuring
the impact of dissatisfaction. More and more quality experts are
measuring patient dissatisfaction with the use of market surveys.

As with output data, the good news is that a tremendous number of
quality measures have been converted to standard values. Some of these
measures are listed in Table 8.4.

TABLE 8.4   Examples of Quality Measures

• Defects	• Patient complaints
• Rework/Readmissions	• Unplanned absences
• Processing errors	• Downtime—equipment
• Infections	• Downtime—systems
• Data errors	• Excessive length of stay
• Medicine errors	• Delays
• Accidents	• Fines
• Incidents	• Penalties
• Injuries	• Legal expenses
• Grievances	• Unbilled services
• Voluntary turnover	• Uncollected billing

CONVERTING EMPLOYEE TIME USING COMPENSATION

Reducing the workforce, controlling employee growth, reducing overtime, minimizing labor costs, or saving employee time are common objectives for healthcare projects. In a team environment, a project may enable the team to complete tasks in less time or with fewer people. A major project could lead to a reduction of several hundred employees. On an individual basis, a technology project may be designed to help professional, administrative, and managerial employees save time when performing daily tasks. The value of the time saved is an important measure, and determining a monetary value for it is relatively easy.

When jobs are eliminated (or prevented), the savings are the salaries plus benefits for the job removed or prevented. When paid work hours or overtime hours are reduced (or prevented), the savings are the fully loaded hourly costs multiplied by hours saved. The most obvious time savings stem from reduced labor costs for performing a given amount of work. The monetary savings are found by multiplying the hours saved (or avoided) by the labor cost per hour. For example, a time-saving process in one organization, participants estimated, saved an average of 74 minutes per day, worth $31.25 per day or $7,500 per year, based on the average salary plus benefits for a typical participant.

The average wage, with a percentage added for employee benefits, will suffice for most calculations. However, employee time may be worth more. For example, additional costs for maintaining an employee (office space, furniture, telephones, utilities, computers, administrative support, and other overhead expenses) could be included in calculating the average labor cost. Thus, the wage rate used in the calculation can escalate quickly. In a large-scale employee reduction effort, calculating the total costs of employees may be more appropriate for showing the value. However, for most projects, the conservative approach of using salary plus employee benefits is recommended.

Beyond reducing the labor cost per hour, time savings can produce benefits such as improved service, avoidance of penalties for late projects, and additional profit opportunities. These values can be estimated using other methods discussed in this chapter.

A word of caution is needed concerning time savings. Savings are realized only when the amount of time saved translates into a cost reduction or a contribution to revenue. Even if a project produces savings in manager time, monetary value is not realized unless the manager puts the time saved to productive use. Having managers estimate the percentage of time saved that is devoted to productive work may be helpful, if it is followed up with a request for examples of how the extra time was used. If a team-based project sparks a new process that eliminates several hours of work each day, the actual savings will be based on the corresponding direct reduction in staff, labor costs, or overtime pay. Therefore, an important preliminary step in figuring time savings is determining whether the expected savings will be genuine.

FINDING STANDARD VALUES

Standard values are available for all types of data. Virtually every major department will develop standard values that are monitored for that area. Typical functions in a major organization where standard values are tracked include:

- Finance and accounting
- Risk management
- Quality
- Operations

- Research

- Information technology (IT)

- Business process improvement

- Administration

- Marketing and patient relations

- Facilities and support

- Procurement

- Biomedical services

- Logistics

- Compliance

- Food services

- Organizational effectiveness

- Human resources (HR)

Thanks to enterprise-wide systems software, standard values are commonly integrated and made available for access by system users. In some cases, access may need to be addressed to ensure that the data can be obtained by those who require them.

WHEN STANDARD VALUES ARE NOT AVAILABLE

When standard values are not available, several alternative strategies for converting data to monetary worth are available. Some are appropriate for a specific type of data or data category, while others may be used with virtually any type of data. The challenge is to select the strategy that best suits the situation.

USING HISTORICAL COSTS FROM RECORDS

Historical records often indicate the value of a measure and the cost (or value) of a unit of improvement. This strategy relies on identifying the appropriate records and tabulating the proper cost components for the item in question.

For example, a large health services firm initiated a project to improve patient and employee safety. The project improved several safety-related performance measures, ranging from amounts spent in response to fines to total worker's compensation costs. From the records for one year of data, the average cost for each safety measure was determined. This value included the direct costs of medical payments, insurance payments and premiums, investigation services, replacement of staff, reserves, costs of safety programs, and lost-time payments to employees, as well as payments for legal expenses, fines, and other direct services. The amount of time used to investigate, resolve, and correct the issues was also factored in. This time involved not only the health and safety staff, but other staff members as well. In addition, the costs of lost productivity, disruption of services, morale, and dissatisfaction were estimated to obtain a full cost. The corresponding costs for each item were then developed.

This example suggests the challenges inherent in maintaining systems and databases to enable the value for a particular data item to be identified. It also raises several concerns about project managers using historical costs as a technique to convert data to money.

TIME

Sorting through databases, cost statements, financial records, and activity reports takes a tremendous amount of time that may not be available for the evaluation of project. It is important to keep this part of the process in perspective. It is only one step in the ROI Methodology (converting data to monetary values) and only one measure among many that may need to be converted. Time resources must be conserved.

AVAILABILITY AND ACCESS

In some cases, data are not readily available to show all of the costs for a particular item. In addition to the direct costs associated with a measure, an equal number of indirect or invisible costs may be present that cannot be obtained easily. Compounding the problem of availability is access. Monetary values may be needed from a system or database that is under someone else's control. In a typical implementation, the project leader or evaluator may not have full access to cost data. These data are more sensitive than other types of data and are often protected for a number of reasons, including competitive advantage. Therefore, access can be difficult and sometimes is even prohibited unless an absolute need to know can be demonstrated.

ACCURACY

Finally, the need for accuracy in this analysis should not be overlooked. A measure provided in current records may appear to be based on accurate data, but may in fact be an illusion. When data are calculated, estimations are involved, access to certain systems is denied, and different assumptions are made (all of which can be compounded by different definitions of systems, data, and measures). Because of these limitations, the calculated values should be viewed as approximate unless means are available to ensure that they are accurate.

WHEN TO DO IT

Calculating monetary value using historical data and records should be pursued with caution and only when these two conditions exist:

- The sponsor has approved the use of additional time, effort, and money to develop a monetary value from the current records and reports.

- The measure is simple and can be found by searching only a few records.

Otherwise, an alternative method is preferred, discussed next.

USING INPUT FROM EXPERTS TO CONVERT DATA

When it is necessary to convert data items for which historical cost data are not available, input from experts on the process might be a consideration, as discussed in Chapter 7. Internal experts can provide the cost (or value) of one unit of improvement. Individuals with knowledge of the situation and the confidence of management must be willing to provide estimates— as well as the assumptions behind the estimates. Internal experts may be found in the department in which the data originated—risk management, procurement, operations, labor relations, business process improvements, or any number of other functions. Most experts have their own methodologies for developing these values. So when their input is required, it is important to explain the full scope of what is needed and to provide as many specifics as possible.

If internal experts have a strong bias regarding the measure or are not available, external experts are sought. External experts should be selected based on their experience with the unit of measure. Fortunately, many external healthcare experts are available who work directly with important measures, such as patient outcomes, patient safety, patient satisfaction, workforce management, safety and health, labor economics, turnover, absenteeism, and wellness, to name a few. They are often willing to provide estimates of the cost (or value) of these intangibles.

External experts—including consultants, professionals, or suppliers in a particular area—can also be found in obvious places. For example, the costs of accidents can be estimated by the worker's compensation carrier, or the cost of a grievance may be estimated by a labor attorney. Savings from a wellness plan may be estimated by health and wellness consultants assisting in the implementation of a wellness center. The process of locating an external expert is similar to the external database search, which is described later.

The credibility of the expert, whether internal or external, is an important issue if the monetary value placed on a measure is to be reliable. Foremost among the factors behind an expert's credibility is the individual's experience with the process or measure at hand. Ideally, he or she should work with this measure routinely through collection, analysis, and reporting. Also, the expert must be unbiased. Experts should be neutral in connection with the measure's value and should have no personal interest in the value being larger or smaller.

In addition, the credentials of external experts—published works, degrees, honors, or awards—are important in validating their expertise. Many of these experts are tapped often, and their track records can and should be checked. An estimate that has been validated in more detailed studies and was found to be consistent can serve as a confirmation of their qualifications in providing such data.

Using Values from External Databases

For some measures, the use of cost (or value) estimates based on the work and research of others may be appropriate. This technique makes use of external databases that contain studies and research projects focusing on the cost of data items. Fortunately, many databases include cost studies of data items related to projects, and most are accessible on the Internet. Data are available on the costs of accidents, incidents, adverse outcomes, turnover, absenteeism, grievances, and even patient satisfaction. The difficulty lies in finding a database with studies or research relevant to the particular project. Ideally, the data should originate from a similar setting in the same industry, but such similarity is not always possible. Sometimes, data on industries or organizations in general are sufficient, with adjustments possibly required to suit the project at hand. Healthcare databases such as the Center for Medicare/Medicaid Services (CMS),[6] Healthcare Cost and Utilization Project,[7] the Agency for Healthcare Research and Quality,[8] the National Institutes of Health[9] can provide useful data and information.

LINKING WITH OTHER MEASURES

When standard values, records, experts, and external studies are not available, a feasible alternative might be to find a relationship between the measure in question and some other measure that can be easily converted to a monetary value. This process involves identifying existing relationships that show a strong correlation between one measure and another with a standard value.

A classic relationship is the correlation between job satisfaction and employee turnover. Suppose that in a project designed to improve job satisfaction, a value is needed to reflect changes in the job satisfaction index. A predetermined relationship showing the correlation between increases in job satisfaction and reductions in turnover can directly link the two measures. Using standard data or external studies, the cost of turnover can easily be determined as described earlier. Therefore, a change in job satisfaction can be immediately converted to a monetary value, or at least an approximate value. The conversion is not always exact because of the potential for error and other factors, but the estimate is sufficient for converting the data to monetary values. Another common relationship is between engagement (physician, nurse, etc.) and gross productivity (patient revenue per employee).

Finding a correlation between a patient satisfaction measure and another measure that can easily be converted to a monetary value is sometimes possible. A strong correlation often exists between patient satisfaction and patient revenue. Connecting these two variables allows the monetary value of customer satisfaction to be estimated.

In some situations, a chain of relationships may establish a connection between two or more variables. A measure that may be difficult to convert to a monetary value is linked to other measures that, in turn, are linked to measures to which values can be assigned. Ultimately, these measures are traced to a monetary value. Figure 8.2 shows a connection between job satisfaction of employees and patient satisfaction, which is directly related to patient revenue growth. The figure shows a relationship between patient satisfaction and patient revenue growth. This figure starts with the employee satisfaction and shows the link between it and patient satisfaction. This classic linkage has been developed in many organizations. Logically, it makes sense. If employees are satisfied with their jobs, work, or career, they are more likely to provide excellent service to patients. As the figure shows, a change in job satisfaction from Y1 to Y2 yields a change in patient satisfaction from X1 to X2. The figure also shows that as patient satisfaction increases, a correlation with patient revenue growth can be demonstrated. As patient satisfaction moves from X1 to X2, patient revenue growth moves from Ya to Yb. Although this correlation certainly has not been developed in a vast number of firms, these types of relationships are becoming more common in the healthcare arena. These links between measures, often called the service-profit chain, offer a promising methodology for applying monetary values to hard-to-quantify measures.[10]

Using Estimates from Participants

In some cases, participants in the project should estimate the value of improvement. This technique is appropriate when participants are capable of providing estimates of the cost (or value) of the unit of measure that has improved as a result of the project. For example, nurse managers may be the most credible sources to provide an estimate of an unplanned absence. They understand the problem the best. With this approach, participants should be provided clear instructions along with examples of the type of information needed. The advantage of this approach is that the individuals who are most closely connected to the improvement are often able to provide the most reliable estimates of its value. As with isolating project effects, when

FIGURE 8.2   Relationship of Patient Satisfaction and Patient Revenue
Growth

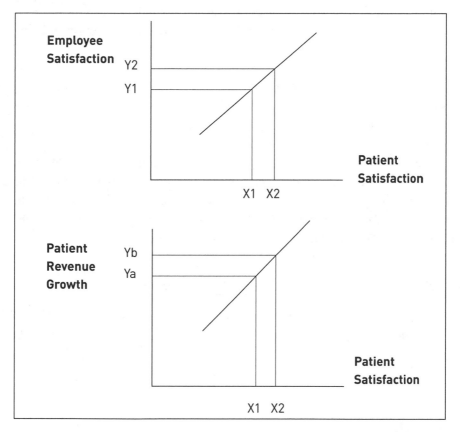

estimates are used to convert measures to monetary values, adjustments are
made to reduce the error in those estimates.

USING ESTIMATES FROM THE MANAGEMENT TEAM

In some situations, participants in a project may be incapable of placing
a value on the improvement. Their work may be so far removed from the
ultimate value of the process that they cannot provide reliable estimates.
For example, nurses may not be capable of accurately estimating the cost
of an adverse patient outcome. In these cases, nurse manager, directors, or
other managers may be able to provide estimates. Thus, they may be asked
to provide a value for a unit of improvement linked to the project.

In other situations, managers are asked to review and approve participants' estimates and confirm, adjust, or reject those values. For example, suppose a project involving patient service representatives was designed to reduce patient complaints. The project did result in a reduction in complaints, but the value of a single patient complaint had to be identified to determine the value of the improvement. Although patient service representatives had knowledge of certain issues surrounding customer complaints, their scope was limited, so their managers were asked to provide a value. These managers had a broader perspective of the impact of a customer complaint.

Senior management can often provide estimates of the value of data. In this approach, senior managers concerned with the project are asked to place a value on the improvement based on their perception of its worth. This approach is used when calculating the value is difficult or when other sources of estimation are unavailable or unreliable.

TECHNIQUE SELECTION AND FINALIZING VALUE

With so many techniques available, the challenge is selecting one or more strategies appropriate for the situation and available resources. Developing a table or list of values or techniques for the situation may be helpful. The guidelines that follow may aid in selecting a technique and finalizing the values.

Choose a Technique Appropriate for the Type of Data

Some strategies are designed specifically for hard data, whereas others are more appropriate for soft data. Thus, the type of data often dictates the strategy. Standard values are developed for most hard data items, and company records and cost statements are used in the process. Soft data often involve the use of external databases, links with other measures, and estimates. Experts are used to convert each type of data to monetary values.

Move from Most Accurate to Least Accurate

The techniques in this chapter are presented in order of accuracy. Standard values are always more accurate and therefore the most credible. But, as mentioned earlier, they are not always readily available. When standard values are not available, the following sequence of operational techniques should be explored:

- Historical costs from company records (be cautious of the time needed for this)

- Internal and external experts

- External databases

- Links with other measures

- Estimates

Each technique should be considered in turn based on its feasibility and applicability to the situation. The technique associated with the highest accuracy is always preferred if the situation allows.

CONSIDER SOURCE AVAILABILITY

Sometimes the availability of a particular source of data determines the method selection. For example, experts may or may not be readily accessible. Some standard values are easy to find; others are more difficult. In other situations, the convenience of a technique is a major factor in the selection. The Internet, for example, has made external database searches more convenient.

As with other processes, keeping the time investment for this phase to a minimum is important so that the total effort directed to the ROI study does not become excessive. Some techniques can be implemented in much less time than others. Devoting too much time to the conversion process may dampen otherwise enthusiastic attitudes about the use of the methodology.

USE THE SOURCE WITH THE BROADEST PERSPECTIVE ON THE ISSUE

According to Guiding Principle 3 in Table 2.1, the most credible data source must be used. The individual providing estimates must be knowledgeable of the processes and the issues surrounding the valuation of the data. For example, consider the estimation of the cost of nurse turnover.

Although a nurse manager may have insight into what caused a particular nurse departure, he or she may have a limited perspective. A high-level manager may be able to grasp the overall impact of the grievance and how it will affect other areas. Thus, a high-level manager would be a more credible source in this situation.

USE MULTIPLE TECHNIQUES WHEN FEASIBLE

The availability of more than one technique for obtaining values for the data is often beneficial. When appropriate, multiple sources should be used to provide a basis for comparison or for additional perspectives. The data must be integrated using a convenient and conservative decision rule, such as the lowest value. The conservative approach of using the lowest value was presented as Guiding Principle 4 in Table 2.1, but it applies only when the sources have equal or similar credibility.

Converting data to monetary values has its challenges. When the particular method has been selected and applied, several adjustments or tests are necessary to ensure the use of the most credible and appropriate value with the least amount of resources.

APPLY THE CREDIBILITY TEST

The discussion of techniques in this chapter assumes that each data item collected and linked to a project can be converted to a monetary value. Highly subjective data, however, such as changes in employee engagement or improvements in reputation, are difficult to convert. Although estimates can be developed using one or more strategies, the estimates may lack credibility with the target audience, which can render their use in analysis questionable.

The issue of credibility in combination with resources is illustrated quite clearly in Figure 8.3. This chart shows a logical way to decide whether to convert data to monetary values or leave them intangible. Essentially, in the absence of standard values, many other ways are available to capture the data or convert them to monetary values. However, a question must be answered: Can it be done with minimum resources? Some of the techniques mentioned in this chapter—such as searching records or maybe even searching the Internet—cannot be performed with minimal use of

FIGURE 8.3 Four-Part Test: To Convert or Not to Convert?

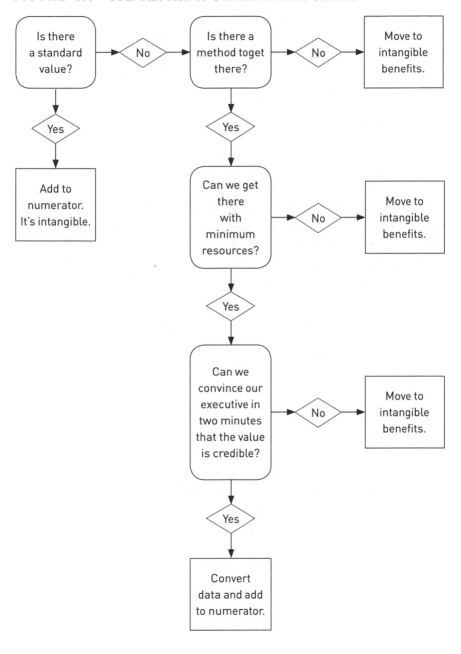

resources. However, an estimate obtained from a group or from a few individuals is available with minimal use of resources. Then we move to the next question: Will the executive who is interested in the project buy into the monetary value assigned to the measure in two minutes? If so, then it is credible enough to be included in the analysis; if not, move it to the intangibles. The intangibles are also important and are covered in much more detail in the next chapter.

CONSIDER THE POSSIBILITY OF A MANAGEMENT ADJUSTMENT

In organizations where soft data are common and values are derived using imprecise methods, senior managers and administrators are sometimes offered the opportunity to review and approve the data. Because of the subjective nature of this process, management may factor (reduce) the data to make the final results more credible to them.

CONSIDER THE SHORT-TERM/LONG-TERM ISSUE

When data are converted to monetary values, usually one year's worth of data is included in the analysis. Guiding Principle 9 (Table 2.1) states that for short-term solutions, only the first year's benefits are used. The issue of whether a project is short-term or long-term depends on the time it takes to complete or implement the project. If one group participating in the project and working through the process takes months to complete it, then it is probably not short-term. Some projects literally take years to implement even for one particular group. In general, it is appropriate to consider a project short-term when the investment is low and it takes one individual a few days to learn what needs to be done to make the project successful. When the lag between project implementation and the consequences is relatively brief, a short-term solution may be appropriate.

When a project is long-term, no time limit for data inclusion is used, but the time value should be set before the project evaluation is undertaken. Input on the time value should be secured from all stakeholders, including the sponsor, champion, implementer, designer, evaluator, and analyst. After some discussion, the estimates of the time factor should be conservative and perhaps reviewed by finance and accounting. When a project is a long-term solution, forecasting will need to be used to estimate multiple years of value. No sponsor will wait several years to see how a project unfolds.

CONSIDER AN ADJUSTMENT FOR THE TIME VALUE OF MONEY

Because investment in a project is made in one time period and the return is realized at a later time, some organizations adjust project benefits to reflect the time value of money using discounted cash flow techniques. The actual monetary benefits of the project are adjusted for the time period. With today's cost of capital, the amount of adjustment, however, is usually small compared with the typical benefits of projects.

Although the time value of money may not be an issue for every project, it should be considered for each project, and some standard discount rate should be used. Consider the following example of how it is calculated. Assume that a project costs $100,000, and it is expected to take two years for the full value of the estimate to be realized. Using a discount rate of 6 percent, the cost for the project for the first year would be $100,000 × 106 percent = $106,000. For the second year it is $106,000 × 106 percent, or $112,360. Thus, the project cost has been adjusted for a two-year value with a 6 percent discount rate. This calculation assumes that the project sponsor could have invested the money in some other project and obtained at least a 6 percent return on that investment.

FINAL THOUGHTS

Showing the real money requires just that—money. Business impact data that have improved as a result of a project must be converted to money. Standard values make this process easier, but easy is not always an option, and other techniques must sometimes be used. However, if a measure cannot be converted with minimum resources or with no assurance of credibility, the improvement in the measure should be reported as an intangible benefit. After the data are converted to monetary values, the next step is collecting the project costs and calculating the ROI, covered in the next chapter.

CHAPTER 9

Measuring the Intangibles

The results from healthcare performance improvement projects include both tangible and intangible measures. Intangible measures are the benefits (or detriments) directly linked to a project that cannot be converted to monetary values credibly, with a reasonable amount of resources. These measures are often monitored after the project has been completed. Although not converted to monetary values, they are an important part of the evaluation process. This chapter explores the role of intangibles, how to measure them, when to measure them, and how to report them.

The range of intangible measures is almost limitless. Although Table 9.1 highlights many examples of these measures, this chapter describes just a few common outcomes of projects. Some measures make the list because of the difficulty in measuring them; others because of the difficulty in converting them to money. Others are on the list for both reasons. Being labeled as intangible does not mean that these items can never be measured or converted to monetary values. In one study or another, each item on the list has been monitored and quantified in financial terms. However, in typical projects, these measures are considered intangible

TABLE 9.1   Common Intangibles

• Accountability	• Leadership
• Accreditation status	• Networking
• Affiliations (religious, etc)	• Nurse engagement
• Alliances	• Organizational commitment
• Awards/recognition	• Patient loyalty
• Branding	• Partnering
• Capacity	• Patient engagement
• Caring	• Patient satisfaction
• Clarity	• Physician engagement
• Communication	• Physician satisfaction
• Corporate social responsibility	• Quality of life
• Creativity	• Rating systems*
• Culture	• Reputation
• Employee satisfaction	• Stress
• Ethics and integrity	• Sustainability
• Human life	• Teamwork
• Image	• Timeliness
• Innovation	• Work/life balance
• Intellectual capital	

*Such as Medicare's star rating system

benefits because of the difficulty in converting them to monetary values, within the resources of the project's budget.

OPENING STORIES

Miami Children's Hospital

Miami Children's Hospital (MCH) faced a hard challenge of doubling of the demand for talented employees in healthcare, coupled with dwindling labor supply.[1] The hospital answered this challenge with a variety of initiatives to attract, train, and retain the kind of talent that the organization must have to lead it into the future. MCH enjoys in important place in the community, with 650 affiliated physicians and 2,750 staff and frontline employees. Its goal is to work together to deliver care and services to families in the Miami area.

One of the initiatives employed was designed to help reduce the excessive turnover of new employees as they become centralized in the organization. As part of the initiative, each new employee was assigned an MCH "buddy." These buddies participated in an eight-hour training session to learn about communication, coaching, learning, mentoring, and engagement strategies. Employees shadowed their MCH buddy for 40 hours, followed by weekly meetings. Buddies were compensated if the new hire rated the on-boarding experience favorably. To date, 288 MCH buddies have been trained and assigned to a new hire. The buddy and manager also met to plan the process to ensure the new employee received the support needed to adjust to the new workplace and culture.

Another program was called "The MCH Way," a comprehensive two-day, culture-shaping process that engages people and affects their spirit and engagement in the organization. MCH president and CEO, Narenda Kini, MD, provided a strong catalyst for this transformational change. He understood that this type of foundational undertaking was needed before major business initiatives could take place, especially those initiatives that would drastically transform the way employees work together to deliver care and services. An important business goal of transforming the culture was to quickly engage people at all levels of MCH, starting with the senior leadership team.

Within 18 months, 70 percent of the hospital staff and leaders had participated in the initial MCH Way culture-shaping sessions. Just as quickly, positive results were seen in a number of areas. MCH saw improvement in medical staff satisfaction, from the fifth percentile, to 94 percent. They also saw improvements in the patient experience and employee engagement in all off-site facilities. Thus, the measures of engagement, culture, patient satisfaction, and staff satisfaction were all huge intangibles connected to these initiatives.

MAJOR PHARMACEUTICAL COMPANY

A major pharmaceutical firm that manufactures drugs to treat colon cancer tried an important experiment with its employees. The firm wanted to show the power of colonoscopy screening, early detection, and prevention to control and avoid healthcare costs. An experiment was conducted with employees in appropriate age groups where a colonoscopy was provided on company time, fully paid for by the company's self-insured medical plan (no deductibles and no copayments applied). The firm wanted this particular age group to participate in the colonoscopy program and did not want cost to be an issue for the employees.

In all, almost 2,500 employees in the over-50 age group took advantage of the program. In 22 of these employees, cancerous polyps were discovered that would likely have quickly deteriorated into colon cancer. Those 22 employees were able to prevent colon cancer with this early detection and removal of the polyps.

The first step in the analysis was to isolate the effects of this program on the data. Some of these 22 employees would have perhaps caught the polyps through routine exams or some other motivation to pursue screening. In direct interviews with the 22 employees, 5 of them indicated that they would probably have sought out a colonoscopy on their own because of other motivation. The other 17 would not have pursued it. The bottom line is that 17 people were spared the pain, suffering, and expense of cancer that is often fatal.

An ROI analysis was conducted where the fully loaded cost of the program was compared to the cost savings derived from the program. Because the sick leave and medical plans were self-funded, the cost was absorbed directly by the company. Instances of colon cancer would cause short- and long-term disability averaging six months, which would also be paid for by the company at the employee's full salary. When these costs were totaled (which were avoided because of this program) and compared to fully loaded costs of the program, the ROI was impressive, convincing other employees to pursue these types of screenings.

In the analysis, the value of the human life, beyond direct costs to the company in terms of life insurance, was not included in the calculation. Essentially, the value of a human life was left as an intangible and a powerful one at that. Even though a monetary value of a human life is routinely developed, it was not included in this study, and will probably not be included in most of the studies in the healthcare area, except for projects involving risk management and adverse patient outcomes.

THE IMPORTANCE OF INTANGIBLES

Although intangible measures are not new, they are becoming increasingly important. Intangibles secure funding and drive the economy, and many healthcare organizations are built on them. In every direction we turn, intangibles are becoming not only increasingly important, but also critical to executives. Here's why they have become so important.

Intangibles: The Invisible Advantage

When examining the success behind many well-known organizations, intangibles are often a common factor. A highly innovative biotech company continues to develop new and improved products; a government health services agency reinvents itself; a hospital with highly involved and engaged employees attracts and keeps talent, and a healthcare research organization shares knowledge with employees. Still another successful healthcare firm is able to develop strategic partners and alliances. These intangibles do not often appear in financial statements and other record keeping, but they are there, and they are differentiators.

Trying to identify, measure, and react to intangibles may be difficult, but the ability to do so exists. Intangibles transform the way organizations work, the way employees are managed, the way products and services are designed, the way services are sold, and the way patients are treated. The implications are profound, and an organization's strategy must be set up to deal with them. Although seemingly invisible, the presence of intangibles is felt and the results are concrete.

The Intangible Economy

The intangible economy has evolved from basic changes that date to the Iron Age, which evolved into the Agricultural Age. In the late nineteenth century and during the early twentieth century the world moved into the Industrial Age. From the 1950s forward, the world has moved into the Technology and Knowledge Age, and these moves translate into intangibles. During this time, a natural evolution of technology has occurred.

During the Industrial Age, companies and individuals invested in tangible assets such as plants and equipment. In the Technology and Knowledge Age, companies invest in intangible assets: brands, talent, or systems. The future holds more of the same as intangibles continue to evolve into an important part of the overall economic system.[2]

Conversion of Intangibles into Tangibles

The good news is that more data once regarded as intangible are now being converted into monetary values. For this reason, classic intangibles are now accepted as tangible measures, and their value is more easily understood. Consider, for example, employee engagement. Just a decade ago, few organizations had a clue as to the monetary value of engagement. Now more firms have taken the extra step to link employee engagement directly to gross productivity (patient revenue divided by employees) and other measures such as turnover. Because Medicare and other payers are linking payment to patient satisfaction, more healthcare providers are converting this measure to money. In the next decade, most large providers will have to make this conversion.

Healthcare organizations are seeing the tremendous value that can be derived from intangibles. As this chapter will illustrate, more data are being accumulated to show monetary values, moving some intangible measures into the tangible category.

Intangibles Drive Projects

Some projects are implemented because of the intangibles. For example, the need to have greater collaboration, partnering, communication, teamwork, or patient satisfaction will drive projects. In the healthcare industry, the need to improve the image, reputation, and corporate social responsibility often drives projects. From the outset, the intangibles are the important drivers and become the most important measures. Consequently, more executives include a string of intangibles on their scorecards, key operating reports, key performance indicators, dashboards, and other routine reporting systems. In some cases, the intangibles represent nearly half of all measures that are monitored.

THE INTANGIBLE INVESTMENT

From the finance and accounting perspective, the investment in intangible assets is huge. In today's knowledge economy, only about 15 percent of the value of a contemporary organization can be tied to tangible assets such as buildings and equipment. For example, companies such as Google and Facebook have worth that adds up to far more than computers and buildings. Intangible assets have become the dominant investment in businesses. They are a growing force in the economy, and measuring their values poses challenges to managers and investors. They can no longer be ignored. They must be properly identified, selected, measured, reported, and in some cases, converted to monetary values.

MEASURING AND ANALYZING INTANGIBLES

In some projects, intangibles are more important than monetary measures. Consequently, these measures should be monitored and reported as part of the project evaluation. In practice, every project, regardless of its nature, scope, and content, will produce intangible measures. The challenge is to identify them effectively, measure them efficiently, and report them appropriately.

MEASURING THE INTANGIBLES

From time to time it is necessary to explore the issue of measuring the difficult-to-measure. Responses to this exploration usually occur in the form of comments instead of questions. "You can't measure it," is a typical response. This statement cannot be true, because anything can be measured. What the frustrated observer suggests by the comment is that the intangible is not something you can count, examine, or see in quantities (e.g., patients admitted to the hospital). In reality, a quantitative value can be assigned to or developed for any intangible. If it exists, it can be measured. For example, the Software Engineering Institute of Carnegie-Mellon University assigns software organizations a score of 1 to 5 to represent their maturity in software engineering. This score has enormous implications for the organizations' business development capabilities, yet the measure goes practically unchallenged. Consider patient satisfaction in another example. Although patient satisfaction is complex and abstract with myriad facets and qualities, patient satisfaction scores are developed and most executives and payees seem to accept them.

MEASUREMENT APPROACHES

Several approaches are available for measuring intangibles. Some intangibles that can be counted include patient complaints, employee complaints, and conflicts. These can be recorded easily, and constitute one of the most acceptable types of measures. Unfortunately, many intangibles are based on attitudes and perceptions that must be measured. The key is in the development of the instrument of measure. The instruments are usually developed around scales of 3, 5, and even 10 to represent levels of perception. The instruments to measure intangibles consist of three basic varieties.

The first lists the intangible items and asks respondents to agree or disagree on a 5-point scale (where the midpoint represents a neutral opinion). Other instruments define various qualities of the intangible, such as its reputation. A 5-point scale can easily be developed to describe degrees of reputation, ranging from the worst rating (a horrible reputation) to the best rating (an excellent reputation). Still other ratings are expressed as an assessment on a scale of 1 to 10, after respondents review a description of the intangible.

Another instrument to measure the intangible connects it, when possible, to a measure that is easier to measure. As shown in Figure 9.1, most hard-to-measure items are linked to an easy-to-measure item. In the classic situation, a soft measure (typically the intangible) is connected to a hard measure (typically the tangible). Although this link can be developed through logical deductions and conclusions, having some empirical evidence through a correlation analysis (as shown in the figure) and developing a significant correlation between the items is the best approach. However, a detailed analysis would have to be conducted to ensure that a causal relationship exists. In other words, just because a correlation is apparent, does not mean that one caused the other. Consequently, additional analysis, other empirical evidence, and supporting data could pinpoint the actual causal effect.

FIGURE 9.1   The Link Between Hard-to-Measure and Easy-to-Measure
Items

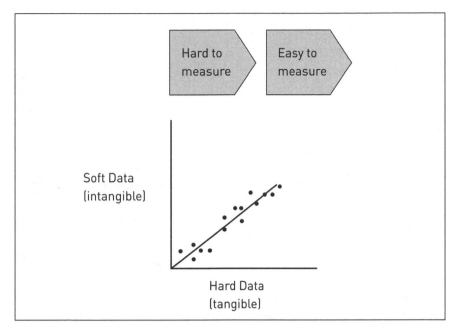

A final instrument for measuring the intangible is the development of
an index of different values. These could be a combination of both hard and
soft data items that make up a particular index value. An index is a single
score representing some complex factor that is constructed by aggregating
the values of several different measures. Measures making up the index are
sometimes weighted based on their importance to the abstract factor being
measured. Some index measures are based strictly on hard data items. For
example, the U.S. poverty level is based on a family income amount equal
to three times the money needed to feed a family as determined by the U.S.
Department of Agriculture, adjusted for inflation using the consumer price
index. Sometimes an index is completely intangible, such as the consumer
satisfaction index developed by the University of Michigan.

Intangibles are often combined with a variety of tangibles to reflect the
performance of a hospital, clinic, business unit, function, or project. Intangibles are also often associated with nonprofit, nongovernment, and public
sector organizations.

Converting to Money

Converting the hard-to-measure to monetary values is sometimes challenging. Examples in this chapter show various attempts to convert these hard-to-value measures to monetary values. When working with intangibles, the interest in the monetary contribution expands considerably. Three major groups have an interest in the monetary value. First are the sponsors who fund a particular project. These individuals almost always seek monetary values for important measures. In the current economic climate, these executives are suggesting that now is the time to connect "these intangibles to money."

Second, the public is involved in some way with many intangibles. Even private sector organizations are trying to improve their image and reputation, and the public's confidence in their organizations. The public is interested in the financial impacts of these organizations. They are no longer willing to accept the notion that the intangibles are enough to justify projects, particularly if the projects are funded by taxpayers.

Third, the individuals who are actively involved with and support the project often need, and sometimes demand, that the monetary value be developed. The "money" helps them understand the importance of the project. They may not appreciate the concept of nurse engagement, for example, but they completely understand the money.

The approaches to convert to monetary values were detailed in Chapter 8. The specific methods used in that chapter represent approaches that may be used to convert the intangibles to monetary values. Although they will not be repeated here, showing the path most commonly used to capture values for the intangibles is helpful. Figure 9.2 shows the typical path of converting intangibles to monetary values, building on the methods in Chapter 8. The first challenge is to locate existing data or measure them in some way, making sure they are accurate and reliable. Next, an expert may be able to place a monetary value on the item based on experience, knowledge, credentials, and track record. Stakeholders may provide their input, although it should be factored for bias. Some stakeholders are biased in one way or the other—they want the value to be smaller or larger depending on their particular motives. The values may have to be adjusted or thrown out all together. Finally, the data are converted using the conservative processes described in Chapter 8, often

FIGURE 9.2 Converting to Money

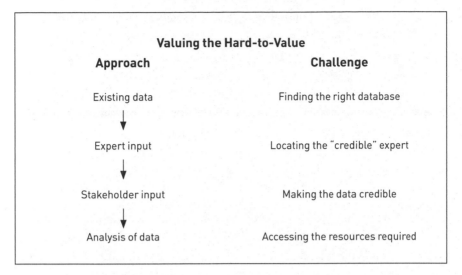

Valuing the Hard-to-Value	
Approach	**Challenge**
Existing data	Finding the right database
↓	
Expert input	Locating the "credible" expert
↓	
Stakeholder input	Making the data credible
↓	
Analysis of data	Accessing the resources required

adjusting for error in the process. Unfortunately, no specific rule exists for when to convert each intangible to monetary value. By definition, an intangible is a measure that is not converted to money. If the conversion cannot be accomplished with minimum resources and with credibility, it is left as an intangible.

IDENTIFYING AND COLLECTING INTANGIBLES

Intangible measures can be taken from different sources and at different times during the project life cycle, as depicted in Figure 9.3. They can be uncovered early in the process, during the needs assessment, and their collection can be planned as part of the overall data collection strategy. For example, a workforce scheduling project has several hard data measures linked to it. Job stress, an intangible measure, is identified and monitored with no plans to convert it to a monetary value. From the beginning, this measure is destined to be a nonmonetary, intangible benefit reported along with the ROI results.

A second opportunity to identify intangible benefits is in the planning process, when clients or sponsors of the project agree on an evaluation plan. Key stakeholders can usually identify the intangible measures they

FIGURE 9.3 Identifying Intangible Measures During the Project Life Cycle

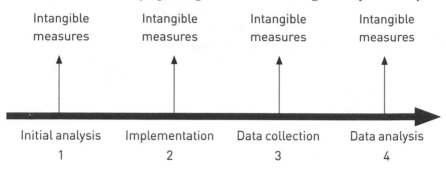

expect to be influenced by the project. For example, a collaborative project in a large healthcare organization was conducted, and an ROI analysis was planned. Project leaders, directors, participants' managers, and subject experts identified potential intangible measures that were perceived to be influenced by the project, including collaboration, communication, and teamwork.

A third opportunity to collect intangible measures presents itself during data collection. Although a measure may not be anticipated in the initial project design, it may surface on a questionnaire, in an interview, or during a focus group. Questions are often asked about other improvements linked to a project, and participants usually provide several intangible measures for which no plans are available to assign a value. For example, in the evaluation of a patient quality project, participants were asked what specifically had improved about their work area and relationships with patients as a result of the project. Participants provided more than a dozen intangible measures that managers attributed to the project.

The fourth opportunity to identify intangible measures is during data analysis and reporting, while attempting to convert data to monetary values. If the conversion loses credibility, the measure should be reported as an intangible benefit. For example, in one project, patient satisfaction was identified early in the process as a measure of project success. A conversion to monetary values was attempted, but it lacked accuracy and credibility. Consequently, patient satisfaction was reported as an intangible benefit.

ANALYZING INTANGIBLES

For each intangible measure identified, some evidence of its connection to the project must be shown. However, in many cases, no specific analysis is planned beyond tabulation of responses. Early attempts to quantify intangible data sometimes resulted in aborting the entire process, with no further data analysis being conducted. In some cases, isolating the effects of the project may be undertaken using one or more of the methods outlined in Chapter 7. This step is necessary when project leaders need to know the specific amount of change in the intangible measure that is linked to the project. Intangible data often reflect improvement; however, neither the precise amount of improvement nor the amount of improvement directly related to a project is always identified or needed. Still, it is important to show the connection between an intangible and the project in a credible way. Such a connection can be demonstrated in a few steps. First, the participants involved in the project are asked to indicate the extent to which a particular intangible measure is connected to the project. The response could be on a 5-point scale with 1 representing no connection and 5 representing a significant connection. Next, the specific intangibles need to be identified to develop the final report. Only those with ratings that indicate a connection to the project are included. For example, on a 1–5 scale, intangibles rated a 3, 4, or, 5 would be considered to be connected to the project. A rule should be stated that indicates what percent of the respondents need to recognize this connection (e.g., 10%) in order for it to be included. Finally, a percent of individuals actually connecting the measure to the project must be defined. For example, if only 1 of 100 participants connected a specific intangible to the project, that measure would not be listed. A cut-off requirement is needed, such as 10 percent: Unless 10 percent of the participants see the connection of an intangible to the project, it will not be listed in the report. These steps are necessary to show the intangible measure's link to the project in a credible way.

Because the value of these data is not included in the ROI calculation, intangible measures are not normally used to justify another project or to justify continuing an existing project. A detailed analysis is not necessary. Intangible benefits are often viewed as additional evidence of the project's success and are presented as supportive qualitative data.

CONFRONTING INTANGIBLES

Because any given project may have many intangibles, addressing them appropriately can be difficult. Many advances have been made in measuring intangibles effectively and in converting them to money. Of course, when they are converted to money, they are no longer intangible—they are tangible. This issue is not easy, but progress is being made and will continue to be made. The following section covers several areas in which organizations focus on measuring intangibles in the public and private sectors. These measures include some of the examples listed in Table 9.1.

BRANDING AND IMAGE

Because of the importance of building and improving perceived quality, reputational clinical excellence, and patient satisfaction, related measures are typically monitored to track project payoff. Several types of projects have a direct influence on these measures. This metric makes our list because it is perceived as difficult to measure and to convert to monetary value. However, in the last two decades, much progress has been made in this area, and some of these measures are routinely considered tangible because they are converted to money using the measures described in Chapter 8, where the technique of linking to other measures clearly illustrates the most common way in which customer service intangible measures are converted to money. This technique follows the sequence shown in Figure 9.4. The first step is to create awareness of a particular medical staff, clinic, brand, or service. The next step is to develop attitudes that define the beliefs, opinions, and intentions regarding the hospital, service, or brand that leads to usage. The final step confirms the purchasing habits and loyalty of the patient.

This important link is ingrained in most marketing and promotion projects and processes and has led to a variety of measures that are becoming standard in the industry. Table 9.2 shows branding and underscores the array of possibilities—all aimed at developing awareness, attitudes, and usage.[3]

PATIENT SATISFACTION

Perhaps the most common intangible is patient satisfaction, which is generally measured on scales of 1 to 5, 1 to 7, or 1 to 10 (although other scales

FIGURE 9.4 Patient Service Linkage

Awareness, Attitudes, and Usage: Typical Questions		
Type	**Measures**	**Typical Questions**
Awareness ↓	Awareness and knowledge	Have you heard of Hospital X? What hospital comes to mind when you think of a top-quality hospital?
Attitudes ↓	Beliefs and intentions	Is Hospital X for me? On a scale of 1 to 5, is Hospital X for senior citizens?
Usage ↓	Purchasing habits and loyalty	Did you use Hospital X this year? What hospital did you last use?

are used, too). A tremendous amount of research has been accumulated about the value of satisfied patients and the loss connected with dissatisfied patients. Using elaborate processes of decision tree analysis, probability theories, expected value, and correlations, organizations have developed detailed monetary values showing that movement in sales and profits is connected to a variety of measures.

Patient satisfaction has become the most critical intangible in the healthcare field. Because Medicare and other providers are now linking payment to patient satisfaction, this intangible has taken on new importance. More healthcare executives and other professionals have bonuses linked to patient satisfaction scores. With this much focus, this measure may move from intangible (not usually converted to money) to tangible (converted to monetary value), at least in places where patients have a choice.

A positive patient satisfaction survey is a highly desirable outcome of the hospital experience. A patient's degree of satisfaction or dissatisfaction is a judgment on the overall quality of the hospital stay. Whatever its strengths and limitations, patient satisfaction is an indicator that should be indispensable to the assessment of the quality of care in hospitals.

Beginning in 2002, the Centers for Medicare and Medicaid Services (CMS) partnered with the Agency for Healthcare Research and Quality to develop and test the Hospital Consumer Assessment of Healthcare Providers and Systems (HCAHPS) survey. In December 2005, the federal

TABLE 9.2 Branding and Image

Metric	Definition	Issues	Purpose
Awareness	Percentage of total population who are aware of a brand or organization	Is awareness prompted or unprompted?	Consideration of who has heard of the brand
Top of mind	May be subject to most recent advertising or experience	Saliency of brand	
Knowledge	Percentage of population who know a service, have recollection of its advertising	Not a formal metric. Is knowledge prompted or unprompted?	Extent of familiarity with service beyond name recognition
Beliefs	Patients'/ consumers' view of service, generally captured via survey responses, often through ratings on a scale	Patients/ consumers may hold beliefs with varying degrees of conviction	Perception of brand by attribute
Purchasing intentions	Probability of intention to purchase	To estimate probability of purchase, aggregate and analyze ratings of stated intentions (e.g., top two boxes)	Measures pre-shopping disposition to purchase

Metric	Definition	Issues	Purpose
Willingness to recommend	Generally measured by ratings on a scale of 1 to 5	Nonlinear in impact	Shows strength of loyalty, potential impact on others
Customer satisfaction	Generally measured on scale of 1 to 5, in which patients declare satisfaction with brand in general or with specific attributes	Subject to response bias; captures views of current patients, not lost patients; satisfaction is function of expectations	Indicates likelihood of repurchase; reports of dissatisfaction show aspects requiring improvement to enhance loyalty
Willingness to search	Percentage of patients willing to delay purchases, change stores, or reduce quantities to avoid switching brands	Hard to capture	Indicates importance of distribution coverage
Loyalty	Measures include willingness to pay premium, to search	"Loyalty" itself is not a formal metric, but specific metrics do measure aspects of this dynamic; new product entries may alter loyalty levels	Indication of base future patient revenue stream

Office of Management and Budget gave its final approval for the national implementation of HCAHPS and the first public reporting results occurred in March 2008. The survey, its methodology, and the results it produces are publicly reported.[4]

The recently enacted Patient Protection and Affordable Care Act of 2010 includes HCAHPS among the measures to be used to calculate value-based incentive payments in the Hospital Value-Based Purchasing program, beginning with discharges in October 2012.

The HCAHPS formal public reporting initiative asks patients to rate their experiences with respect to various healthcare delivery systems. The survey asks discharged patients 27 questions about their recent hospital stay. These ratings are shared with the public and can potentially affect the hospital's reputation and standing in the community and additionally will be used in calculating value-based purchasing payments going forward.

Patient satisfaction surveys are valuable tools healthcare providers can use to identify areas that need improvement. By extracting accurate, measurable data, patient satisfaction surveys can help assess the quality of care and service from patients' perspectives.

Taking this type of patient-centered approach to quality management is vital in today's competitive healthcare environment. Patient satisfaction surveys demonstrate to patients and the community at large that quality is important and that the industry is proactively searching for ways to provide them with better service. These surveys empower patients and provide organizations with honest, insightful feedback that can be interpreted and acted upon.

INNOVATION

Although innovation is critical to most organizations, it is particularly important to healthcare. Just how important is innovation? Let's put it in perspective. If it were not for the intellectual curiosity of employees— thinking things through, trying out new ideas, and taking wild guesses in all the R&D labs across the country—the United States would have half the economy it has today. In a recent report on R&D, the American Association for the Advancement of Science estimated that as much as 50 percent of U.S. economic growth in the last 50 years came into existence is the result of advances in technology.[5]

After a few years' retrenchment and cost cutting, senior executives from a variety of industries now share the conviction that innovation—the ability to define and create new products and services and quickly bring them to market—is an increasingly important source of competitive advantage. Executives are setting aggressive performance goals for their innovation and product development organizations, targeting 20 to 30 percent improvements in such areas as time to market, development cost, product and service cost, and customer value.

A vast disconnect lies between hope and reality, however. A recent survey of 50 companies conducted by Booz Allen Hamilton shows that companies are only marginally satisfied that the innovations in their organizations are delivering at maximum potential. Worse, executives say that only half the improvement efforts they launch end up meeting expectations. Several waves of improvement in innovation and product development have already substantially enhanced companies' abilities to deliver differentiated, higher-quality products to markets faster and more efficiently. However, the degree of success achieved has varied greatly among companies and among units within companies. The differences in success stem from the difficulty in managing change in the complex processes and organizations associated with innovation and product development.

Some companies have managed to assemble an integrated "innovation chain" that is truly global and allows them to outflank competitors that innovate using knowledge in a single cluster. They have been able to implement a *process* for innovating that transcends local clusters and national boundaries, becoming "meta-national innovators." This strategy of using localized pockets of technology, market intelligence, and capabilities has provided a powerful new source of competitive advantage: more higher-value innovation at lower cost.

Innovation is both easy and difficult to measure. Measuring the outcomes in areas such as new products and processes, improved products and processes, copyrights, patents, inventions, and employee suggestions is easy. Many companies track these items. They can be documented to reflect the innovative profile of an organization. Unfortunately, comparing these data with previous data or benchmarking with other organizations is difficult because these measures are typically unique to each organization.

Perhaps the most obvious measure is tracking patents that are both used internally and licensed for others' use through a patent and license exchange. For example, pharmaceutical manufacturer Pfizer has been granted a large number of U.S. patents, most of which have a 20-year expiration term including the clinical trial period. Pfizer's licensing of patents and technology generates more than $60 billion in profits each year. Pfizer is at the top of the pharmaceutical list, but most healthcare organizations in the new economy monitor trademarks, patents, and copyrights as important measures of the innovative talent of its employees.[6]

It is helpful to remember that the registration of patents stems from employees' inventive spirit. The good news is that employees do not have to be highly degreed scientists or engineers to be inventive. Although invention is often thought of in the context of technology, computing, materials, or energy, in fact it spans all disciplines and can therefore be extracted from any technological realm for application to problems in any area.

Through the years, inventors have been viewed as "nerds," with much of their inventiveness explained by their quirky personality makeup. History is laced with well-known inventors endowed with an eccentric personality; but in actuality, inventors are usually ordinary people who possess extraordinary imagination. Many modern organizations of wide-ranging focus are devoting resources to encouraging employee creativity as a way to gain advantage over their competition. Organizations intent on sparking ingenuity will consider innovation, monitor it, and take action to enhance it.

CREATIVITY

Creativity, often considered the precursor to innovation, encompasses the creative experience, actions, and input of organizations. Measuring the creative spirit of employees is potentially more difficult. An employee suggestion system, a long-time measure of the creative processes of the organization, flourishes today in many organizations and is easily measured. Employees are rewarded for their suggestions if they are approved and implemented. Tracking the suggestion rates and comparing them with other organizations is an important benchmarking item for creative capability. Other measures that can be monitored are the number of new ideas, comments, or complaints. Formal feedback systems often contain creative suggestions that can lead to improved processes.

Some organizations measure the creative capabilities of employees using inventories and instruments that may be distributed at meetings and training sessions. In other organizations, a range of statements about employee creativity is included in the annual employee feedback survey. Using scaled ratings, employees either agree or disagree with the statements. Comparing actual scores of groups of employees over time reflects the degree to which employees perceive improvement in creativity in the workplace. Having consistent and comparable measures is still a challenge. Other organizations monitor the number, duration, and participation rate of creativity training projects. The last decade has witnessed a proliferation of creativity tools, projects, and activity.

EMPLOYEE SATISFACTION

An important item monitored by most organizations is employee job satisfaction. Using feedback surveys, executives can monitor the degree to which employees are satisfied with their employer's policies, work environment, and supervision and leadership; with the work itself; and with other factors. A composite rating may be developed to reflect an overall satisfaction value or an index for the organization, division, department, or region.

Whereas job satisfaction has always been an important factor in employee relations, in recent years it has taken on a new dimension because of the link between job satisfaction and other measures. The relationship between job satisfaction and the attraction and retention of employees is classic. Healthcare firms with excellent job satisfaction ratings have better success in attracting the most desirable employees. Job satisfaction ratings high enough that companies can be titled among the "Employers of Choice" or "Best Places to Work" become a subtle but powerful recruiting tool. The recent emphasis on the relationship between job satisfaction and employee retention arose out of the growing importance of turnover and retention issues. These relationships are now easily developed using human capital management systems featuring modules to calculate the correlation between turnover rates and job satisfaction scores for various job groups, divisions, and departments.

Job satisfaction has taken on new dimensions in connection with patient satisfaction as well. Dozens of applied research projects are beginning to show a significant correlation between job satisfaction scores and patient satisfaction scores. Intuitively, this correlation is logical because a more satisfied employee is likely to provide more productive, friendly, and appropriate patient service. Likewise, a disgruntled employee will provide less than desired patient service. Research has established that job attitudes (job satisfaction) relate to patient satisfaction, which relates to patient revenue growth. Therefore, the conclusion follows that if employee attitudes improve, revenues increase. These links, often referred to as a service profit chain, described in Chapter 8, create a promising way to identify important relationships between attitudes within an organization and the profits the organization earns.

ORGANIZATIONAL COMMITMENT

In recent years, organizational commitment (OC) measures have complemented or replaced job satisfaction measures. OC measures go beyond employee satisfaction to include the extent to which the employees identify with the organization's goals, mission, philosophy, values, policies, and practices. The concept of involvement and commitment to the organization is a key issue. OC more closely correlates with productivity and other performance improvement measures, whereas job satisfaction usually does not. OC is often measured in the same way as job satisfaction, using attitude surveys based on a 5-point or 7-point scale, and administered directly to employees. As organizational commitment scores (taken as a standard index) improve, a corresponding improvement in productivity should also be seen.

EMPLOYEE ENGAGEMENT

A different twist to the OC measure is one that reflects employee engagement. This measure indicates the extent to which employees are actively engaged in the organization. Research on engagement demonstrates that increased physician engagement enhances interaction with nursing and other office staff, improves overall physician alignment, and may heighten physicians' willingness to participate with hospital administration and policy development. Data support these findings and further describe the importance of engagement in quality improvement activities, whether it be through assembling and working on a team, analyzing hospital systems, navigating existing institutional linkages, or simply driving the creative initiative on a quality improvement project.[7]

Hundreds of organizations now use engagement data, reflecting the extent to which employees are engaged and how their engagement connects with productivity (defined as patient revenue divided by the number of employees) and employee turnover.

Leadership

Leadership is perhaps the most intriguing measure to address. On the surface, it would seem easy to measure the outcome because effective leadership leads to an effective organization. However, putting a monetary value on the consequences of new leadership behavior is not as easy as it appears. Leadership can (and usually does) determine the success or failure of an organization. Without appropriate leadership behaviors throughout an organization, resources can be misapplied or wasted, and opportunities can be missed. The news and literature are laced with examples of failed leadership at the top, and accounts of mismanaged employees, shareholders, investors, and the public. Some of these high-profile failed leadership stories have been painful.

At the same time, positive examples exist of leaders who have won extraordinary success at many levels of their organization over a sustained period. These leaders are often documented in books, articles, and lists of admiration. They clearly make the difference in their organizations. Obviously, the ultimate measure of leadership is the overall success of the organization. Whenever overall measures of success have been achieved or surpassed, they are always attributed to great leadership—perhaps rightfully so. However, attempting to use overall success as the only measure of leadership is a cop-out in terms of accountability. Other measures must be in place to develop systemwide monitoring of leaders and leadership in the organization.

360° FEEDBACK

Leadership can be measured in many different ways, perhaps the most common of which is known as 360° feedback. Here, a prescribed set of leadership behaviors desired in the organization is assessed by different sources to provide a composite of overall leadership capability and behavior. The sources often consist of the immediate manager of the leader being assessed, a colleague in the same area, the employees directly supervised by the leader, internal or external customers, and the leader's self-assessment. Combined, these assessments form a circle of influence (360°). The measure is basically an observation of behavior captured in a survey, often reported electronically. This 360° feedback has been growing rapidly in the United States, Europe, and Asia as an important way to capture overall leadership behavior change. Because the consequences of behavior change are usually measured as business impact, leadership improvement should be linked to the business in some way.

LEADERSHIP INVENTORIES AND ASSESSMENT

Another way to measure leadership is to require the management team to participate in a variety of leadership inventories, assessing predetermined leadership competency statements. The inventories reflect the extent to which a particular leadership style, approach, or even success is in place. These inventories, although popular in the 1970s and 1980s, are today often being replaced by the 360° feedback process.

LEADERSHIP PERCEPTION

It is also useful to capture the quality of leadership from the perspective of employees. In a few organizations, employees rate the quality of their leadership. Top executives and middle managers are typically the subjects of this form of evaluation. The measure is usually taken in conjunction with the annual feedback survey in the form of direct statements about the executive or immediate manager with which respondents agree or disagree using a 5-point scale. This survey attempts to measure how the followers in a particular situation perceive the quality, effectiveness, and appropriateness of leadership as exercised by their managers.

BUSINESS IMPACT

The outcomes of leadership development are clearly documented in many case studies involving ROI analysis. Of the thousands of studies conducted annually, leadership development ROI studies are at the top of the list—not because conducting them is easier but because of the uncertainty and the unknown aspects of investing in leadership development. Most leadership development will have an impact in a particular leader's area. Leadership development produces new skills that are applied on the job and lead to improvements in the leader's particular work unit. These improvements can vary significantly. The best way to evaluate a general leadership development project involving executives and leaders from a variety of areas is with respect to the monetary impact. When particular measures are improved, examining those measures individually makes little sense. Examining the monetary value of each measure as a whole is more worthwhile. The measures are converted to monetary values using one of the methods discussed in Chapter 8. The monetary values of the improvements from the first year are combined into a total value, ultimately leading to an ROI calculation. Leadership development projects aimed at improving leadership behavior and driving business improvement often yield high payoff, with ROI values that range from 500 percent to 1,000 percent, primarily because of the multiplicative effect as changes in leader behavior influence important measures in the leaders' teams.[8]

HUMAN LIFE

Seeing human life listed as an intangible may be surprising to some. It's not intangible because of the difficulty in measuring it—obviously, bodies can be counted. Human life is often considered to be intangible because of the difficulty in converting the value of life to money. Yet, this value is required in many projects and has been used in hundreds of studies. The issue spans both the private sector and the public sector.

Consider, for example, a recommendation by federal health officials that 11- and 12-year-old girls be routinely vaccinated against the sexually transmitted human papilloma virus (HPV) that causes cervical cancer. This recommendation has been endorsed by several federal health agencies and by insurance companies. One health insurance company, Wellpoint, Inc., announced its intention to cover the vaccine. What would lead Wellpoint to this decision? Insurance companies are willing to pay for the vaccine because it can reduce the number of claims, and ultimately the number of deaths, caused by cervical and vaginal cancers. Each year in the United States alone, approximately 4,000 women die from cervical cancer. The HPV vaccine Gardasil is expected to dramatically reduce this number. The results are even more staggering when it is considered that one or more types of HPV will infect more than 50 percent of sexually active women in their lifetimes. On the logic of the situation, covering the vaccination pays off for insurance companies, but only if monetary values are established for the cost of treating cancer (which should exist in insurance company records), and for the cost of a death (which also should exist in company records). Compensation limits are often defined by the amount of life insurance carried by the person who dies.

The value of a life comes into question more clearly in public policy projects, as when the government acts to try to prevent death. A cost-benefit analysis can quickly show what is economically sound to attempt. An example is the valuation of a life according to the U.S. Environmental Protection Agency, which places the value at $6.1 million. This estimate was developed in 2000 to evaluate the benefits of removing arsenic from drinking water. Since then, many government studies have placed a value on a human life, and the results vary considerably, ranging from $1.5 million to $5.8 million. The factors involved in placing a value on a human life include the person's age, economic status, education, and potential. Consequently, not every life is of equal value.

The private sector is especially interested in this issue because of the risks associated with everyday dangers in the safety and health sectors of the economy. Employers must be concerned about casualties that may result from on-the-job accidents, and about their liability exposure. The value of a human life is a constant concern in the arena of risk management. Consider, for example, a healthcare chain that is considering a new risk management procedure that would reduce the likelihood of acts of infant abduction. Although the infant may not be killed during the act of abduction, assumptions must be made about such costs. To conduct this type of analysis, the probability of infant abduction without the risk management procedure is compared to the probability of infant abduction with the procedure in place, based on assumptions made by those who understand such processes well. The cost of the risk management procedure, which would be accounted for as an extra direct expense, is known. What must be identified to make the estimate complete is the cost of an abduction. Previous liability claims can be reviewed to estimate what it would cost the hospital should an abduction occur, based on the value of the human life. When this number is known, it is a matter of using the ROI Methodology to determine whether the risk management procedure is economically justified. To some, such a calculation would seem absurd, and no amount of money would be considered too great to prevent the abduction or even the death of an infant. However, organizations have limits on what they can afford and are willing to pay.

As with many intangibles, this one generates others. For example, loss of life not only generates pain and suffering for the family, but can also lower morale and can even tarnish the image of an organization. For example, the energy company British Petroleum (BP) saw its stock price nosedive when unsafe conditions led to fatalities. BP's safety record was among the worst in the industry. After an explosion on an oil platform, investors grew alarmed and began to sell shares. It was an image problem that spooked investors. A damaged public image is an expensive intangible that can generate other economic impacts as well.

In summary, human life is considered an intangible primarily because of the perceived difficulty of placing a monetary value on it. However, a human life *can be valued* and human life *is being valued* routinely, making it more likely to be measured as a tangible in the future.

FINAL THOUGHTS

Get the picture? Intangible measures are crucial in reflecting the success of a project. Although they may not carry the weight of measures expressed in monetary terms, they are nevertheless an important part of the overall evaluation. Intangible measures should be identified, explored, examined, and monitored for changes linked to projects. Collectively, they add a unique dimension to the project report because most, if not all, projects involve intangible variables. Although several common intangible measures are explored in some detail in this chapter, the coverage is woefully incomplete. The range of intangible measures is practically limitless. With the data converted to monetary values and intangible measures identified, the next step is to capture the costs and calculate ROI. This step is covered in the next chapter.

CHAPTER 10

Monitoring Project Costs and Calculating ROI

This chapter explores the costs of healthcare improvement projects and the steps taken to calculate ROI. Specific costs that should be captured are identified along with economical ways in which approaches for measuring various aspects can be developed. One of the challenges addressed in this chapter is deciding which costs should be captured or estimated. For major projects, some costs are hidden and usually not counted. The conservative philosophy presented here is to account for all costs, direct and indirect. Several checklists and guidelines are included.

The monetary values for the benefits of a project (after converting data to money) are combined with project cost data to calculate the return on investment. This chapter explores the various techniques, processes, and issues involved in calculating and interpreting the financial ROI.

OPENING STORIES

HOMETOWN CARE

Hometown Care is a senior services organization in rural Pennsylvania. This long-term care facility is a skilled nursing and rehabilitative division associated with a retirement community that offers a continuum of care. The health center offers three levels of skilled nursing care: comprehensive, rehabilitative, and memory support. The facility consists of 90 beds and 168 employees.[1]

Healthcare organizations such as Hometown Care are constantly looking for ways to improve quality and efficiency through new and innovative initiatives. Along with this movement, return on investment (ROI) has also become a topic of interest across the healthcare system, particularly with top executives in this facility. Executives wanted to see the ROI calculation on three projects that were being undertaken by eight employees at Hometown Care. These projects used the concept of lean technology, which consists of a variety of tools and processes for problem analysis and measurement. These eight employees tackled three projects in the healthcare area. The first project involved dressing change delays and the concerns when a patient required a dressing change. The second project targeted times for short-term rehab discharge to home. The organization was experiencing delays when short-term rehab patients were discharged to home. The third project was a chart-to-go project and addressed the documentation system used by the certified nurse assistants (CNAs) to capture activities of daily living (ADL) for each resident in the long-term care unit.

The individuals explored these three healthcare improvement projects using a conservative approach, the ROI Methodology. Each project captured the impact of the major measures, isolated the effects of the programs on the impact, and converted the data to money to get a total benefit. This figure was then compared to the total cost of the project including the cost of the training to learn how to apply these principles. These projects generated ROI results of 590 percent, 154 percent, and 31 percent, respectively. The results of the studies were communicated to a variety of stakeholders, starting with the senior leadership. The leadership team was impressed to the point of making the program the primary quality initiative in their organization. They also assigned a senior leader the responsibility of coordinating and tracking each project to create a database that documents a long-term care organization's transformation to a lean enterprise.

Healthcare Fraud

In a recent announcement from the Obama administration, investigators recovered a record-breaking $4.1 billion in healthcare fraud money during 2011, a reflection of the Obama administration's increased focus on fighting fraud. In a recent article, *USA Today* notes that the federal government collected $7.20 for every dollar spent on fighting fraud according to the department of Health and Human Services (HHS) inspector general.[2] This ratio translates to an ROI calculation of 620 percent, representing an impressive return on investment of expenditures in tackling healthcare fraud. The officials attributed much of the progress to nine enforcement action teams in cities such as Chicago and Miami. The government increased funding to Senior Medicare Patrol teams from $9 million in 2010 to $18 million in 2011 in the form of Administration on Aging grants in fraud-heavy states such as California and Michigan.

With this impressive ROI came much scrutiny. Some of the critics of this program asked for an account of the benefits to see whether conservative assumptions were made in the analysis. The critics wanted to understand whether all of the costs to capture the fraud were included, including costs with justice systems' time and direct expenses. Sometimes these factors are underestimated in calculations. Finally, they wanted to know whether other factors outside of these patrol teams could have reduced the expenditures. At the last count, the Justice Department and HHS had not provided clear answers to these questions.

These two stories point out the importance of having a project or program culminate with an actual ROI calculation. These powerful data are likely to be scrutinized. It is the one measure that is often emotional; if the measure is too high it becomes unbelievable, if the measure is too low or negative, top executives want to place blame and use the information as punitive, rather than as a process improvement tool.

THE IMPORTANCE OF COSTS AND ROI

One of the main reasons for monitoring costs is to create budgets for healthcare improvement projects. The initial costs of most projects are usually estimated during the proposal process and are often based on experience with previous projects. Costs are monitored in an ongoing effort to control expenditures, plan for cash flow, and keep the project within budget. Monitoring costs not only reveals the status of expenditures but also increases the visibility of expenditures and encourages the project team to spend wisely. And, of course, monitoring costs in an ongoing fashion is much easier, more accurate, and more efficient than trying to reconstruct events to capture costs retrospectively. Developing accurate costs by category builds a database for understanding and predicting costs in the future.

Monitoring project costs is an essential step in developing the ROI calculation because it represents the denominator in the ROI formula. ROI has become a critical measure demanded by many stakeholders, including clients and senior executives. It is the ultimate level of evaluation, showing the actual payoff of the project, expressed as a percentage and based on the same formula as the evaluation for capital investments.

A brief example will highlight the importance of costs and ROI. To control healthcare costs, a new creativity program was implemented in a hospital network. This new program provided cash awards for employees when they submitted ideas that, when implemented, resulted in cost savings. The project was undertaken to help lower the costs of this publicly owned healthcare provider. As the project was rolled out, the project team captured reaction to ensure that the employees perceived the program as fair, equitable, motivating, and challenging. At Level 2, they measured learning to ensure that the employees understood how to document their ideas and how and when the awards were made. Application data (Level 3) were the actual submission of the ideas, and the hospital network had the goal of a 10 percent participation rate. Level 4 data corresponded to the actual monetary savings from the implemented ideas. In this case, $1.5 million was saved over a two-year period.

In most organizations, the evaluation would have stopped there. The project appeared to be a success, with objectives met at each of the four levels. Bring on the champagne! However, the costs of the project for the same two-year period totaled $2.1 million. Thus, the hospital network spent $2.1 million to have $1.5 million returned. This negative ROI would not have been recognized if the ultimate measure, the ROI, had not been developed. A negative ROI might be acceptable to some executives. After all, the intangibles in this example showed increased creativity, engagement, ownership, teamwork, cooperation, and communications. However, if the objective was a positive ROI, this program failed to achieve it, primarily because of excessive administrative costs. With this analysis, the project leader was able to reduce costs going forward, generating a positive ROI.

FUNDAMENTAL COST ISSUES

The first step in monitoring costs is to define and address issues relating to cost control. Several rules apply to tabulating costs. Consistency and standardization are necessary. All costs should be monitored and disclosed, even if they are not needed. Although costs must be realistic and reasonable, they will not always be precise; estimates are okay. Other key issues are detailed in this section.

FULLY LOADED COSTS

When a conservative approach is used to calculate the ROI, costs should be fully loaded, which is Guiding Principle 10 (see Chapter 2). With this approach, all costs (direct and indirect) that can be identified and linked to a particular project are included. The philosophy is simple: For the denominator of the ROI formula, "when in doubt, put it in" (i.e., if any question arises as to whether a cost should be included, include it, even if the cost guidelines for the organization do not require it). When an ROI is calculated and reported to target audiences, the process should withstand even the closest scrutiny to ensure its credibility. The only way to meet this test is to include all costs. Of course, from a realistic viewpoint, if the controller or chief financial officer insists on not using certain costs, then leaving them out or reporting them in an alternative way is best.

COSTS REPORTED WITHOUT BENEFITS

Because costs can easily be collected, they are presented to management in many ingenious ways, such as in terms of the total cost of the project, cost per day, cost per unit, and cost per participant. While these data may be helpful for efficiency comparisons, presenting them without identifying the corresponding benefits may be problematic. When most executives review a healthcare improvement project's cost, a logical question is raised: What benefit was received from the project? This management reaction is typical, particularly when costs are perceived to be high.

Unfortunately, many organizations have fallen into this trap. For example, in one hospital chain, the CEO asked for all the costs associated with a physician leadership conference. The costs were tabulated and reported to the CEO, reflecting the total investment in the project. From the executive perspective, the total figure exceeded the perceived value of the project, and the CEO's immediate reaction was to request a summary of (monetary and nonmonetary) benefits derived from the conference. Because the evaluation was not planned, the results were hard to identify. The conclusion was that few, if any, economic benefits were achieved from the project. Consequently, budgets for similar projects were reduced in the future. Although this example may be extreme, it shows the danger of presenting only half the equation. For this reason, some organizations have developed a policy of not communicating cost data unless the benefits can be captured and presented along with the costs, even if the benefits are subjective and intangible. Even when time is not available to develop the benefits, at least a plan is presented to develop them, if desired. This approach helps maintain a balance between the two components.

Develop and Use Cost Guidelines

When multiple projects are being evaluated, it may be helpful to detail the philosophy and policy on costs in the form of guidelines for the evaluators or others who monitor and report costs. Cost guidelines detail specifically which cost categories are included with projects and how the data are captured, analyzed, and reported. Standards, unit cost guiding principles, and generally accepted values are included in the guidelines. Cost guidelines can range from a 1-page brief to a 100-page document in a large, complex organization. The simpler approach is better. When fully developed, cost guidelines should be reviewed and approved by the finance and accounting staff. The final document serves as the guiding force in collecting, monitoring, and reporting costs. When the ROI is calculated and reported, costs are included in summary or table form, and the cost guidelines are usually referenced in a footnote or attached as an appendix.

Sources of Costs

It is sometimes helpful to first consider the sources of project costs. Four major categories of sources are illustrated in Table 10.1. The charges and expenses from the project team represent the major segment of costs. This group leads and implements the project, including the evaluation effort. A second major cost category relates to the vendors or suppliers who assist with the project. A variety of expenses, such as consulting or advisory fees, may be in this category. A third major cost category includes those expenses borne by the department, function, or organization where the project is being implemented. Contained in this category are the participants who must make the project successful. In many projects, these costs are not identified but nevertheless are part of the costs of the project. The final cost category involves expenses not covered in the other three categories, such as payments for equipment and services needed for the project. Finance and accounting records should track and reflect the costs from these different sources, and the process presented in this chapter can help track these costs.

TABLE 10.1 Sources of Project Costs

Source of Costs	Cost Reporting Issues
Project team expenses	• Costs are usually accurate • Variable expenses are usually underestimated
Vendor/suppliers fees and expenses	• Costs are usually accurate • Variable expenses are usually underestimated
Participants' expenses, direct and indirect	• Direct expenses are usually not fully loaded • Indirect expenses are rarely included in costs
Equipment, services, and other expenses	• Costs are sometimes understated • Expenses as reported may lack accountability

Prorated versus Direct Costs

Usually all costs related to a project are captured and expensed to that project. However, some costs are prorated over a longer period. Equipment purchases, software development and acquisitions, and the construction of facilities are all significant costs with a useful life that may extend beyond the project. Consequently, a portion of these costs should be prorated to the project. Under a conservative approach, the expected life of the project is fixed. Some organizations will assume a period of one year of operation for a simple project. Others may consider three to five years appropriate. In rare occasions, the proration time may be more. If a question is raised about the specific time period to be used in this calculation, the finance and accounting staff should be consulted, or appropriate guidelines should be developed and followed.

Employee Benefits Factor

Employee time is valuable, and when time is required for a project, the costs must be fully loaded, representing total compensation, including employee benefits. The employee benefits factor is usually well known in the healthcare organization and is used in other costing formulas. It represents the cost of all employee benefits expressed as a percentage of payroll. In some organizations, this value is as high as 60 to 70 percent. In others, it may be as low as 25 to 30 percent. The average in the United States is 49 percent.[3]

SPECIFIC COSTS TO INCLUDE

Table 10.2 shows the recommended cost categories for a fully loaded, conservative approach to estimating project costs. Consistency in capturing all these costs is essential, and standardization adds credibility. Each category is described in this section.

Initial Analysis and Assessment

One of the most underestimated items is the cost of conducting the initial analysis and assessment that leads to the project. In a comprehensive

TABLE 10.2 Project Cost Categories

Cost Item	Prorated	Expensed
Initial analysis and assessment to determine need for project	✓	
Development of improvement project including content	✓	
Acquisition of technology, materials, content	✓	
Implementation costs:		
• Salaries/benefits for project team time		✓
• Salaries/benefits for coordination time		✓
• Salaries/benefits for participant time		✓
• Project materials and supplies		✓
• Hardware/software, if appropriate	✓	
• Travel/lodging/meals		✓
• Use of facilities		✓
• Capital expenditures, if appropriate	✓	
Maintenance and monitoring		✓
Administrative support and overhead	✓	
Evaluation and reporting		✓

project, it involves data collection, problem solving, assessment, and analysis. In some projects, its cost is near zero because the project is conducted without an appropriate assessment. However, as project sponsors place increased attention on needs assessment and analysis in the future, this item will become a significant cost.

DEVELOPMENT OF PROJECT

Also significant are the costs of designing and developing the project. These costs include time spent in both the design and development and the purchase of supplies, materials, and other items directly related to project development. As with needs assessment costs, design and development costs are usually charged to the project. However, if the solution can be used in other projects, the major expenditures can be prorated.

Acquisition Costs

In lieu of development costs, some project leaders use acquisition costs connected to the purchasing of solutions from other sources to use directly or in a modified format. For example, the purchase of a workforce management system would be prorated over the life of the system. The costs for these solutions include the purchase price, support materials, and licensing agreements. Some projects have both acquisition costs and solution development costs. Acquisition costs can be prorated if the acquired solutions can be used in other projects.

Implementation Costs

The largest cost segment in a project is associated with implementation and delivery. The time (salaries and benefits), travel, and other expenses of all involved in the project in any way should be included. This category encompasses the project team, the participants, and any local coordinators. When a project is targeted for an ROI calculation, participants may provide their salaries directly in a confidential manner. If not, these costs can be estimated using average or midpoint salary values for corresponding job classifications. Project materials, such as field journals, instructions, reference guides, case studies, surveys, and participant workbooks, should be included in the implementation costs, along with license fees, user fees, and royalty payments. Supporting hardware, software, podcasts, and videos should also be taken into account.

The cost for the use of facilities needed for the project should be included. For external meetings, the direct charge for the conference center, hotel, or motel would be included. If the meetings are conducted in-house, the conference room represents a cost for the organization, and the cost should be estimated for time of use even if it is uncommon to include facilities costs in other cost reporting. If a facility or building is constructed or other capital equipment is purchased for the project, it is included as a capital expenditure.

Maintenance and Monitoring

Maintenance and monitoring involve routine expenses necessary to maintain and operate the project. These ongoing expenses allow the new project to continue and may involve staff members and additional expenses. This particular category may be significant for some projects.

SUPPORT AND OVERHEAD

The cost of support and overhead includes the additional costs not directly charged to the project—any project cost not considered in the previous calculations. Typical items are the cost of administrative/clerical support, telecommunication expenses, office expenses, salaries of client managers for the time involved in the project, and other fixed costs. Usually, this figure is provided in the form of an estimate allocated in some convenient way.

EVALUATION AND REPORTING

The total evaluation and reporting cost completes the fully loaded costs. Activities under evaluation costs include developing the evaluation strategy, designing instruments, collecting data, analyzing data, preparing a report, and communicating the results. Cost categories include time, materials, purchased instruments, surveys, and any consulting fees.

COST CLASSIFICATIONS

Project costs can be classified in two basic ways. One is with a description of the expenditures, such as labor, materials, supplies, or travel. These expense account classifications are standard with most accounting systems. The other way to classify costs is to use the categories in the project steps, such as initial analysis and assessment, development, implementation, and evaluation. An effective system monitors costs by account category according to the description of those accounts, but also includes a method for accumulating costs in the process/functional category. Many systems stop short of this second step. Although the first grouping adequately states the total project costs, it does not allow for a useful comparison with other projects to provide information on areas where costs might be excessive.

THE ROI CALCULATION

The term *return on investment* for healthcare projects and programs is occasionally misused, sometimes intentionally. In this misuse, a broad definition for ROI is reported that includes any benefit from the project. In such a case, ROI becomes a vague concept where even subjective data linked to a program are called ROI. In this book, the return on investment is defined more precisely and represents a value determined by comparing project costs to benefits. The two most common measures are the benefits/costs ratio (BCR) and the ROI formula. Both are presented along with other approaches to calculate the return or payback.

Using annualized values is an accepted practice for developing the ROI. The formulas presented in this chapter use annualized values so that the first-year impact of the investment can be calculated for short-term projects. This approach is a conservative way to develop the ROI, because many short-term projects have added value in the second or third year. For long-term projects, longer time frames should be used. For example, in an ROI analysis of a project involving major purchases for an enterprise-wide system (ERP), a five-year time frame was used. However, for short-term projects that take only a few weeks to implement (such as a simple change in a medical procedure), first-year values are appropriate.

When selecting the approach to measure ROI, the formula used and the assumptions made to arrive at the decision to use this formula should be communicated to the target audience. It helps prevent misunderstandings and confusion surrounding how the ROI value was developed. Although several approaches are described in this chapter, two stand out as preferred methods: the benefits/costs ratio and the basic ROI formula. These two approaches are described next.

BENEFITS/COSTS RATIO

One of the original methods for evaluating projects was the benefits/costs ratio, used for centuries by governments to make decisions about spending money for projects. This method compares the benefits of the project with the costs, using a simple ratio. In formula form,

$$BCR = \frac{\text{Project Monetary} - \text{Benefits}}{\text{Project Costs}}$$

In simple terms, the BCR compares the economic benefits of the project with the costs of the project. A BCR of 1 means that the benefits equal the costs. A BCR of 2, usually written as 2:1, indicates that for each dollar spent on the project, two dollars were generated in benefits.

The following example illustrates the use of the BCR. A work modification project was implemented for employees who had been injured on the job in a hospital. This project allowed employees to continue work in a limited capacity. In a follow-up evaluation, action planning and business performance monitoring were used to capture the benefits. The first-year payoff for the program was $1,554,000. The total, fully loaded implementation costs were $248,000. Thus, the ratio was

$$BCR = \frac{\$1,554,000}{\$248,000} = 6.3:1$$

For every dollar invested in the project, $6.30 in benefits were generated.

ROI Formula

Perhaps the most appropriate formula for evaluating project investments is net program benefits divided by costs. This traditional financial ROI is directly related to the BCR. The ROI ratio is usually expressed as a percentage where the fractional values are multiplied by 100. In formula form,

$$ROI\ (\%) = \frac{Net\ Project\ Benefits}{Project\ Costs} \times 100$$

Net project benefits are project benefits minus costs. For a shortcut, subtract 1 from the BCR and multiply by 100 to get the ROI percentage. For example, a BCR of 2.45 is the same as an ROI value of 145 percent (1.45 × 100%). This formula is essentially the same as the ROI for capital investments that has been used in businesses for more than 200 years. For example, when a hospital purchases new medical equipment, the ROI is developed by dividing annual earnings by the investment. The annual earnings are comparable to net benefits (annual benefits minus the cost). The investment is comparable to the fully loaded project costs.

An ROI of 50 percent means that the costs were recovered and an additional 50 percent of the costs were returned. A project ROI of 150 percent indicates that the costs have been recovered and an additional 1.5 times the costs are returned.

An example illustrates the ROI calculation. Public and private sector hospital groups concerned about the shortage of doctors in certain areas have developed a variety of projects to address the issue. One project involved the use of nurse practitioners to perform some portions of the physicians' routine duties. The results of the project were impressive. Productivity and quality alone yielded an annual value of $2,700,000. The total, fully loaded costs for the project were $1,150,000. Thus, the return on investment was

$$\text{ROI (\%)} = \frac{\$2,700,000 - \$1,150,000}{\$1,150,000} \times 100 = 135\%$$

For each dollar invested, this project received $1.35 in return after the costs of the project were recovered.

Investments in plants, equipment, subsidiaries, or other companies are not usually evaluated using the benefits/costs method. Using the ROI formula to calculate the return on project investments essentially places these investments on a level playing field with other investments whose valuation uses the same formula and similar concepts. The ROI calculation is easily understood by key management and financial executives who regularly work with investments and their ROIs.

BASIS FOR MONETARY BENEFITS

Profits can be generated through increased sales or cost savings. In practice, more opportunities are generally available for cost savings than for profits. Cost savings can be realized when improvements in productivity, patient outcomes, quality, safety, efficiency, cycle time, or actual cost reduction occur. In a review of almost 500 studies, the vast majority of them were based on cost savings or cost avoidance. Approximately 85 percent of the studies used monetary benefits based on cost savings or avoidance from output, quality, efficiency, time, or a variety of soft data measures. The others used monetary benefits based on patient revenue increases, where the earnings were derived from the profit margin. Cost savings are important for nonprofits and public sector organizations, where opportunities for profit are often unavailable. Because most projects are connected directly to cost savings, ROIs can still be developed in these settings.

The formula provided here should be used consistently throughout an organization. Deviations from or misuse of the formula can create confusion, not only among users but also among the finance and accounting team. The chief financial officer (CFO) and the finance and accounting team should become partners in the implementation of the ROI Methodology. The staff must use the same financial terms as those used and expected by the CFO. Without the support, involvement, and commitment of these individuals, a broader use of ROI will be unlikely.

Table 1.6 shows some financial terms that are misused in the literature. Terms such as *return on intelligence* (or *information*), abbreviated as ROI, do nothing but confuse the CFO, who assumes that ROI refers to the return on investment. Sometimes *return on expectations* (ROE), *return on anticipation* (ROA), and *return on client expectations* (ROCE) are used, also confusing the CFO, who assumes the abbreviations refer to return on equity, return on assets, and return on capital employed, respectively. The use of these terms in the payback calculation of a project will also confuse and perhaps lose the support of the finance and accounting staff. Other terms such as *return on people, return on resources, return on technology, return on web, return on marketing, return on objectives,* and *return on quality* are often used with almost no consistency in terms of financial calculations. The bottom line: Don't confuse the CFO. Consider this person an ally, and use the same terminology, processes, and concepts when applying financial returns for projects.

ROI OBJECTIVES

Specific expectations for ROI should be developed before an evaluation study is undertaken. Although no standard amounts exist, four strategies have been used to establish a minimum expected ROI amount. This ROI objective for a project or program is sometimes called the target or hurdle rate. The first approach is to set the ROI using the same values used for investing in capital expenditures, such as equipment, facilities, and new companies. For North America, Western Europe, South America, and most of the Asia-Pacific area, including Australia and New Zealand, the cost of capital is quite low, and the internal hurdle rate for ROI is usually in the 15 to 20 percent range. Thus, using this strategy, organizations would set the expected ROI for a project at the same value expected from other investments.

A second strategy is to use an ROI minimum value that is above the percentage expected for other types of investments. The rationale is that the ROI process for healthcare projects and programs is still relatively new and often involves subjective input, including estimations. For this reason, a higher standard is required or suggested.

A third strategy is to set the ROI value at a breakeven point. A 0 percent ROI represents breakeven and is equivalent to a BCR of 1. This approach is used when the goal is to recapture the cost of the project only. This ROI objective is used for many public sector organizations, where all of the value and benefit from the program come through the intangible measures that are not converted to monetary values. Thus, an organization will use a breakeven point for the ROI based on the reasoning that it is not attempting to make a profit from a particular project.

A fourth, and often the recommended, strategy is to let the client or program sponsor set the minimum acceptable ROI value. In this scenario, the individual who initiates, approves, sponsors, or supports the project establishes the acceptable ROI. Almost every project has a major sponsor, and that person may be willing to specify an acceptable value that links the expectations for financial return directly to the expectations of the sponsor.

OTHER ROI MEASURES

In addition to the traditional ROI formula, several other measures are occasionally used under the general heading of return on investment. These measures are designed primarily for evaluating other financial measures but sometimes work their way into project evaluations.

Payback Period (Breakeven Analysis)

The payback period is commonly used for evaluating capital expenditures. With this approach, the annual cash proceeds (savings) produced by an investment are compared against the original cash outlay for the investment to determine the multiple of cash proceeds that is equal to the original investment. Measurement is usually in terms of years and months. For example, if the cost savings generated from a project are constant each year, the payback period is determined by dividing the original cash investment (including development costs, expenses, etc.) by the expected or actual annual savings. The net savings are found by subtracting the project expenses.

To illustrate this calculation, assume that the initial cost of a project is $100,000 and the project has a three-year useful life. Annual net savings from the project are expected to be $40,000. Thus, the payback period is

$$\text{Payback Period} = \frac{\text{Total Investment (\$100,000)}}{\text{Annual Savings (\$40,000)}} = 2.5 \text{ Years}$$

The project will "pay back" the original investment in 2.5 years.

The payback period method is simple to use but has the limitation of ignoring the time value of money. It has not enjoyed widespread use in the evaluation of healthcare project investments.

DISCOUNTED CASH FLOW

Discounted cash flow is a method of evaluating investment opportunities in which certain values are assigned to the timing of the proceeds from the investment. The assumption behind this approach is that a dollar earned today is more valuable than a dollar earned a year from now, based on the accrued interest possible from investing the dollar.

Using the discounted cash flow concept to evaluate a project investment can be approached in several ways. The most common approach uses the net present value of an investment. The savings each year are compared with the outflow of cash required by the investment. The expected annual savings are discounted based on a selected interest rate, and the outflow of cash is discounted by the same interest rate. If the present value of the savings exceeds the present value of the outlays, after the two have been discounted by the common interest rate, the investment is usually considered acceptable by management. The discounted cash flow method has the advantage of ranking investments, but it requires calculations that can become difficult to use. Many healthcare improvement projects do not have a constant flow of savings each year.

INTERNAL RATE OF RETURN

The internal rate of return (IRR) method determines the interest rate necessary to make the present value of the cash flow equal zero. It represents the maximum rate of interest that could be paid if all project funds were borrowed and the organization was required to break even on the project. The IRR considers the time value of money and is unaffected by the scale of the project. It can be used to rank alternatives and to accept or reject decisions when a minimum rate of return is specified. A major weakness of the IRR method is that it assumes all returns are reinvested at the same internal rate of return. This assumption can make an investment alternative with a high rate of return look even better than it really is and make a project with a low rate of return look even worse. In practice, the IRR is rarely used to evaluate healthcare improvement project investments.

FINAL THOUGHTS

ROI, the final evaluation level, compares costs with benefits. Costs are important and should be fully loaded in the ROI calculation. From a practical standpoint, some costs may be optional and depend on the healthcare organization's guidelines and philosophy. However, because of the scrutiny ROI calculations typically receive, all costs should be included, even going beyond the requirements of the organization's policy. After the impact measures are collected and converted to monetary values and the project costs are tabulated, the ROI calculation itself is easy. Plugging the values into the appropriate formula is the final step. This chapter presented the two basic approaches for calculating return: the ROI formula and the benefits/costs ratio. Each has its advantages and disadvantages. Alternatives to the standard ROI determination were also briefly discussed.

Now that the process has been fully laid out, the next chapter details how to forecast the value of a project, including its ROI.

CHAPTER 11

Reporting Results

With the ROI results in hand, what's next? Should the results be used to modify the healthcare improvement project, change the internal processes, explain the contribution, justify new projects, gain additional support, or build goodwill? How should the data be presented? The worst course of action is to do nothing, except, of course, providing the data to the project sponsor. Achieving results without communicating them to other stakeholders is like planting seeds and failing to fertilize and cultivate the seedlings—the yield will be less than optimal. This chapter provides useful information for presenting evaluation data to various audiences in the form of both oral and written reports.

OPENING STORIES

CLEVELAND CLINIC

Of all factors that lead to premature deaths, smoking is the deadliest. Tobacco is addictive, damaging, and deadly, causing 450,000 deaths each year, or 1 in every 5, often from early heart attacks, chronic lung diseases, and cancers. For a healthcare institution whose inherent mission is healing the sick and promoting health, it would not make sense to support a habit that leads to disease, disability, and death. Cleveland Clinic took this point one step further by adopting a smoke-free campus in 2005 and, in 2007, deciding to no longer hire smokers. Job candidates are told they will be subject to urine tests to check for nicotine. If a candidate tests positive for nicotine, the job offer is rescinded and he or she is offered a free tobacco cessation program and may reapply in 90 days.

If that policy sounds unreasonable, consider the toxic nature of cigarette smoke, which contains hundreds of chemicals and compounds, at least 69 of which cause cancer. Smoking puts these chemicals directly into the body, which leads to lung disease, heart disease, cancer, diminished immune system, and other deadly issues. By ignoring these issues, Cleveland Clinic's commitment to health and wellness would be undermined and the healthy environment for employees, patients, and visitors would be compromised.

This program has a tremendous payoff for Cleveland Clinic in terms of medical costs for employees, reduction in sick days, short- and long-term disability, even a reduction in incidents and increased productivity. Cleveland Clinic began amassing the statistics for the program, both from the perspective of cost savings and the negative impact it would have on recruiting job applicants. Since this program was instituted, less than 2 percent of job offers (about 300 out of 20,000) have been rescinded due to positive nicotine tests.

The reporting of results of this program was critical. A variety of communication methods were in place, reporting not only the rationale for the program, but also the results anticipated in the beginning and the results achieved during the program. Because this issue is politically sensitive, communications were chosen carefully. The new employee policy was published online and messages to the employees and the public came directly from the Hospital CEO and the medical director for Employee Health Services.

Cleveland Clinic sees their vital role in educating patients and employees about lifestyle choices. It is only right to practice what they preach according to Dr. Paul Terpeluk, Cleveland Clinic's medical director of Employee Health Services. Part of this communication campaign involved taking the message to the national media, letting others know what the clinic stands for and its stand on this particular issue. Part of the communication was to include an opinion piece in the *USA Today* weekly international edition, published in February 2012.[1] The Cleveland Clinic has since been awarded the Tom Hurst Award for Smoke-Free Hospitals.

SOUTHERN HEALTHCARE ORGANIZATION

Southern Healthcare, controlled by a religious organization, was facing a persistent and nagging issue. The number of sexual harassment complaints was excessive and increasing. An analysis showed that the principle reason resulted from physicians, directors, administrators, and team leaders not being fully aware of what constitutes sexual harassment. At the same time, they were unaware of all the aspects of the healthcare chain's sexual harassment policy. To correct this problem, the organization implemented a sexual harassment prevention program that included workshops with physicians, directors, administrators, and team leaders throughout the system. This program was followed with meetings with all employees. The focus was on what constitutes sexual harassment and the policy in place to discourage and prevent it.

After the program was implemented, the sexual harassment complaints dropped dramatically. The ROI study, based on the average cost of a sexual harassment complaint was impressive, yielding greater than 1,000 percent ROI. The communication plan around the program was critical. It began with briefings with senior executives of the hospital chain, the hospital administrators, and their direct reports, informing them about the ROI study, with a purpose of underscoring that these types of programs, although undertaken to prevent problems, also result in a huge business value.

Next, information was reported to the team leaders, supervisors, managers, and directors in the form of meetings at each hospital and regularly scheduled staff meetings. Face-to-face meetings were preferred to discuss the issues and the methodology used to conduct the study. Finally, in light of a sensitive issue such as sexual harassment, the results were communicated to all employees, some of whom were the victims of sexual harassment. The information pointed out dramatic evidence that the activities were almost nonexistent now (Level 3) and the claims filed with the HR director were dramatically reduced (Level 4).

It was determined not to communicate the ROI to all employees for two reasons. First, unless the organization is willing to take the time to fully explain what ROI means to all employees, it may not be completely understood. Second, some individuals may get the wrong impression and may think the organization would not address this issue unless it created a positive ROI, although the presence of sexual harassment is not only illegal, but also unethical and immoral.

These two stories show the importance of planning the communication after the results of the study and executing the communication plan. This task involves a variety of audiences with different communication and timing needs.

THE IMPORTANCE OF COMMUNICATING RESULTS

Communicating results, the final step in the ROI Methodology, is critical to project success. The results achieved must be conveyed to stakeholders not just at project completion but throughout the project. Continuous communication maintains the flow of information so that adjustments can be made and all stakeholders are kept up to date on the status of the project.

Mark Twain once said, "Collecting data is like collecting garbage—pretty soon we will have to do something with it." Measuring project success and collecting evaluation data mean nothing unless the findings are communicated promptly to the appropriate audiences so that they are apprised of the results and can take action in response if necessary. Communication is important for many reasons, some of which are detailed next.

COMMUNICATION IS NECESSARY TO MAKE IMPROVEMENTS

Information is collected at different points during the ROI study, and providing feedback to involved groups enables them to take action and make adjustments if needed. Thus, the quality and timeliness of communication are critical to making improvements. Even after the project is completed, communication is necessary to make sure the target audiences fully understand the results achieved, and how the results may be enhanced in future projects or in the current project, if it is still operational. Communication is the key to making important adjustments at all phases of the project.

COMMUNICATION IS NECESSARY TO EXPLAIN THE CONTRIBUTION

The overall contribution of the project, as determined from the six types of outcome measures, is unclear at best. The different target audiences will each need a thorough explanation of the results. The communication strategy—including message, media, and timing—will determine the extent to which each group understands the contribution. Communicating results, particularly in terms of business impact and ROI, can quickly overwhelm even the most sophisticated target audiences. Communication must be planned and implemented with the goal of making sure the respective audiences understand the full contribution.

COMMUNICATION IS A POLITICALLY SENSITIVE ISSUE

Because healthcare is a political issue, communication can cause problems. The results of a project may be closely linked to political positions within an organization and communicating the results can upset some individuals while pleasing others. If certain individuals do not receive the information, or if it is delivered inconsistently between groups, problems can quickly surface. Not only must the information be understood, but issues relating to fairness, quality, and political correctness make it crucial that the communication be constructed and delivered effectively to all key individuals.

DIFFERENT AUDIENCES NEED DIFFERENT INFORMATION

With so many potential target audiences requiring communication on the success of a project, the communication must be individually tailored to their needs. A varied audience has varied needs. Planning and effort are necessary to ensure that each audience receives all the information it needs, in the proper format, at the proper time. A single report for presentation to all audiences is usually inappropriate. The scope, the format, and even the content of the information will vary significantly from one group to another. Thus, the target audience is the key to determining the appropriate method of communication.

Even though communication of results is a critical need, it is often overlooked or underfunded in projects. This chapter presents a variety of techniques for accomplishing communication of all types for various target audiences.

PRINCIPLES OF COMMUNICATING RESULTS

The skills needed to communicate results effectively are almost as sensitive and sophisticated as those necessary for obtaining results. The style of the communication is as important as the substance. Regardless of the message, audience, or medium, a few general principles apply.

COMMUNICATION MUST BE TIMELY

In general, project results should be communicated as soon as they become known. From a practical standpoint, however, it is sometimes best to delay the communication until a convenient time, such as the publication of the next newsletter or the next executive group meeting. Several questions are relevant to the timing decision. Is the audience ready for the results in view of other issues that may have developed? Is the audience expecting results? When will the delivery have the maximum impact on the audience? Do circumstances dictate a change in the timing of the communication?

COMMUNICATION SHOULD BE TARGETED TO SPECIFIC AUDIENCES

Because communication is usually more effective when designed for the specific group being addressed, the message should be tailored to the interests, needs, and expectations of the audience. The results of the project should reflect outcomes at all levels, including the six levels presented in this book. Some of the data are developed earlier in the project and communicated during the implementation of the project. Other data are collected after project implementation and communicated in a follow-up study. The results, in their broadest sense, may incorporate early feedback in qualitative form all the way to ROI values expressed in varying quantitative terms.

Media Should Be Carefully Selected

Certain media may be more appropriate for a particular group than others. Face-to-face meetings may be preferable to special bulletins. A memo distributed exclusively to top executives may be a more effective outlet than the hospital administrator's newsletter. The proper format of communication can determine the effectiveness of the process.

Communication Should Be Unbiased and Modest in Tone

For communication to be effective, fact must be separated from fiction and accurate statements distinguished from opinions. Some audiences may approach the communication with skepticism, anticipating the presence of biased opinions. Boastful statements can turn off recipients, and most of the content will be lost. Observable phenomena and credible statements carry much more weight than extreme or sensational claims. Although these claims may get an audience's attention, they often detract from the importance of the results.

Communication Must Be Consistent

The timing and content of the communication should be consistent with past practices. A special presentation at an unusual time during the course of the project may provoke suspicion. Also, if a particular group, such as top management, regularly receives communication on outcomes, it should continue receiving communication even if the results are not positive. Omitting unfavorable results leaves the impression that only positive results will be reported.

Testimonials Are More Effective When They Come from Respected Individuals

Opinions are strongly influenced by other people, particularly those who are respected and trusted. Testimonials about project results, when solicited from individuals who are respected within the organization, can influence the effectiveness of the message. This respect may be related to leadership ability, position, special skills, or knowledge. A testimonial from an individual who commands little respect and is regarded as a substandard performer can have a negative impact on the message.

THE AUDIENCE'S OPINION OF THE PROJECT WILL INFLUENCE THE COMMUNICATION STRATEGY

Opinions are difficult to change, and a negative opinion toward a project or project team may not change with the mere presentation of facts. However, the presentation of facts alone may strengthen the opinions held by those who already support the project. Presentation of the results reinforces their position and provides them with a defense in discussions with others. A project team with a high level of credibility and respect may have a relatively easy time communicating results. Low credibility can create problems when one is trying to be persuasive.

These general principles are vital to the overall success of the communication effort. They should serve as a checklist for the project team planning the dissemination of project results.

THE PROCESS FOR COMMUNICATING RESULTS

The communication of project results must be systematic, timely, and well planned, and the process must include seven components in a precise sequence. The first step is critical and consists of an analysis of the need to communicate the results from a project. Possibly, a lack of support for the project was identified, or perhaps the need for adjusting or maintaining the funding for the project was uncovered. Instilling confidence or building credibility for the project may be necessary. It is important first of all to outline the specific reasons for communicating the results.

The second step focuses on the plan for communication. Planning should include numerous agenda items to be addressed in all communications about the project. Planning also covers the actual communication, detailing the specific types of data to be communicated, and when and to which groups the communication will be presented.

The third step involves selecting the target audiences for communication. Audiences range from top management to past participants, and each audience has its own special needs. All groups should be considered in the communication strategy. An artfully crafted, targeted delivery may be necessary to win the approval of a specific group.

The fourth step is developing a report, the written material explaining project results. A report can encompass a wide variety of possibilities, from a brief summary of the results to a detailed research document on the evaluation effort. Usually, a complete report is developed, and selected parts or summaries from the report are used for different media.

Media selection is the fifth step. Some groups respond more favorably to certain methods of communication. A variety of approaches, both oral and written, are available to the project leaders.

The presentation of information represents the sixth step. In the execution of the plan, the communication is delivered with the utmost care, confidence, and professionalism.

The last step, but certainly not the least significant, is analyzing reactions to the communication. Positive reactions, negative feedback, and a lack of comments are all indicators of how well the information was received and understood. An informal analysis may be appropriate for many situations. For an extensive and more involved communication effort, a formal, structured feedback process may be necessary. The nature of the reactions could trigger an adjustment to the subsequent communication of results for the same project or provide input for adapting future project communications.

The various steps are discussed further in the following sections.

THE NEED FOR COMMUNICATION

Because of the various reasons behind communicating results, a list should be tailored to the healthcare organization and adjusted as necessary. The reasons for communicating results depend on the specific project, the setting, and the unique needs of each party. Some of the most common reasons are

- Securing approval for the project and the allocation of time and money
- Gaining support for the project and its objectives
- Securing agreement on the issues, solutions, and resources

- Enhancing the credibility of the project leader
- Reinforcing the processes used in the project
- Driving action for improvement in the project
- Preparing participants for the project
- Optimizing results throughout the project
- Improving the quality of future feedback
- Showing the complete results of the project
- Underscoring the importance of measuring results
- Explaining techniques used to measure results
- Motivating participants to become involved in the project
- Demonstrating accountability for expenditures
- Marketing future projects

Other reasons for communicating results are possible as well, and the list should be tailored to the needs of each organization.

THE COMMUNICATION PLAN

Any activity must be carefully planned to achieve maximum results. This careful planning is a critical part of communicating the results of the project. The planning of the communication is important to ensure that each audience receives the proper information at the right time and that necessary actions are taken. Several issues are crucial in planning the communication of results:

- What will be communicated?
- When will the data be communicated?
- How will the information be communicated?
- Where will the information be communicated?
- Who will communicate the information?

- Who is the target audience?

- What are the specific actions required or desired?

The communication plan is usually developed when the project is approved. This plan details how specific information is to be developed and communicated to various groups and the expected actions. In addition, this plan details how the overall results will be communicated, the time frame for communication, and the appropriate groups to receive the information. The project leader, key managers, and stakeholders need to agree on the degree of detail in the plan.

An impact study can be used to present the results of a project. Such a study is developed when a major project is completed and the overall, detailed results are known. Among the major questions to be answered in an impact study are who should receive the results and in what form. The impact study is more specialized than the plan for the overall project because it involves the final results of the project.

THE AUDIENCE FOR COMMUNICATIONS

The following questions should be asked about each potential audience to whom project results are communicated:

- Are they interested in the project?

- Do they really want to receive the information?

- Has a commitment been made to include them in the communications?

- Is the timing right for this audience?

- Are they familiar with the project?

- How do they prefer to have results communicated?

- Do they know the project leader? The project team?

- Are they likely to find the results threatening?

- Which medium will be most convincing to this group?

For each target audience, three steps are necessary. To the greatest extent possible, the project leader should get to know and understand the target audience. Also, the project leader should find out what information is needed and why. Each group will have its own required amount of information; some will want detailed information while others will prefer a brief overview. Rely on the input from others to determine the audience's needs. Finally, the project leaders should take into account audience bias. Some audiences will immediately support the results, others may oppose them, and still others will be neutral. The staff should be empathetic and try to understand the basis for the differing views. Given this understanding, communications can be tailored to each group, which is critical when the potential exists for the audience to react negatively to the results.

The target audiences for information on project results are varied in terms of job levels and responsibilities. Determining which groups will receive a particular item of communication requires careful thought, because problems can arise when a group receives inappropriate information or is overlooked altogether. A sound basis for audience selection is to analyze the reason for the communication, as discussed earlier. Table 11.1 identifies common target audiences and the basis for audience selection. Several audiences stand out as critical. Perhaps the most important audience is the sponsor or client. This group (or individual) initiates the project, reviews data, usually selects the project leader, and weighs the final assessment of the effectiveness of the project. Another important target audience is top management. This group is responsible for allocating resources to the project and needs information to help them justify expenditures and gauge the effectiveness of the efforts.

Participants need feedback on the overall success of the effort. Some individuals may not have been as successful as others in achieving the desired results. Communicating the results creates additional pressure to implement the project effectively and improve results in the future. For those achieving excellent results, the communication will serve as reinforcement. Communication of results to participants is often overlooked, with the assumption that when the project is completed, they do not need to be informed of its success.

Also, an important audience is the future (prospective) participants, those individuals who may be involved in the project in the future. Communication with this group can create the desire to participate and prepare them to be successful with the project.

TABLE 11.1 Common Target Audiences

Primary Target Audience	Reason for Communication
Client/sponsor	To secure approval for the project results and actions
Top executives	To enhance the credibility of the project
Managers and directors	To gain support for the project
Participants	To secure agreement with the issues; to improve the results, to improve the quality of future feedback
Immediate managers of participants	To reinforce the need for results; to underscore the importance of measuring results
Project team	To drive action for improvement; to explain the techniques used to measure results
Prospective participants	To prepare participants for the project; to create the desire for a participant to be involved
Stakeholders	To show the results of the project
All employees	To highlight accountability for expenditures
Prospective clients, sponsors	To market future projects
Physicians	To initiate new systems, gain support, engage
Board members	To demonstrate accountability with projects
Regulators	To gain approval for new processes or services
Media	To announce best practices or new advancements
Community	To announce new services or tell how you will meet community needs

Communicating with the participants' immediate managers is essential. In many cases, these managers must encourage participants to implement the project. Also, they are key in supporting and reinforcing the objectives of the project. An appropriate return on investment strengthens the commitment to projects and enhances the credibility of the project.

The project team must receive information about results. Whether for small projects in which team members receive a project update, or for larger projects where a complete team is involved, those who design, develop, facilitate, and implement the project require information on the project's effectiveness. Evaluation data are necessary so that adjustments can be made if the project is not as effective as it was projected to be.

In addition, a variety of other stakeholders need to see the results of the project. All employees might need general information about the success of projects to underscore the need to show accountability for expenditures. Prospective clients and sponsors may be another audience. These individuals might want to have the project implemented in their hospital or clinic in the future. Physicians need to see the importance of these projects, which may motivate them to explore new systems and processes, build support for the projects, and perhaps even increase engagement in projects in the future. Board members, regulators, and the media all need to see that the expenditures are proper, new processes are being implemented, and the organization is using best practices.

INFORMATION DEVELOPMENT: THE IMPACT STUDY

A complete and comprehensive impact study report is usually necessary. The type of formal evaluation report to be issued depends on the degree of detail in the information presented to the various target audiences. Brief summaries of project results with appropriate charts may be sufficient for some communication efforts. In other situations, particularly those involving major projects requiring extensive funding, a detailed evaluation report is crucial. This report can then be used as the basis for more streamlined information aimed at specific audiences and using various media. One possible format for an impact study report is presented in Figure 11.1.

Although the impact study report is an effective, professional way to present ROI results, several cautions are in order. Because this report documents the success of other people, credit for the success must go completely to the participants and their immediate leaders. Their performance generated the success. It is important to avoid boasting about results. Grand claims of overwhelming success can quickly turn off an audience and interfere with the delivery of the desired message. Also, individual names should be omitted to protect the confidentiality of the data sources.

FIGURE 11.1   Format of an Impact Study Report

- General information
  - ○ Background
  - ○ Need for study
  - ○ Objectives for study
  - ○ Rationale for ROI analysis
- Methodology for impact study
  - ○ Levels of data and results
  - ○ The ROI Methodology
  - ○ Data collection
  - ○ Isolating the effects of the project
  - ○ Converting data to monetary values
  - ○ Guiding principles
- Data collection and analysis issues
- Project costs
- Results: General information
  - ○ Response profile
  - ○ Inputs: volume and time
- Results: Reaction
  - ○ Data sources
- Results summary
  - ○ Key issues
- Results: Learning
  - ○ Data sources

- Results summary
  - ○ Key issues
- Results application and implementation
  - ○ Data sources
- Results summary
  - ○ Key issues
- Results: Impact
  - ○ General comments
- Results summary
  - ○ Isolating the effects of the project
  - ○ Converting data to money
  - ○ Key issues
- Results: ROI and its meaning
- Results: Intangible measures
- Barriers and enablers
  - ○ Barriers
  - ○ Enablers
- Conclusions and recommendations
  - ○ Conclusions
  - ○ Recommendations

The methodology should be clearly explained, along with the assumptions made in the analysis. The reader should easily see how the values were developed and how specific steps were followed to make the process more conservative, credible, and accurate. Detailed statistical analyses should be placed in an appendix.

MEDIA SELECTION AND PRESENTING RESULTS

Many options are available for the dissemination of the results. In addition to the impact study report, commonly used media are meetings, interim and progress reports, organization publications, and case studies. Table 11.2 lists a variety of options.

TABLE 11.2 How to Communicate Results

Meetings	Detailed Reports	Brief Reports	Electronic Reporting	Mass Publications
Sponsor/ client	Impact study	Executive summary	Website	Announce- ments
Senior executives or adminis- trators	Case study (internal)	Slide overview	E-mail	Bulletins
Staff meetings	Case study (external)	One-page summary	Blog	Newsletters
Team meetings	Major articles	Brochure	Video	Brief articles

MEETINGS

If used properly, meetings are fertile ground for the communication of project results. All organizations hold a variety of meetings, and some may provide the proper context to convey project results.

The most important meeting is with the project sponsor (or client) who initiated the ROI study. This face-to-face briefing is critical for explaining results and the ROI Methodology. Because of its importance, it will be discussed in more detail later in the chapter. Along the chain of command, staff meetings are held to review progress, discuss current problems, and distribute information. These meetings can be an excellent forum for discussing the results achieved in a project that relates to the group's activities. Project results can be sent to executives for use in a staff meeting, or a member of the project team can attend the meeting to make the presentation.

Regular meetings with management groups are a common practice. Typically, discussions will focus on items that might be of help to work units. The discussion of a project and its results can be integrated into the regular meeting format. A few organizations have initiated the use of periodic meetings for all key stakeholders, where the project leader reviews progress and discusses next steps. A few highlights from interim project results can be helpful in building interest, commitment, and support for the project.

INTERIM AND PROGRESS REPORTS

A highly visible way to communicate results, although usually limited to large projects, is the use of interim and routine memos and reports. Published or disseminated by e-mail on a periodic basis, these communications are designed to inform management about the status of the project, to communicate interim results of the project, and to spur needed changes and improvements.

A secondary reason for the interim report is to enlist additional support and commitment from the management group and to keep the project intact. This report is produced by the project team and distributed to a select group of stakeholders in the organization. The report may vary considerably in format and scope and may include a schedule of planned steps or activities, a brief summary of reaction evaluations, initial results achieved from the project, and various spotlights recognizing team members or participants. Other topics may also be appropriate. When produced in a professional manner, the interim report can boost management support and commitment.

ROUTINE COMMUNICATION TOOLS

To reach a wide audience, the project leader can use internal, routine publications. Whether a newsletter, magazine, newspaper, or electronic file, these media usually reach all employees or stakeholders. The content can have a significant impact if communicated appropriately. The scope should be limited to general-interest articles, announcements, and interviews.

Results communicated through these types of media must be important enough to arouse general interest. For example, a story with the headline "New Procedures Reduce Infections" will catch the attention of many readers because they can appreciate the relevance of the results. Reports on the accomplishments of a group of participants may not generate interest if the audience cannot relate to the accomplishments.

For many projects, results are not achieved until weeks or even months after the project is completed. Participants need reinforcement from many sources. Communicating results to a general audience may lead to additional pressure to continue the project or introduce similar ones in the future.

Stories about participants involved in a project and the results they have achieved can help create a favorable image. Employees are made aware that the organization is investing time and money to improve healthcare and prepare for the future. This type of story provides information about a project that employees otherwise may be unfamiliar with, and it sometimes creates a desire in others to participate if given the opportunity.

General-audience communication can bring recognition to project participants, particularly those who excel in some aspect of the project. Public recognition of participants who deliver exceptional performance can enhance their self-esteem and their drive to continue to excel. A project can generate many human interest stories. A rigorous project with difficult challenges can provide the basis for an interesting story on participants who made the extra effort.

E-Mail and Electronic Media

Internal and external Internet pages, companywide intranets, and e-mails are excellent vehicles for releasing results, promoting ideas, and informing employees and other target groups of project results. E-mail, in particular, provides a virtually instantaneous means of communicating results to and soliciting responses from large groups of people. For major projects, some organizations create blogs to present results and elicit reactions, feedback, and suggestions.

Project Brochures and Pamphlets

A brochure might be appropriate for a project conducted on a continuing basis or where the audience is large and continuously changing. The brochure should be attractive and present a complete description of the project, with a major section devoted to results obtained with previous participants, if available. Measurable results and reactions from participants, or even direct quotes from individuals, can add spice to an otherwise dull brochure.

Case Studies

Case studies represent an effective way to communicate the results of a project. A typical case study describes the situation, provides appropriate background information (including the events that led to the project), presents the techniques and strategies used to develop the study, and highlights the key issues in the project. Case studies tell an interesting story of how the project was implemented and the evaluation was developed, including the problems and concerns identified along the way. For example, the VA Health System provided its own book of case studies.

Routine Feedback on Project Progress

A primary reason for collecting reaction and learning data is to provide feedback so that adjustments can be made throughout the project. For most projects, data are routinely collected and quickly communicated to a variety of groups. A feedback action plan designed to provide information to several audiences using a variety of media may be an option. These feedback sessions may point out specific actions that need to be taken. This process becomes complex and must be managed in a proactive manner. The following steps are recommended for providing feedback and managing the overall process. Many of the steps and concepts are based on the recommendations of Peter Block in his successful book *Flawless Consulting*.[2]

- *Communicate quickly.* Whether the news is good or bad, it should be passed on to individuals involved in the project as soon as possible. The recommended time for providing feedback is usually a matter of days and certainly no longer than a week or two after the results become known.

- *Simplify the data.* Condense the data into an easily understandable, concise presentation. It is not the appropriate situation for detailed explanations and analysis.

- *Examine the role of the project team, participants, and the client in the feedback process.* The project leader is often the judge, jury, prosecutor, defendant, and/or witness. On the other hand, sometimes the client fills these roles. These respective functions must be examined in terms of reactions to the data and the actions that are called for.

- *Use negative data in a constructive way.* Some of the data will show that things are not going so well, and the fault may rest with the project leader or the client. In this case, the story basically changes from "Let's look at the success we've achieved" to "Now we know which areas to change."

- *Use positive data in a cautious way.* Positive data can be misleading, and if they are communicated too enthusiastically, they may create expectations that exceed what finally materializes. Positive data should be presented in a cautious way—almost in a discounting manner.

- *Choose the language of the meeting and the communication carefully.* The language used should be descriptive, focused, specific, short, and simple. Language that is too judgmental, macro, stereotypical, lengthy, or complex should be avoided.

- *Ask the client for reactions to the data.* After all, the client is the number one customer, and it is most important that the client be pleased with the project.

- *Ask the client for recommendations.* The client may have some good suggestions for what needs to be changed to keep a project on track, or to put it back on track should it derail.

- *Use support and confrontation carefully.* These two actions are not mutually exclusive. At times, support and confrontation are both needed for a particular group. The client may need support and yet be confronted for lack of improvement or sponsorship. The project team may be confronted regarding the problem areas that have developed, but may need support as well.

- *React to and act on the data.* The different alternatives and possibilities should be weighed carefully to arrive at the adjustments that will be necessary.

- *Secure agreement from all key stakeholders.* It is essential to ensure that everyone is willing to make any changes that may be necessary.

- *Keep the feedback process short.* Allowing the process to become bogged down in long, drawn-out meetings or lengthy documents is a bad idea. If this occurs, stakeholders will avoid the process instead of being willing participants.

Following these steps will help move the project forward and generate useful feedback, often ensuring that adjustments are supported and can be executed.

PRESENTATION OF RESULTS TO SENIOR MANAGEMENT

Perhaps one of the most challenging and stressful types of communication is presenting an impact study to the senior management team, which often serves as the client for a project. The challenge is convincing this highly skeptical and critical group that outstanding results have been achieved (assuming they have) in a reasonable time frame, addressing the salient points, and making sure the managers understand the process. Two potential reactions can create problems. First, if the results are especially impressive, making the managers accept the data may be difficult. On the other extreme, if the data are negative, ensuring that managers don't overreact to the results and look for someone to blame is important. Several guidelines can help ensure that this process is planned and executed properly.

Arrange a face-to-face meeting with senior team members to review the first one or two major impact studies. If they are unfamiliar with the ROI Methodology, this meeting is necessary to make sure they understand the process. The good news is that they will probably attend the meeting because they have never seen ROI data developed for this type of project. The bad news is that it takes a lot of time, usually about 30 minutes to one hour, for this presentation. After the meeting with a couple of presentations, an executive summary may suffice. At this point, the senior members will understand the process, so a shortened version may be appropriate. When the target audience is familiar with the process, a brief version may be developed, including a one- or two-page summary with charts and graphs showing the six types of measures.

The results should not be distributed before the initial presentation or even during the session, but should be saved until the end of the session. Waiting will allow enough time to present the results and collect reactions to it before the target audience sees the ROI calculation quickly. Present the ROI Methodology, showing how the data were collected, when they were collected, who provided them, how the effect of the project was isolated from other influences, and how data were converted to monetary values. The Guiding Principles are briefly discussed because they explain the various assumptions, adjustments, and conservative approaches taken. It is recommended that two conservative principles are illustrated as they relate to the project. For example, it would be helpful to show that for a short-term project, only one year of data is used in the analysis, which is Guiding Principle 9. Also, if data were collected from a group of people and not everyone responded, it would be helpful to highlight Guiding Principle 6, which says that only the data provided are used in the analysis, which results in missing data being calculated as zero value. These Guiding Principles are executive-friendly and help achieve buy-in from the target audience.

When the data are actually presented, the results are presented one level at a time, starting with Level 1, moving through Level 5, and ending with the intangibles. This progression allows the audience to observe the reaction, learning, application and implementation, business impact, and ROI procedures. After some discussion of the meaning of the ROI, the intangible measures are presented. Allocate time for each level as appropriate for the audience. The first two levels are often of little value to executive groups. They should be presented in two to three minutes. Level 3 is more important but should not be allocated more than five minutes. The bulk of the discussion should be centered on Levels 4 and 5, as questions from the audience typically arise here. This logical sequence of analysis will help to diffuse the potential emotional reactions to an extreme positive or negative ROI.

Show the consequences of additional accuracy if accuracy is an issue. The trade-off for more accuracy and validity often is more expense. Address this issue when necessary, agreeing to add more data if they are required. Collect concerns, reactions, and issues involving the process and make adjustments accordingly for the next presentation.

Collectively, these steps will help in the preparation and presentation of one of the most important meetings in the ROI process. Figure 11.2 shows the recommended approach to an important meeting with the sponsor. Out of the five purposes for the meeting, only two will be addressed directly: to communicate the results of the study and to drive improvement for results. The other three items are more hidden but will be discussed in the context of the meeting. Essentially, this meeting provides an opportunity to educate

FIGURE 11.2   Presenting the Impact Study to Executive Sponsors

Purpose of the Meeting
- Create awareness and understanding of ROI.
- Build support for the ROI Methodology.
- Communicate results of study.
- Drive improvement from results.
- Cultivate effective use of the ROI Methodology.

Meeting Ground Rules
- Do not distribute the impact study until the end of the meeting.
- Be precise and to the point.
- Avoid jargon and unfamiliar terms.
- Spend less time on the lower levels of evaluation data.
- Present the data with a strategy in mind.

Presentation Sequence
1. Describe the program and explain why it is being evaluated.
2. Present the methodology process.
3. Present the reaction and learning data.
4. Present the application data.
5. List the barriers and enablers to success.
6. Address the business impact.
7. Show the costs.
8. Present the ROI.
9. Show the intangibles.
10. Review the credibility of the data.
11. Summarize the conclusions.
12. Present the recommendations.

the audience about the ROI Methodology, although they may not want to be "taught" about ROI. The ground rules are consistent with any executive meeting. The important point is not to distribute the results until the end of the meeting. If the senior executives or board requires an advance distribution, it is recommended that the actual ROI calculation be withheld until the meeting, and the group should do the calculation together. This approach helps avoid an emotional reaction to the ROI, either positive or negative, before the rest of the data have been seen. The presentation sequence is based on best practice, as thousands of individuals have presented this critical meeting.

REACTIONS TO COMMUNICATION

The best indicator of how effectively the results of a project have been communicated is the level of commitment and support from the managers, executives, and sponsors. The allocation of requested resources and voiced commitment from top management are strong evidence of management's positive perception of the results. In addition to this macro-level reaction, a few techniques can also be helpful in measuring the effectiveness of the communication effort.

When results are communicated, the reactions of the target audiences can be monitored. These reactions may include nonverbal gestures, oral remarks, written comments, or indirect actions that reveal how the communication was received. Usually, when results are presented in a meeting, the presenter will have some indication of how they were received by the group. Usually, the interest and attitudes of the audience can be quickly evaluated. Comments about the results—formal or informal—should be noted and tabulated.

Project team meetings are an excellent arena for discussing the reaction to communicated results. Comments can come from many sources depending on the particular target audience. When major project results are communicated, a feedback questionnaire may be administered to the entire audience or a sample of the audience. The purpose of the questionnaire is to determine the extent to which the audience understood and/or believed the information presented, but it is practical only when the effectiveness of the communication will have a significant impact on future actions by the project team.

FINAL THOUGHTS

The final step in the ROI Methodology, communication of results, is a crucial step in the overall evaluation process. If this step is not executed adequately, the full impact of the results will not be recognized, and the study may amount to a waste of time. The chapter began with general principles and steps for communicating project results, which can serve as a guide for any significant communication effort. The various target audiences were then discussed, with emphasis on the executive group because of its importance. A suggested format for a detailed evaluation report was also provided. The chapter presented the most commonly used media for communicating project results, including meetings, client publications, and electronic media.

A final issue regarding the ROI Methodology will be discussed in the next chapter: overcoming barriers to implementing and sustaining the use of the methodology.

CHAPTER 12

Implementing and Sustaining ROI

Even the best-designed evaluation process, model, or technique is worthless unless it is effectively and efficiently integrated into the organization. This level of accountability represents significant change for healthcare organizations. This change leads to resistance to the use of ROI. Some of this resistance is based on fear and misunderstanding. Some is real, based on actual barriers and obstacles. Although the ROI Methodology presented in this book is a step-by-step, methodical, and simplistic procedure, it can fail if it is not integrated properly, fully accepted, and supported by those who must make it work within the organization. This chapter focuses on some of the most effective means of overcoming resistance to implementing the use of ROI in an organization and shows how to sustain its use for years.

OPENING STORIES

VETERANS HEALTH ADMINISTRATION

When the VA system decided to embrace the ROI Methodology in 1999, it was initially organized by the Employee Education System (EES) with a goal of using ROI to measure all types of learning and development programs in the VA medical centers. As this implementation began to spread, it moved into other areas, which ultimately involved all types of studies throughout the medical centers and clinics.

Implementation began by having groups of people develop capability in the ROI Methodology. These individuals were pursuing the designation of Certified ROI Professional. In total, over an eight-year period, more than 150 people participated in certification, with two-thirds of them obtaining the CRP designation. The results of the studies that were conducted were published on their website. At one point, 45 ROI studies were on the VA website. In addition, one- and two-day workshops were conducted with all types of teams, introducing them to the concept of ROI. Individuals were trained to conduct the two-day workshops to help with implementation.

This structure of delivering ROI was developed with a goal of having a core team of ROI specialists in headquarters, and with ROI certified professionals in each of the regional delivery systems knows as VISNs. This goal was achieved and as studies were conducted, analyses were performed to see how the results crossed different areas and to gain more insight into how ROI is making a difference.

As data from the studies were accumulated, improvement actions were initiated. Each study sparked improvement for the same or similar studies in the future. Improvements were captured and summarized on the website. In essence, the VA system was showing the value of this level of accountability and what it meant to the organization. Issues were identified and addressed throughout the process. Finally, the VA captured the ROI on the ROI, showing how the use of the ROI Methodology had added value in excess of what it cost.

GUTHRIE HEALTHCARE SYSTEM

Guthrie Healthcare System (GHS) serves as a regional health center for a sparsely populated area of Pennsylvania and New York. This multispecialty system is a not-for-profit healthcare organization that includes primary care and specialty physicians, community hospitals, a tertiary trauma center, and a research institute as well as home care. More than 450,000 patients come from a 130-mile span east and west and a 60-mile span north and south to seek treatment for healthcare needs.[1]

Like many healthcare organizations, Guthrie was concerned about the efficiency and effectiveness of the organization. The president and CEO observed that Guthrie's previously successful business practices were becoming quickly outdated and a new vision was created for GHS to become a high-performance organization. To accomplish this goal, the top executive team pursued the implementation of an ROI strategy.

After searching for an appropriate strategy, the team focused on the ROI Methodology offered by the ROI Institute. Their implementation efforts began with the following:

- Obtaining ROI certification for 12 key staff members

- Creating a task force to implement ROI, which included the 12 participants plus others

- Developing a partnership with the finance and accounting team to support ROI implementation

- Communicating the purpose and scope of the implementation to a large audience

- Developing goals and timetables for implementing ROI in different projects and programs

The first project focused on measuring ROI to increase retention of aides in the Ancillary Aides Program at the Tioga Nursing Facility. The second project involved measuring ROI on the Management Development Technology Initiative, designed to provide all members of the Guthrie management and leadership team access to technology to facilitate decision making, enhance communication, and improve management performance.

To ensure that appropriate team members had adequate skills, the initial task force developed briefings and workshops to help others understand the ROI process and what it means to the organization.

As implementation progressed, the team:

- Developed and delivered briefings for managers, directors, and administrators.

- Delivered workshops on ROI to all team members.

- Captured the ROI on the ROI to understand the return on investment for implementing ROI in the organization.

SUSTAINING THE USE OF ROI

Almost any new process or change will encounter resistance. Resistance may be especially great when implementing a process that is often perceived as complex. To implement ROI and sustain it as an important accountability tool, the resistance must be minimized or removed. Successful implementation essentially equates to overcoming resistance. Explained next are four key reasons to have a detailed plan in place to overcome resistance.

Resistance Is Always Present

Resistance to change is a constant. Sometimes resistance arises out of good reasons, but often it exists for the wrong reasons. The important point is to sort out both kinds of resistance and try to dispel the myths. When legitimate barriers are the basis for resistance, minimizing or removing them altogether is the challenge.

Implementation Is Key

As with any process, effective implementation overcomes the resistance when the new technique, tool, or process is integrated into the routine framework. The stakeholders understand it and embrace their role with it. Without effective implementation, even the best process will fail. A process that is never removed from the shelf will never be understood, supported, or improved. Clear-cut steps must be in place for designing a comprehensive implementation process that will overcome resistance.

Consistency Is Needed

Consistency is an important consideration as the ROI process is implemented. With consistency come accuracy and reliability. The only way to make sure consistency is achieved is to follow clearly defined processes and procedures each time the ROI Methodology is used. Proper effective implementation will ensure this greater consistency.

Efficiency

Cost control and efficiency will be significant considerations in any major undertaking, and the ROI Methodology is no exception. During implementation, tasks must be completed efficiently and effectively. Doing so will help ensure that process costs are kept to a minimum, that time is used economically, and that the process remains affordable.

One of the most important issues is to set the investment for measurement and evaluation. Most organizations pursuing these types of projects invest little in the evaluation, often less than 1 percent of the total budget for the project. Ideally, this methodology can be implemented for about 5 percent of the total budget of the project or program. In essence, it is helpful to spend the 5 percent to see how the other 95 percent is working.

IMPLEMENTING THE PROCESS: OVERCOMING RESISTANCE

Resistance appears in varied ways: in the form of comments, remarks, actions (or inactions), or behaviors. Table 12.1 lists representative comments that indicate open resistance to the ROI process. Each comment signals an issue that must be resolved or addressed in some way. A few are based on realistic barriers, whereas others are based on myths that must be dispelled. Sometimes, resistance to the process reflects underlying concerns. For example, the project owners involved may fear losing control of their processes, and others may feel vulnerable to whatever action may follow if the project is not successful. Still others may be concerned about any process that brings change or requires the additional effort of learning.

Project managers and participants may resist the ROI process and openly make comments similar to those listed in Table 12.1. It may take heavy persuasion and evidence of tangible benefits to convince team members that it is in their best interest to make the project a success. Although most clients and sponsors do want to see the results of the project, they may have concerns about the information they are asked to provide and about whether their personal performance is being judged while the project is undergoing evaluation. Participants may express fears similar to those listed in the table.

The challenge is to implement the methodology systematically and consistently so that it becomes normal business behavior and a routine and standard process built into healthcare projects and programs. The implementation necessary to overcome resistance covers a variety of areas. Figure 12.1 shows actions outlined in this chapter that are presented as building blocks to overcoming resistance. They are all necessary to build the proper base or framework to dispel myths and remove or minimize

TABLE 12.1   Typical Objections to the Use of the ROI Methodology

1. It costs too much.
2. It takes too much time.
3. Is this really needed?
4. Who is asking for this?
5. This is not in my job description.
6. I did not have input on this.
7. I do not understand this.
8. What happens when the results are negative?
9. How can we be consistent with this?
10. This is not appropriate when lives are at stake.
11. The ROI looks too subjective.
12. Our managers will not support this.
13. ROI is too narrowly focused.
14. This is not practical.
15. This won't work in governments and nonprofits.

barriers. The remainder of this chapter presents specific strategies and techniques devoted to each building block identified in Figure 12.1. They apply equally to the evaluation team and the client organization, and no attempt is made to separate the two in this presentation. In some situations, a particular strategy would work best with the evaluation team. In certain cases all strategies may be appropriate for both groups.

ASSESSING THE CLIMATE

As a first step toward implementation, some organizations assess the current climate for achieving results. One place to start is to develop a survey to determine current perspectives of the evaluation team and other stakeholders (for an example, see appendix). Another way is to conduct interviews with key stakeholders to determine their willingness to follow the project through to ROI. With an awareness of the current status, the project leaders can plan for significant changes and pinpoint particular issues that need support as the ROI process is implemented.

FIGURE 12.1   Building Blocks to Overcome Resistance

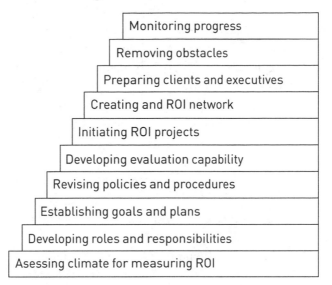

```
                          Monitoring progress
                        Removing obstacles
                      Preparing clients and executives
                    Creating and ROI network
                  Initiating ROI projects
                Developing evaluation capability
              Revising policies and procedures
            Establishing goals and plans
          Developing roles and responsibilities
        Asessing climate for measuring ROI
```

DEVELOPING ROLES AND RESPONSIBILITIES

Defining and detailing specific roles and responsibilities for different groups and individuals address many of the resistance factors and help pave a smooth path for implementation. Several issues are at stake.

IDENTIFYING A CHAMPION

As an early step in the process, one or more individuals should be designated as the internal leader or champion for the ROI Methodology. As in most change efforts, someone must take responsibility for ensuring that the process is implemented successfully. This leader serves as a champion for ROI and is usually the one who understands the process best and sees vast potential for its contribution. More important, this leader is willing to teach others and will work to sustain sponsorship.

DEVELOPING THE ROI LEADER

The ROI leader is usually a member of the evaluation team who has the responsibility for evaluation. For large organizations, the ROI leader may be part of the support services for project management, business process improvement, or business analytics. This person holds a full-time position in larger project teams or a part-time position in smaller teams. The typical job title for a full-time ROI leader is "manager of measurement and evaluation." Some organizations assign this responsibility to a team and empower it to lead the ROI effort.

In preparation for this assignment, individuals usually receive special training that builds specific skills and knowledge of the ROI process. The role of the implementation leader is quite broad and serves a variety of specialized duties. In some organizations, the implementation leader can take on many roles, ranging from problem solver to communicator to cheerleader.

Leading the ROI process is a difficult and challenging assignment that requires unique skill. Fortunately, programs are available that teach these skills. For example, one such program is designed to prepare individuals who will be assuming leadership roles in the implementation of the ROI Methodology. Ultimately, individuals become certified ROI professionals (CRP) when they complete an ROI study. (For more detail, see www.roiinstitute.net.) This ROI certification is built around 10 specific skill sets linked to successful ROI implementation, focusing on the critical areas of data collection, isolating the effects of the project, converting data to monetary value, presenting evaluation data, and building capability. This process is quite comprehensive but may be necessary to build the skills essential for taking on this challenging assignment.

ESTABLISHING A TASK FORCE

Making the ROI Methodology work well may require the use of a task force. A task force usually comprises a group of individuals from different parts of the organization who are willing to develop the ROI Methodology and implement it in the organization. The selection of the task force may involve volunteers, or participation may be mandatory depending on specific job responsibilities and expectations. The task force should represent the cross-section necessary for accomplishing stated goals. Task forces have the additional advantage of bringing more people into the process and developing more ownership of and support for the ROI Methodology. The task force must be large enough to cover the key areas but not so large that it becomes too cumbersome to function. Six to 12 members is a good size.

ASSIGNING RESPONSIBILITIES

Determining specific responsibilities is critical because confusion can arise when individuals are unclear about their specific assignments in the ROI process. Responsibilities apply to two general areas. The first is the measurement and evaluation responsibility of the individuals involved in healthcare improvement projects in a particular functional area (nursing, laps, outpatient, etc.). Everyone involved in projects must have some responsibility for measurement and evaluation. These responsibilities include providing input on designing instruments, planning specific evaluations, analyzing data, and interpreting the results. Typical responsibilities include:

- Ensuring that the initial analysis for the project includes specific business impact measures

- Developing specific application and impact objectives for the project

- Keeping participants focused on application and impact objectives

- Communicating rationale and reasons for evaluation

- Assisting in follow-up activities to capture application and impact data

- Providing assistance for data collection, data analysis, and reporting

Although involving each member of the project team in all these activities may not be appropriate, each individual should have at least one responsibility as part of his or her routine job duties. This assignment of responsibility keeps the ROI Methodology from being disjointed and separated during projects. More important, it brings accountability to those directly involved in project implementation.

Another issue involves technical support. Depending on the size of the ROI effort, establishing a group of technical experts to provide assistance with the ROI process may be helpful. For example, the VA medical centers have trained more than 100 of these experts who have a certified ROI professional designation. When the group is established, the project team must understand that the experts have been assigned not for the purpose of relieving the team of its evaluation responsibilities, but to supplement its ROI efforts with technical expertise. These technical experts are typically the individuals who participated in the certification and training process to build special skills. Responsibilities of the technical support group involve seven key areas:

1. Designing data collection instruments

2. Providing assistance for developing an evaluation strategy

3. Analyzing data, including specialized statistical analyses

4. Interpreting results and making specific recommendations

5. Developing an evaluation report or case study to communicate overall results

6. Presenting (or assisting in the presentation of) an ROI study to an executive group

7. Providing technical support in all phases of the ROI Methodology

The assignment of responsibilities for evaluation requires attention throughout the evaluation process. Although the project team must be assigned specific responsibilities during an evaluation, requiring others to serve in support functions to help with data collection is not unusual. These responsibilities are defined when a particular evaluation strategy plan is developed and approved.

ESTABLISHING GOALS AND PLANS

Establishing goals, targets, and objectives is critical to the implementation, particularly when several projects are planned. The establishment of goals can include detailed planning documents for the overall process and for individual ROI projects. The next sections discuss aspects of the establishment of goals and plans.

SETTING EVALUATION TARGETS

Establishing specific targets for evaluation levels is an important way to make progress with measurement and evaluation. As emphasized throughout this book, not every project should be evaluated to ROI. Knowing in advance to which level the project will be evaluated helps in planning which measures will be needed and how detailed the evaluation must be at each level. Table 12.2 presents examples of targets set for evaluation at each level. The targets are the percent of projects or programs evaluated at each level for Scripps Health, one of the most successful hospital networks in the United States. The setting of targets should be completed early in the process with the full support of the entire project team. If practical and feasible, the targets should also have the approval of key managers—particularly the senior management team.

DEVELOPING A PLAN FOR IMPLEMENTATION

An important part of implementation is establishing a timetable for the complete implementation of the ROI process. This document becomes a master plan for completion of the different elements presented earlier. Beginning with forming a team and concluding with meeting the targets previously described, this schedule is a project plan for transitioning from the present situation to the desired future situation. Items on the schedule include developing specific ROI projects, building staff skills, developing policy, and teaching managers the process. Figure 12.2 is an example of an implementation plan. The more detailed the document, the more useful it becomes. The project plan is a living, long-range document that should be reviewed frequently and adjusted as necessary. More important, those engaged in work on the ROI Methodology should always be familiar with the implementation plan.

REVISING OR DEVELOPING POLICIES AND PROCEDURES

Another part of planning is revising or developing the organization's policy on measurement and evaluation. The policy statement contains information

TABLE 12.2 Evaluation Targets in a Scripps Health Organization with Many Projects

Level	Target*
Level 1, Reaction	100%
Level 2, Learning	80
Level 3, Application and Implementation	40
Level 4, Impact	25
Level 5, ROI	10

*Percent of projects evaluated at this level

developed specifically for the measurement and evaluation process. It is developed with input from the project team and key managers or stakeholders. Sometimes, policy issues are addressed during internal workshops designed to build measurement and evaluation skills. The policy statement addresses critical matters that will influence the effectiveness of the measurement and evaluation process and may include adopting the five-level framework presented in this book, requiring Level 3 and 4 objectives for some or all projects, and defining responsibilities for the project team.

Policy statements are important because they provide guidance and direction for the staff and others who work closely with the ROI Methodology. These individuals keep the process clearly focused and enable the group to establish goals for evaluation. Policy statements also provide an opportunity to communicate basic requirements and fundamentals of performance and accountability. More than anything else, they serve as learning tools to teach others, especially when they are developed in a collaborative way. If policy statements are developed in isolation, staff and management will be denied the sense of their ownership, making them neither effective nor useful.

Guidelines for measurement and evaluation are important for showing how to use the tools and techniques, guide the design process, provide consistency in the ROI process, ensure that appropriate methods are used, and place the proper emphasis on each of the areas. The guidelines are more technical than policy statements and often include detailed procedures showing how the process is undertaken and developed. They often include specific forms, instruments, and tools necessary to facilitate the process.

FIGURE 12.2 Implementation Plan for a Large Organization with Many Projects

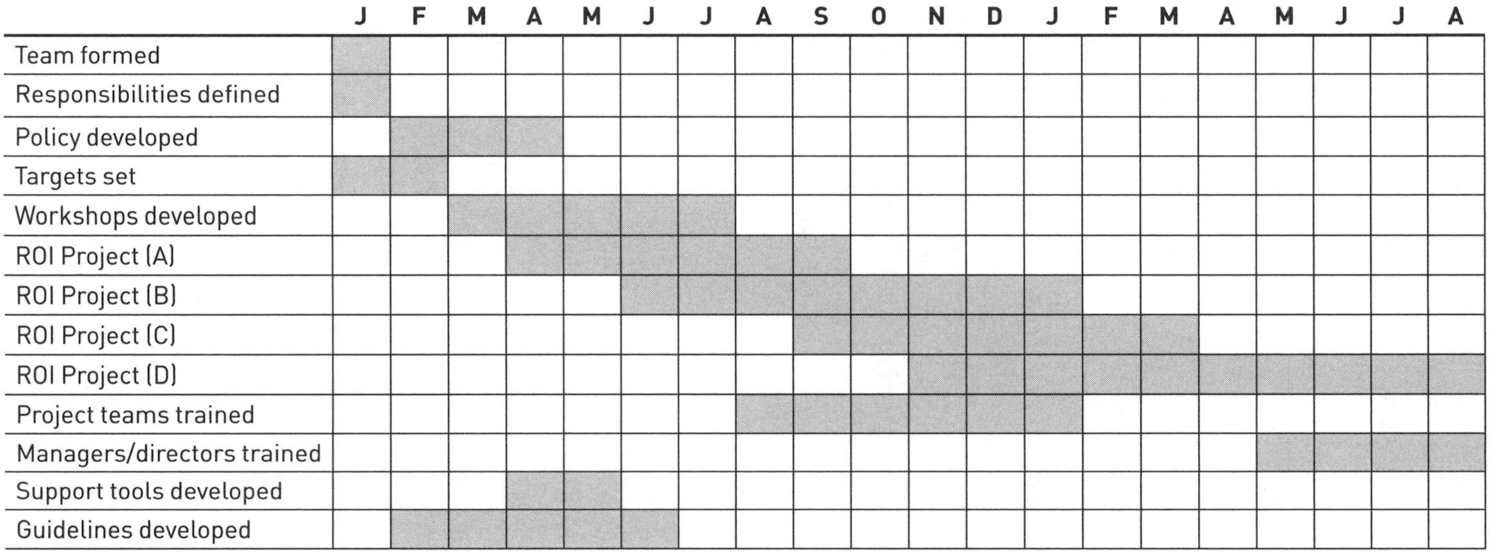

DEVELOPING EVALUATION CAPABILITY

Evaluation team members may resist the ROI Methodology. They often see evaluation as an unnecessary intrusion into their responsibilities that absorbs precious time and stifles creative freedom. The cartoon character Pogo perhaps characterized it best when he said, "We have met the enemy, and he is us." Several issues must be addressed when preparing the project team for ROI implementation.

INVOLVING THE EVALUATION TEAM

For each key issue or major decision involving ROI implementation, the evaluation team should be involved in the process. As policy statements are prepared and evaluation guidelines developed, team input is essential. Resistance is more difficult if the team helped design and develop the ROI process. Convene meetings, brainstorming sessions, and task forces to involve the team in every phase of developing the framework and supporting documents for ROI.

USING ROI AS A LEARNING TOOL

One reason the project team may resist the ROI process is that the projects' effectiveness will be fully exposed, placing the reputation of the team on the line. They may have a fear of failure. To overcome this resistance, the ROI Methodology should be clearly positioned as a tool for learning, not a tool for evaluating project team performance (at least not during the early years of project implementation). Team members will not be interested in developing a process that may reflect unfavorably on their performance.

Evaluators can learn as much from failures as from success. If the project is not working, it is best to find out quickly so that issues can be understood firsthand, not from others. If a project is ineffective and not producing the desired results, the failure will eventually be known to clients and the management group (if they are not aware of it already). A lack of results will make managers less supportive of immediate and future projects. If the projects' weaknesses are identified and adjustments quickly made, not only can more effective projects be developed, but the credibility of and respect for project implementation will be enhanced.

Teaching the Team

The project evaluators usually have inadequate skills in measurement and evaluation and will need to develop some expertise. Measurement and evaluation are not always a formal part of their job preparation. Consequently, the project team leader must learn ROI Methodology and its systematic steps, and the evaluator must learn to develop an evaluation strategy and specific plan, to collect and analyze data from the evaluation, and to interpret results from data analysis. A one- or two-day workshop can help build the skills and knowledge needed to understand the process and appreciate what it can do for project success and for the client organization. A teach-the-team workshop can be a valuable tool in ensuring successful implementation of ROI Methodology.

INITIATING ROI PROJECTS

The first tangible evidence of the value of using the ROI Methodology may be seen at the initiation of the first project where an ROI calculation is planned. The next sections discuss aspects of identifying appropriate projects and keeping them on track.

Selecting the Initial Projects

It is critical that appropriate projects be selected for ROI analysis. Only certain types of projects qualify for comprehensive, detailed analysis. Characteristic of projects that are suitable for analysis are those that (1) will be linked to major operational problems; (2) are important to strategic objectives; (3) are expensive; (4) are time-consuming; (5) have high visibility; (6) involve large groups of participants; (7) are expected to have a long life cycle; and (8) have the interest of management in performing their evaluation. Using these or similar criteria, the project leader must select the appropriate projects to consider for ROI evaluation. Ideally, sponsors should agree with or approve the criteria.

Developing the Planning Documents

Perhaps the two most useful ROI documents are the data collection plan and the ROI analysis plan. The data collection plan shows what data will be collected, the methods used, the sources, the timing, and the assignment of responsibilities. The ROI analysis plan shows how specific analyses will be conducted, including how to isolate the effects of the project and how to convert data to monetary values. Each evaluator should know how to develop these plans. These documents were discussed in detail in Chapter 2.

Reporting Progress

As the projects are developed and the ROI implementation gets under way, status meetings should be conducted to report progress and discuss critical issues with appropriate team members. These meetings keep the project team focused on the critical issues, generate the best ideas for addressing problems and barriers, and build a knowledge base for better implementation evaluation of future projects. Sometimes these meetings are facilitated by an external consultant, perhaps an expert in the ROI process. In other cases, the project leader may facilitate. In essence, the meetings serve three major purposes: reporting progress, learning, and planning.

Establishing Discussion Groups

Because the ROI Methodology is considered difficult to understand and apply, establishing discussion groups to teach the process may be helpful. These groups can supplement formal workshops and other learning activities and are often flexible in format. Groups are usually facilitated by an external ROI consultant or the project leader. In each session, a new topic is presented for a thorough discussion that should extend to how the topic applies to the organization. The process can be adjusted for different topics as new group needs arise, driving the issues. Ideally, participants in group discussions will have an opportunity to apply, explore, or research the topics between sessions. Group assignments such as reviewing a case study or reading an article are appropriate between sessions to further the development of knowledge and skills associated with the process.

CREATING AN ROI NETWORK

Because the ROI Methodology is new to many individuals, it is helpful to have a supportive peer group among those who are experiencing similar issues and frustrations. One way is to tap into a network already created, either in a local community, state, or country. Perhaps the best way to utilize the network is to create an internal ROI network. The experience with networks—in organizations where the idea has been tried—shows that these communities of practice are a powerful tool, both accelerating evaluation skill development and cultivating a culture of accountability.

The concept of a network is simplicity itself. The idea is to group people who are interested in ROI together throughout the organization to work under the guidance of trained ROI evaluators. Typically, the network would rise within the department where the program was initiated.

PREPARING THE CLIENTS AND EXECUTIVES

Perhaps no group is more important to the ROI process than the management team that must allocate resources for the project and support its implementation. In addition, the management team often provides input to and assistance for the ROI process. Preparing, training, and developing the management team should be carefully planned and executed.

One effective approach for preparing executives and managers for the ROI process is to conduct a briefing on ROI. Varying in duration from one hour to half a day, this kind of practical briefing can provide critical information and enhance support for ROI use. Managers leave these briefings with greater appreciation of the use of ROI and its potential impact on projects, and with a clearer understanding of their role in the ROI process. More important, they often renew their commitment to react to and use the data collected by the ROI Methodology.

A strong, dynamic relationship between the project team and key managers is essential for successful implementation of the ROI Methodology. A productive partnership is needed that requires each party to understand the concerns, problems, and opportunities of the other. The development of such a beneficial relationship is a long-term process that must be deliberately planned for and initiated by key project team members. The decision to commit resources and support to a project may be based on the effectiveness of this relationship.

REMOVING OBSTACLES

As the ROI Methodology is implemented, obstacles to its progress will inevitably crop up. The obstacles are based on concerns discussed in this chapter, some of which may be valid, others of which may be based on unrealistic fears or misunderstandings.

DISPELLING MYTHS

As part of the implementation, attempts should be made to dispel the myths and remove or minimize the barriers or obstacles. Much of the controversy regarding ROI stems from misunderstandings about what the process can and cannot do and how it can or should be implemented in an organization. After years of experience with ROI, and having noted reactions during hundreds of projects and workshops, observers recognize many misunderstandings about ROI. These misunderstandings, listed here, are the basic myths about the ROI Methodology:

- ROI is too complex for most users.
- ROI is expensive and consumes too many critical resources.
- If senior management does not require ROI, it is not necessary to pursue it.
- ROI is a passing fad.
- ROI is only one type of data.
- ROI is not future-oriented; it only reflects past performance.
- ROI is rarely used by organizations.
- The ROI Methodology cannot be easily replicated.

- ROI is not a credible process; it is too subjective.

- ROI cannot be used with soft projects.

- Isolating the influence of other factors is not always possible.

- ROI is appropriate only for large organizations.

- No standards exist for the ROI Methodology.

For more information on these myths, see www.roiinstitute.net.

DELIVERING BAD NEWS

One of the obstacles perhaps most difficult to overcome is receiving inadequate, insufficient, or disappointing news. Addressing a bad-news situation is an issue for most project leaders and other stakeholders involved in a project. Table 12.3 presents the guidelines to follow when addressing bad news. As the table makes clear, the time to think about bad news is early in the process, but without ever losing sight of the value of the bad news. In essence, bad news means that things can change and need to change and that the situation can improve. The team and others need to be convinced that good news can be found in a bad-news situation.

USING THE DATA

It is unfortunately too often the case that projects are evaluated and significant data are collected, but nothing is done with the data. Failure to use data is a tremendous obstacle because once the project has concluded, the team has a tendency to move on to the next project or issue and get on with other priorities. Table 12.4 shows how the different levels of data can be used to improve projects. It is critical that the data be used—the data were essentially the justification for undertaking the project evaluation in the first place. Failure to use the data may mean that the entire evaluation was a waste. As the table illustrates, many reasons exist for collecting the data and using them after collection. They can become action items for the team to ensure that changes and adjustments are made. Also, the client or sponsor must act to ensure that the uses of data are appropriately addressed.

TABLE 12.3 How to Address Bad News

- Never fail to recognize the power to learn from and improve with a negative study.
- Look for red flags along the way.
- Lower outcome expectations with key stakeholders along the way.
- Look for data everywhere.
- Never alter the standards.
- Remain objective throughout the process.
- Prepare the team for the bad news.
- Consider different scenarios.
- Find out what went wrong.
- Adjust the story line to "Now we have data that show how to make this program more successful." In an odd way, this puts a positive spin on data that are less than positive.
- Drive improvement.

TABLE 12.4 How Data Should Be Used

Action	Appropriate Level of Data				
	1	2	3	4	5
Adjust project design	√	√			
Improve implementation			√	√	
Influence application and impact			√	√	
Improve management support for the project			√	√	√
Improve stakeholder satisfaction			√	√	√
Recognize and reward participants		√	√	√	
Justify or enhance budget				√	√
Reduce costs		√	√	√	√
Market projects in the future	√	√	√	√	√

MONITORING PROGRESS

A final element of the implementation process is monitoring the overall progress made and communicating that progress. Although often overlooked, an effective communication plan can help keep the implementation on target and can let others know what the ROI Methodology is accomplishing for project leaders and the client.

The initial schedule for implementation of ROI is based on key events or milestones. Routine progress reports should be developed to communicate the status of these events or milestones. Reports are usually developed at six-month intervals but may be more frequent for short-term projects. Two target audiences—the project team and senior managers— are critical for progress reporting. All project team members should be kept informed of the progress, and senior managers should know the extent to which ROI is being implemented and how it is working within the organization.

FINAL THOUGHTS

Even the best model or process will die if it is not used and sustained. This chapter explored the implementation of the ROI process and ways to sustain its use. If not approached in a systematic, logical, and planned way, the ROI process will not be an integral part of project evaluation, and project accountability will consequently suffer. Smooth implementation is the most effective means of overcoming resistance to ROI. The result provides a complete integration of ROI as a mainstream component of major projects. Good luck with this methodology.

Do Your Healthcare Improvement Projects Focus on Results?

A SELF-ASSESSMENT SURVEY FOR CLIENTS

Instructions. For each of the following statements, please circle the response that best matches the situation for healthcare improvement activities and philosophy in your organization. If none of the answers describe the situation, select the one that best fits. Please be candid with your responses.

1. The direction and goals of healthcare improvement at your organization:

    a. Shifts with trends, fads, and industry issues.
    b. Is determined by managers of departments and adjusted as needed.
    c. Is based on a mission and a strategic plan for healthcare improvement.

2. The primary mode of operation of healthcare improvement consultants is:

   a. To respond to requests by managers and other employees to solve problems and deliver solutions.
   b. To help management react to crisis situations and reach solutions.
   c. To implement solutions in collaboration with management to prevent problems and crisis situations.

3. Healthcare improvement solutions usually focus on:

   a. Changing perceptions and opinions.
   b. Enhancing skills and job performance.
   c. Driving business measures and enhancing job performance.

4. Most healthcare improvement solutions are initiated:

   a. When a solution appears to be successful in another organization.
   b. By request of management.
   c. After analysis has indicated that the solution is needed.

5. To determine healthcare improvement solutions:

   a. Management is asked to choose a solution from a list of existing packaged solutions.
   b. Employees and unit managers are asked about needs.
   c. Needs are systematically derived from a thorough analysis of healthcare performance problems and issues.

6. When determining the healthcare improvement solutions needed for target audiences:

   a. Nonspecific solutions for large audiences are offered.
   b. Specific needs of specific individuals and groups are addressed.
   c. Highly focused projects are implemented only with those people who need it and can use it.

7. The responsibility for results from healthcare improvement:

   a. Rests primarily with the healthcare improvement consultants.
   b. Is shared with consultants and clients, who jointly ensure that results are obtained.
   c. Rests with consultants, participants, managers, and clients all working together to ensure accountability.

8. Systematic, objective evaluation, designed to ensure that healthcare improvement adds value:

   a. Is never accomplished. Evaluations are conducted during the project and they focus on how much the participants are satisfied with the project.
   b. Is occasionally accomplished. Participants are asked if the healthcare improvement project was effective on the job.
   c. Is frequently and systematically pursued. Business impact is evaluated after the project is completed.

9. Healthcare improvement projects are staffed:

   a. Primarily with internal healthcare improvement consultants.
   b. With one preapproved major healthcare improvement firm.
   c. In the most economical and practical way to meet deadlines and cost objectives, using internal staff and a variety of healthcare improvement firms.

10. The objectives for healthcare improvement solutions are:

    a. Nonspecific and based on subjective input.
    b. Based on learning, application, and implementation.
    c. Based on business impact, application, implementation, and satisfaction.

11. Costs for healthcare improvement are accumulated:

    a. On a total aggregate basis only.
    b. On a project-by-project basis.
    c. By specific process components such as initial analysis and implementation, in addition to a specific project.

12. Management involvement in healthcare improvement is:

    a. Low with only occasional input.
    b. Moderate, usually by request, or on an as-needed basis.
    c. Deliberately planned for all major healthcare improvement projects to ensure a partnership arrangement.

13. To ensure that healthcare improvement projects are translated into performance on the job, we:

    a. Encourage participants to apply what they have learned and report results.
    b. Ask managers to support and reinforce project results.
    c. Utilize a variety of implementation strategies appropriate for each situation.

14. The healthcare improvement consultant's interaction with management is:

    a. Rare. Healthcare improvement consultants almost never discuss issues with them.
    b. Occasional, during activities such as needs analysis or project coordination.
    c. Regular, to build relationships as well as to develop and deliver solutions.

15. The investment in healthcare improvement projects is measured primarily by:

    a. Subjective opinions and relationships.
    b. Observations by management, reactions from participants.
    c. ROI through improved productivity, costs, quality, or patient satisfaction.

16. New healthcare improvement projects, with no formal method of evaluation, are implemented at my organization:

    a. Regularly.
    b. Seldom.
    c. Never.

17. The results of healthcare improvement projects are communicated:

    a. When requested, to those who have a need to know.
    b. Occasionally, to members of management only.
    c. Routinely, to a variety of selected target audiences.

18. Management responsibility for healthcare improvement:

    a. Is minor, with no specific responsibilities.
    b. Consists of informal responsibilities for selected healthcare improvement projects.
    c. Is very specific. Managers have some responsibilities for projects in their business units.

19. During a business decline at my organization, healthcare improvement will:

    a. Be the first to have its budget reduced.
    b. Be retained at the same budget level.
    c. Go untouched in reductions and possibly increased.

20. Budgeting for healthcare improvement is based on:

    a. Last year's budget.
    b. Whatever the healthcare improvement consultant can "sell."
    c. A zero-based system based on the need for each project.

21. The principal group that must justify healthcare improvement expenditures is:

    a. The healthcare improvement consultants.
    b. The consultants and managers of the unit where the project is initiated.
    c. Senior management over the area where the healthcare improvement project is implemented.

22. Over the last two years, the healthcare improvement budget as a percent of operating expenses has:

    a. Decreased.
    b. Remained stable.
    c. Increased.

23. Senior management's involvement in healthcare improvement projects:

    a. Is limited to introductions, announcements, and offering challenges
    b. Includes reviewing status, opening/closing meetings, discussions of status, and presentation on the outlook of the organization.
    c. Includes participation in the project, monitoring progress, and requiring key managers to be involved.

24. When an employee is directly involved in a healthcare improvement project, he or she is required to:

    a. Follow instructions.
    b. Ask questions about the project and use the projects materials and learning.
    c. Implement the project successfully, encourage others to implement it, and report success.

25. Most managers in your organization view the healthcare improvement function as:

    a. A questionable activity that wastes too much of employees' time.
    b. A necessary function that probably cannot be eliminated.
    c. An important resource that can be used to improve healthcare and the organization.

Score the assessment instrument as follows.
Allow:

1 point for each (a) response.
3 points for each (b) response.
5 points for each (c) response.

The total will be between 25 and 125 points.

The interpretation of scoring is provided here. The explanation is based on the input from dozens of organizations.

Score Range	*Analysis of Score*
99–125	**Outstanding Environment** for achieving results with healthcare improvement. Great management support. A truly successful example of results-based healthcare improvement.
76–100	**Above Average** in achieving results with healthcare improvement. Good management support. A solid and methodical approach to results-based healthcare improvement projects.
51–75	**Needs Improvement** to achieve desired results with healthcare improvement. Management support is ineffective. Healthcare improvement projects do not usually focus on results.
25–50	**Serious Problems** with the success and status of healthcare improvement. Management support is non-existent. Healthcare improvement projects are not producing results.

Notes

CHAPTER 1

1. www.scripps.org.
2. American Hospital Association Committee on Performance Improvement (Jeannette Clough, Chairperson), *Hospitals and Care Systems of the Future* (Chicago: American Hospital Association, September 2011).
3. *Value in Healthcare: Current State and Future Directions* (Westchester: Healthcare Financial Management Association, June 2011). Accessed www.hfma.org on February 16, 2012.
4. "Leadership for the Triple Aim," *Healthcare Executive* (March–April 2012): 80–83.
5. Marshall Goldsmith and Mark Reiter, *What Got You Here Won't Get You There: How Successful People Become Even More Successful* (New York: Hyperion, 2007).
6. Jeffrey Pfeffer and Robert I. Sutton, *Hard Facts, Dangerous Half-Truths and Total Nonsense: Profiting from Evidence-Based Management* (Boston: Harvard Business School, 2006).
7. *Value in Healthcare* (June 2011).
8. Robert S. Kaplan and David P. Norton. *The Balanced Scorecard: Translating Strategy into Action* (Boston: Harvard Business School, 1996).
9. *Value in Healthcare* (June 2011).
10. Healthcare Financial Management Association Value Project Survey (January 2011).
11. SullivanCotter, "Survey of Executive Compensation in Hospitals and Health Systems" (HFMA, 2007–2009).

CHAPTER 2

1. Hannah Wolfson, "Program Reduces Blood Infections in Alabama Hospitals," *The Birmingham News* (October 25, 2011). Accessed www.al.com on April 4, 2012.
2. Jack J. Phillips and Patricia Pullliam Phillips, *Show Me the Money: How to Determine the ROI in People, Projects, and Program* (San Francisco: Berrett-Koehler, 2007).

CHAPTER 3

1. Yale New Haven Health, Annual Report 2011.

CHAPTER 4

1. *The Millennium Development Goals Report* (New York: United Nations, 2011).
2. W. Miller, "Building the Ultimate Resource: Today's Competitive Edge Comes from Intellectual Capital," *Management Review* (January 1999): 42–45.

CHAPTER 5

1. http://www.ncqa.org/Portals/0/HEDISQM/HEDIS2010/2010 _Measures.pdf.
2. Michael E. Porter, "What Is Value in Healthcare?" *The New England Journal of Medicine* 363 (January 2, 2012): 2477–481.

CHAPTER 6

1. http://www.greenwaymedical.com/dynamicData/pdf/casestudies /birmingham_heart_clinic_case_study.pdf.
2. Haig R. Nalbantian, Richard A. Guzzo, Dave Kieffer, and Jay Doherty, *Play to Your Strengths: Managing Your Internal Labor Markets for Lasting Competitive Advantage* (New York: McGraw-Hill, 2004).

3. Robert S. Kaplan and David P. Norton, *The Balanced Scorecard: Translating Strategy into Action* (Boston: Harvard Business School Press, 1996).
4. Noah J. Goldstein, Steve J. Martin, and Robert B. Cialdini, *Yes! 50 Scientifically Proven Ways to Be Persuasive* (New York: Free Press, 2010).

CHAPTER 7

1. http://www.albertahealthservices.ca/.
2. http://www.va.gov/health/aboutVHA.asp.
3. James Surowiecki, *The Wisdom of Crowds* (New York: Anchor Books, 2005).

CHAPTER 8

1. Healthcare Financial Management Association, *Value in Healthcare: Current State and Future Directions* (Westchester, NY: Healthcare Financial Management Association, June 2011). Accessed http://www.hfma.org/HFMA-Initiatives/Value-Project/Value-in-Health-Care-Current-State-and-Future-Directions/ on February 16, 2012.
2. http://eric.ed.gov/.
3. Patricia Pulliam Phillips, and Jack J. Phillips, *Proving the Value of HR: ROI Case Studies*, 2nd ed. (Birmingham, AL: ROI Institute, 2010).
4. Paul W. Farris, Neil T. Bendle, Phillip E. Pfeifer, and David J. Ribstein, *Marketing Metrics: 50+ Metrics Every Executive Should Master* (Upper Saddle River, NJ: Wharton School Publishing, 2006).
5. *Value in Healthcare: Current State and Future Directions* (June 2011).
6. http://www.cms.gov/.
7. http://www.hcup-us.ahrq.gov/tech_assist/centdist.jsp.
8. http://www.ahrq.gov/data/datameet.htm.
9. http://www.nih.gov/.
10. http://hbr.org/2008/07/putting-the-service-profit-chain-to-work/ar/1.

Chapter 9

1. "2012 Top 125 Organizations," *Training Magazine* (January–February 2012): 44–48.
2. Richard E. S. Boulton, Barry D. Libert, and Steve M. Samek, *Cracking the Value Code* (New York: HarperBusiness, 2000).
3. Paul W. Farris, Neil T. Bendle, Phillip E. Pfeifer, and David J. Ribstein, *Marketing Metrics: 50+ Metrics Every Executive Should Master* (Upper Saddle River, NJ: Wharton School Publishing, 2006), p. 16.
4. http://www.hcahpsonline.org/home.aspx.
5. Alexander Kandybihn and Martin Kihn, "Raising Your Return on Innovation Investment," *Strategy + Business* 35 (2004).
6. http://www.pfizer.com/files/annualreport/2010/financial/financial2010.pdf.
7. Kelly J. Caverzagie, Elizabeth C. Bernabeo, Siddharta G. Reddy, and Eric S. Holmboe, "The Role of Physician Engagement on the Impact of the Hospital-Based Practice Improvement Module (PIM)," *Journal of Hospital Medicine* 4, 8 (2009): 466–70. Accessed Medscape.com on March 7, 2012.
8. Jack J. Phillips, Patricia Pulliam Phillips, and Rebecca Ray, *Measuring Leadership Development: Quantify Your Program's Impact and ROI on Organizational Performance* (New York: McGraw-Hill, 2012).

Chapter 10

1. Patricia Pulliam Phillips, *Measuring ROI in Learning and Development: Case Studies from Global Organizations* (Alexandria, VA: ASTD Press, 2012).
2. Kelly Kennedy, "Fight Against Health Care Fraud Recovers $4.1B," *USA Today* (February 14, 2012): 4A. Accessed www.usatoday.com/news/washington/story/2012-02-14/sebelius-holder-announce-health-care-fraud-money/53097474/1 on March 12, 2012.
3. http://www.shrm.org/Research/SurveyFindings/Articles/Documents/2011_Emp_Benefits_Report.pdf.

CHAPTER 11

1. Paul Terpeluk, "Why We Won't Hire Smokers," *USA Today Weekly International Edition* (February 3–5, 2012): 7W.
2. Peter Block, *Flawless Consulting: A Guide to Getting Your Expertise Used*, 3rd ed. (San Francisco: Pfeiffer, 2011).

CHAPTER 12

1. Pauline Stamp, "The Role of ROI in a High-Performance Learning Organization," *Implementing Evaluation Systems and Processes*. Ed. Jack J. Phillips (Alexandria, VA: ASTD Press, 1998).

Index

About the Authors

Prior to coming to Scripps Health, **Victor Buzachero** held top executive level positions at organizations such as Providence Health System, Banner Health System, and Baptist Health System. During his tenure at these organizations, Buzachero developed and successfully implemented programs including leadership development, service excellence, reduction in employee turnover, and improved employee satisfaction. Addititonally, he served as vice president of Marketing (hospital acquisitions) for Quinn Health and was coowner and principal of a national labor relations and executive compensation consultancy. In 1999, Franklin Covey honored Buzachero with the "Organization of Excellence" award for his prominent efforts in organizational development and effectiveness and, in 2011, he was honored by *HR Executive* magazine as a top HR Executive for the year. He is frequently sought out to speak at the national level on ROI in healthcare, workforce initiatives, and labor initiatives, among other topics. Buzachero is former chairman of the American Hospital Association Solutions Board and current senior vice president of Scripps Health.

Dr. Jack J. Phillips is chairman of the ROI Institute and a world-renowned expert on measurement and evaluation. Phillips provides consulting services for Fortune 500 companies and workshops for major conference providers worldwide. Phillips is also the author or editor of more than 30 books and more than one hundred articles. His work has been featured in the *Wall Street Journal*, *Bloomberg Businessweek*, *Fortune*, and on CNN.

Dr. Patricia Pulliam Phillips is an internationally recognized author, consultant, and president and CEO of the ROI Institute, Inc. Phillips provides consulting services to organizations worldwide. She helps organizations build capacity in the ROI Methodology by facilitating the ROI certification process and teaching the ROI Methodology through workshops and graduate level courses.

With more than 20 years of experience in the healthcare industry, **Zack Phillips** is currently the director of Cardiopulmonary Services at Emory Johns Creek Hospital in Johns Creek, Georgia. Phillips has served at nearly every level of the healthcare industry. As a senior-level director of the world's largest healthcare organization, he has experience with and accountability for the profitability and efficiency of the service lines he oversees. His broad base of professional experience is fortified by his interest and advanced certifications in emergency medicine and response for hospitals and government organizations. Phillips offers a unique blend of expertise and experience in the field of healthcare. He has a keen understanding of what it means for a hospital to operate efficiently, even in the face of pending legislation that is likely to change the operating paradigm for healthcare industry-wide. Phillips is a trusted colleague, an engaged leader, and a gifted motivator for his staff and peers. His perspective is a valuable asset as healthcare organizations work not only to become more efficient, but also to show verifiable return on investment in human resources, technology, and services.